36th EDITION
2015–2016

A STUDENT'S GUIDE TO
FIRST-YEAR WRITING

HAYDEN
HM
McNEIL

Hayden-McNeil Sustainability

Hayden-McNeil's standard paper stock uses a minimum of 30% post-consumer waste. We offer higher % options by request, including a 100% recycled stock. Additionally, Hayden-McNeil Custom Digital provides authors with the opportunity to convert print products to a digital format. Hayden-McNeil is part of a larger sustainability initiative through Macmillan Higher Ed. Visit http://sustainability.macmillan.com to learn more.

Printed in the United States of America

10 9 8 7 6 5 4 3 2 1

ISBN 978-0-7380-7433-7

Hayden-McNeil Publishing
14903 Pilot Drive
Plymouth, MI 48170
www.hmpublishing.com

HallA 7433-7 F15

printed on 100% recycled paper

Acknowledgements

Writing is a social act, and this book would not be possible without the collaboration of UA faculty, graduate students, and first-year writing students. Now in its 36th edition, *A Student's Guide to First-Year Writing* is more than just a guide to writing—it is a reflection of over three decades of conversations about writing in the university and world. We wish to thank all of the contributors to these pages over the years and those who have offered constructive feedback in meetings, surveys, emails, and hallway chats. These ongoing conversations help this text remain relevant as the work of writing evolves.

We would like to begin the 36th edition by thanking our Writing Program Director, Dr. Amy C. Kimme Hea, and our Writing Program Associate and Assistant Directors, Dr. Christine Tardy and Dr. Aimee Mapes, for their administrative guidance, constant support, and continued efforts to improve the University of Arizona's Writing Program and its curriculum.

We also extend our thanks to the Writing Program's exceptional faculty, course directors, and staff. We are especially grateful to our adviser, D.R. Ransdell, who offered practical suggestions and unending support throughout the revision process. In addition, the program course directors—Jo Anne Behling, Dev Bose, Sean Bottai, Jeremy Godfrey, Keith Harms, Aimee Mapes, Carol Nowotny-Young, Kara Reed, and Erec Toso—offered valuable suggestions at all stages of the process. Without your generous and thoughtful feedback, we would not be able to ensure the integrity of our text and its usefulness to UA students and instructors. Additionally, we would like to thank the talented Writing Program staff who manage everything behind the scenes. Thank you, Monica Vega, Sara Soto, and Sara Vickery, for everything you do. Special thanks go to Lizzy Bentley for contributing the innovative design you see on the cover and within the pages of this book.

We also owe many thanks to our publisher Hayden-McNeil and especially to our outstanding editor Lisa Wess and our layout designers Christine Victor and Amanda Humphrey. Thank you so much, Lisa, Christine, and Amanda, for always answering our emails, offering insightful ideas, and helping guide us to the completion of this project. We also wish to acknowledge Hayden-McNeil's financial support of our annual essay contest: we could not recognize the excellent work by the writers in our program without your gracious contributions.

Your 36th edition editors,
Brad Jacobson, Madelyn Tucker Pawlowski, and Emma Miller

Artist's Statement

For this year's cover, I playfully present the potential expansiveness of foundational concepts like "writing," "text," and "literacy"—all of which are central to the first-year writing curriculum at the University of Arizona. Writing is historicized through communication technologies, such as Peruvian *quipu* and Egyptian hieroglyphics, and represented in different genres including personal journals, academic essays, protest posters, and news articles. Text is expanded beyond the written word to include images and sound, a move visually represented in the sketches of comic books, music albums, and film reels. Hopefully, you will finish your first-year writing sequence with a more complex understanding of the literacies that you possess and those that surround you.

—*Lizzy Bentley*

Table of Contents

Craft Boxes

Tips & Strategies Boxes

Close Reading Strategies for Multimodal Texts 19
What to Do with Writer's Block 48
Tips for Writing Introductions 52
Tips for Writing Conclusions 56
Ways and Means of Transitions 58
Reviewing Explanations 64
Getting the Most from Your Workshop Experience 70
Approaching Instructor Feedback 72
Writing with Integrity: Intentional vs. Unintentional Plagiarism 81
The Research Checklist 98
Interviews: Bringing Your Research Topic to Life 104
Evaluating Internet Sources 106
Writing the Annotation 112
Literacy Narrative as Analysis 136
Reverse Outlining 147
From Reactions to Analysis 148
Anticipating Reader Concerns 173
Reading Visual Rhetoric 186
Avoiding the "*Ethos, Logos, Pathos*" Five-Paragraph Essay 196
Evaluating Potential Research Questions 208
Finding Sources 210
Thesis Statement for the Controversy Analysis 215
Guidelines for Recognizing Bias in Your Writing 216
Creating Your Own Video Public Argument 224
Software, Programs, and Apps for Your Public Argument 236
Developing Thesis Statements for Public Arguments 239
Tips for Giving Oral Presentations 240
Evidence in Reflective Writing 253

Acknowledgements iii

Part I Introduction to First-Year Writing

Part II Strategies and Concepts

PART III Assignments

PART IV Student Writing and Awards

PART I

INTRODUCTION TO FIRST-YEAR WRITING

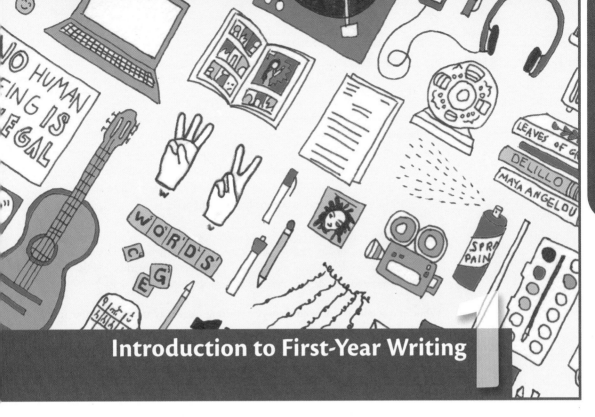

Introduction to First-Year Writing

1.1 Writing at the University of Arizona: An Overview

Welcome to the University of Arizona! By enrolling in your first-year writing courses, you are taking the first step in your journey toward becoming a stronger, more confident writer.

Being a writer means different things in different writing situations. The strategies offered in this text will help you to prepare for these situations by thinking about your writing as a series of choices based on several factors. One of these factors is your **purpose**: the reason you are writing and what you hope to accomplish with your writing. Another factor is your **audience**. You might ask yourself, "Who is going to read my writing?" As a writer, you must make choices that correspond to your purpose and audience. That is why a reporter for the *Arizona Daily Star* will use a distinctly different writing style from the author of a history textbook. Even if these two writers were recounting the same events, the **texts** would look quite different because the writers have different purposes and audiences in mind as they write and revise. Your first-year writing courses are designed to guide you to evaluate **rhetorical situations** (purpose, audience, and context), practice critical analysis, and respond accordingly.

> The magenta terms you'll find throughout this book are **glossary terms**. See the Glossary near the end of the book for definitions.

First-year writing classes, also known as composition classes, are usually much smaller than your other general education classes. In addition, many instructors make use of full-class and small-group discussion, so you will have more of an opportunity to get to know your classmates and instructor. In this setting, your responsibilities as an individual student will be more clearly defined. We find UA student Ray Hum's advice especially pertinent here:

> ❝ The true value of an English composition class depends largely on the student. If the student approaches the class with high motivation, then the class will certainly be enjoyable and valuable. If, on the other hand, the student approaches the class with an uninterested attitude, then the class will inevitably be a waste of time. ❞

While the small size of your first-year writing class may mean that your instructor has high expectations for your participation and work, there are many benefits to this smaller group. Some of these benefits include the opportunity to receive feedback and assistance from your instructor and your peers. UA student Chris Clark provides the following advice to fellow students:

> ❝ The most important thing all freshmen should know in order to succeed is that you have to go to class. English is probably the most common course at UA, and success later starts in the beginning. You will find that the majority of students taking first-year writing are freshmen just like yourself, and going through the same things you are. It's a good chance for you to make friends while starting college out on the right foot. First-year writing instructors are also well aware that you are going through a big adjustment and are sensitive to that. Not only have I found that the English instructors go out of their way to help accommodate new students, but they also act as advisors if you need help. ❞

One important way that your first-year writing classes will aid in a smooth transition into the university is by teaching you a variety of writing techniques that will help you in your future classes, including your NATS classes, TRAD classes, and even your upper-division classes. Attending your first-year writing class, doing the work, and applying it elsewhere will set you up for a successful career at the UA. Good luck!

1.2 A Guide to the *Guide*

The *Student's Guide* offers useful information specific to the University of Arizona's first-year writing program.

Part I (Chapter 1) of the *Guide* gives an overview of first-year writing at the UA. This first chapter is a general introduction and examines some basic assumptions of college writing. It also discusses grades and provides an overview of the kinds of assignments you can expect to encounter in the first-year writing sequence.

Part II (Chapters 2–6) introduces you to reading and writing strategies. It guides you through various writing processes you will need to practice to improve your writing skills. In these chapters, you will learn how to do a close-reading of a text, how to engage in the research process, how to get started writing, how to effectively participate in peer review, and how to use feedback to revise your writing.

Part III (Chapters 7–12) explains how to apply the strategies discussed in Part II to the specific assignments you will encounter in first-year writing. Each chapter has subsections that outline different ways to think about an assignment as well as specific strategies for effective writing.

Part IV (Chapter 13) describes the *Student's Guide* Essay Contest and the Hayden-McNeil Difference and Inequality Essay Contest. It also lists the winners and judges for the previous year's contest. In addition, this chapter also provides a collection of sample essays written by students in the Writing Program.

You will also notice that the *Student's Guide* includes references to your handbook, *Rules for Writers*, and your English 102/108 textbook, *Writing Public Lives*, in the margins and within the text. All of these materials will guide you through your first-year writing courses and can be used as references throughout your academic career.

1.3 High School vs. College Writing

By Faith Kurtyka

Although the course you are in is listed as an English course, it will likely be very different from the English courses you took in high school. This section encourages you to think about ways your high school English classes might be similar to or different from your college English classes. The section also presents recommendations from interviews with several groups of first-year UA students. The students were asked about their high school and college experiences, and what advice they would offer to incoming first-year students. The following are some of their responses:

Tips for Success from Student Writers
On Time Management:

> Start writing early. Don't procrastinate. Even if it's a month away. You can wait a week, but make sure [you get started], even if it's a simple step such as writing an outline really quick.

1.4

On Early Drafts:

> Writing good first drafts helps a lot. For the first essay in our class, my rough draft was terrible. I didn't try on it at all. It was like 'Whatever, I just want to get this done.' And then when I had to write my final, I had to work so hard and it was so annoying. So for this second essay, I tried a lot harder on my outline, so writing the final wasn't as stressful.

On Effort:

> One paper can make or break your grade. So you want to do your best on every assignment, because you can't just make it up just like that.

On Preparing to Write:

> In high school, I would turn in papers and show up for tests, it's just the preparation in the meantime I never did. I would always just wing papers the night before and get high C's or B's on them. And so I settled on those grades, but here I can't settle on that. So I just do an outline just to get thoughts going, and then a few days later expand on it, three points for each major point. Just simple stuff—it really helps.

> See pages 13–17 in *Rules for Writers* for help on exploring ideas.

The above quotes show how close attention to your writing process will likely be a major component of your first-year writing courses. Your instructor may assign **invention** activities that prompt you to generate ideas for your paper—an outline, a discussion or journal post, or even just time to write freely. Beginning the day the project is assigned, these activities can be instrumental in avoiding procrastination and allowing yourself the time to spread out your effort.

To reflect on your own transition from high school to college writing and clarify some of your expectations for this class, discuss the following with your classmates and your instructor:

- Describe some of the writing assignments you did in high school. What were the requirements? What was your writing process?

- What did you learn about writing in high school?

- What do you expect to learn about writing in college?

- How did your high school experience differ from the descriptions above?

- What kind of student were you in high school and what kind of student do you want to be in college?

1.4 Grading and Rubrics in First-Year Writing

The previous section's focus on writing as an ongoing process is important for understanding the function of grading in your first-year writing classes. When assigning a grade, your instructor evaluates how well your writing achieves the goals of a particular assignment. This feedback can offer areas of focus for future writing assignments in your first-year writing courses and beyond. Grades are meant to help your writing improve over the entirety of a course, not to punish you for mistakes you make in a particular essay.

A rubric is a tool that your instructor may use when grading your essays, offering feedback on a draft, or explaining the assignment guidelines and expectations. Many rubrics look like a chart with rows describing writing criteria and columns describing achievement levels. The following sample rubric indicates the standards of the Writing Program broadly defined as content, organization, expression, and mechanics.

Content: This category focuses on the ideas and information present in your writing. It usually includes a strong **thesis**, developed **arguments**, and a clear understanding of the assignment.

Organization/Form: This category focuses on how clearly organized your essay and paragraphs are and how effectively you have transitioned between different thoughts.

Expression/Style: This category focuses on the development of tone or voice appropriate to the assignment, as well as accurate and precise diction. It also takes into account a well-developed writing persona.

Mechanics/Conventions: While this category includes Standard Written English (SWE) grammatical conventions, it also focuses on proper MLA formatting, in-text citations, and the Works Cited page.

When instructors create rubrics, they typically fill in areas on the rubric with their own descriptions of each type of achievement. For example, they will use your assignment sheet to determine the required form or the necessary content for that specific essay. The completed section here focuses on the "Mechanics" row and shows the shifting level of achievement in each progressive column. Keep in mind that the rubric your instructor uses may differ from this sample rubric, or he or she may choose tools other than rubrics to assign grades.

Sample Grading Rubric—Mechanics Category

	Superior	Strong	Competent	Weak	Unacceptable
Mechanics	No errors in standard grammar, spelling, or punctuation to distract readers. Flawless use of MLA formatting.	Very few errors in standard grammar, spelling, or punctuation to distract readers. One or two minor errors in formatting.	Occasional errors in standard grammar, spelling, or punctuation that may distract readers. Three or more errors in formatting.	Frequent errors in standard grammar, spelling, or punctuation that distract readers. Frequent minor errors or one to two major errors in formatting.	Serious problems with grammar, spelling, or punctuation. Not formatted according to MLA guidelines.

After your instructor has graded your essay, you may see something similar to the circle on the sample rubric. This shows where your essay scored in that category. Notice that the "Mechanics" category in this rubric has similar language in each box. The column furthest to the right indicates the most problems in that category, with improvements represented in each shift to the left. This is how the rubric functions in each row. Remember that the middle column indicates competence. This column is used when a student shows adequate achievement in that category. Every move to the left of that column shows significant achievements above a competent performance.

Remember that writing is a process, as is your progress through first-year composition. The quality of your writing will improve as the course progresses if you use these rubrics as a tool to assist your learning instead of concentrating on one or two errors that you believe lowered your grade. Look at the categories where you scored lowest overall and focus on improving in those areas on your next assignment. Finally, your instructor is likely to offer written comments on each of your essays whether or not they choose to use a rubric. You should read all comments with an eye to how they'll help you with your future writing. Feel free to ask questions about your grades and get clarification from your instructor on how you can improve your writing after reflecting on their comments and your grade. For more information on grading criteria, speak to your instructor directly.

Grade Appeals

The Writing Program is committed to providing you with fair, clear, and useful responses to your writing, and will process grade appeals in an efficient and objective fashion. A grade appeal is based on the quality of the writing produced by the student and the grades awarded to that writing by the instructor. If you disagree with a specific grade or if you have questions about the grading policy outlined in the course syllabus, speak with your instructor immediately. You may then speak with your instructor's faculty supervisor or the Course Director, but neither will become involved in considering changes in grades until you file a grade appeal after the end of the semester. If you believe your final grade in a writing course was unfairly or incorrectly assigned, you should first meet with your instructor and then with the Course Director. Go to the Writing Program office in Modern Languages for complete instructions.

Rubric Model

	Superior	Strong	Competent	Weak	Unacceptable
Thesis/Content					
Organization					
Style					
Mechanics					

1.5 Overview of the First-Year Writing Sequence

The UA Writing Program brings together students and instructors from a variety of cultures, languages, and academic disciplines. Instructors in the Writing Program come from various sub-disciplines within English studies, including creative writing, literature, applied linguistics, and **rhetoric** and writing studies, and some instructors have degrees in disciplines outside of English. In addition, your peers represent the many possible majors around the university. Both instructors and students come from across the country and from around the world. Writing courses are designed to challenge you to explore such diversity. All of these sources of difference lead to an exciting variety of materials, class activities, discussions, and assignments.

Instructors may encourage you to explore issues or **topics** that are challenging or even troublesome in order to push you to examine your ideas in writing. Sometimes you might struggle with the material because it conflicts with your personal belief system, but working with controversial issues can help you define and articulate your own position in relation to the complex **context** surrounding those issues. You may even find that topics or issues that initially created discomfort end up leading you to produce your most interesting or thoughtful writing.

The Assignments

You should expect to encounter a range of assignments in your first-year writing classes. For each major assignment, you will complete rough drafts, peer reviews, and final drafts. Short in-class and out-of-class writing assignments will help you prepare for these major projects. While your instructor will certainly not assign all of these different assignments in one semester, the following list offers an overview of the kinds of assignments you can expect:

- **Textual Analysis Essays**: These assignments require a sustained focus on a text in a limited context. For instance, you might analyze the literary, textual, or cultural features that impact a reader's response to a text, including images, sound, videos, or spaces. You might also compare the strategies or features evident in two different texts or explore your personal reactions to the text(s). Yet another type of textual analysis will explore the rhetorical strategies employed by the author (as described below). See Chapter 7 for more about analysis.

- **Text-in-Context Essays:** These assignments, sometimes referred to as contextual analyses, focus on a text and its relationship to a larger context, such as the author's biography, the historical or cultural situation surrounding the text, a particular theoretical approach such as feminism or psychoanalysis, or a related set of texts. Text-in-context essays depend on close reading, research, argument, revision, and synthesis skills. Research for this paper will be limited in focus; your instructor may even provide a few sources for you to use. These assignments emphasize your ability to evaluate and incorporate sources effectively. See Chapter 8 for more about the Text-in-Context Assignment.

- **Literacy Narratives:** For these assignments, you will analyze personal experiences with language or literacy in an effort to present a complex understanding of the social and personal purposes of literacy. See Chapter 7 for more about Literacy Narratives.

- **Rhetorical Analyses:** For these assignments, you will pay close attention to how a writer or speaker achieves a particular purpose for a specific audience. Your instructor will introduce various lenses to help you read and respond to different texts. For example, you may apply a classical rhetorical lens to explore how the writer uses logos, ethos, and pathos to persuade an audience, or you might perform genre analysis in order to identify patterns across multiple texts and explore the relationship between a genre and its social context. See Chapter 9 for more about Rhetorical Analysis.

- **Controversy Analyses:** You may be required to conduct library and/ or field research on a controversial topic of your choice, culminating in an analysis of multiple perspectives on your chosen controversy. This assignment requires you to do more than simply summarize the arguments. Instead, you will be expected to use rhetorical analysis in order to evaluate and critique the arguments on both sides of the issue. See Chapter 10 for more about the Controversy Analysis.

- **Public Arguments:** For these assignments, you will advocate for a specific position on a topic of public interest. You will use research and your understanding of rhetoric as you compose your argument for an audience. You may be required to write an academic essay, or your argument may take on other forms depending on your instructor's directions. See Chapter 11 for more about Public Arguments.

- **Final Projects:** At the end of each course in the sequence, you will complete a final project. Your instructor may ask you to reflect on or revise an assignment or to reflect on your experience in first-year writing. For example, you may be asked to revise your public argument for a different rhetorical situation and write an analysis of your revision process, or your instructor may ask you to write a rhetorical analysis of your own public argument. A reflection assignment might ask you to track your progress over the course of the semester or both of your first-year writing courses. See Chapter 12 for more on the final project.

1.5

Developing different methods or styles of reading will help you deal with the large amount of reading you'll be asked to do in college and in the workplace. See Chapter 2 for more on close-reading strategies.

Conclusion

In summary, your first-year writing courses will help you build the skills to analyze texts, compose arguments about texts, conduct detailed and relevant research on texts and their contexts, revise your work, and reflect on your writing process. UA student Adrian Sotomayor offers the following advice about the importance of analysis:

> Get ready for a year full of analysis! Whether you like it or hate it, you will have to analyze everything you read. The first essay, textual analysis, was both the easiest and the hardest to write. It was easy because I had the option of choosing a story that interested me from several that were presented; thus, it helped me form a relatively strong argument about the text. On the other hand, I had previously taken English 100 but had taken a semester break from English. This created my initial struggle in which I was lost and forgot most, if not all, of what I had learned. To get by, I started to read the *Student's Guide* to see what other students had to say (yep, the same thing you are reading now). It helped me see that I wasn't alone and actually helped with the tips that some students gave.

PART II

STRATEGIES AND CONCEPTS

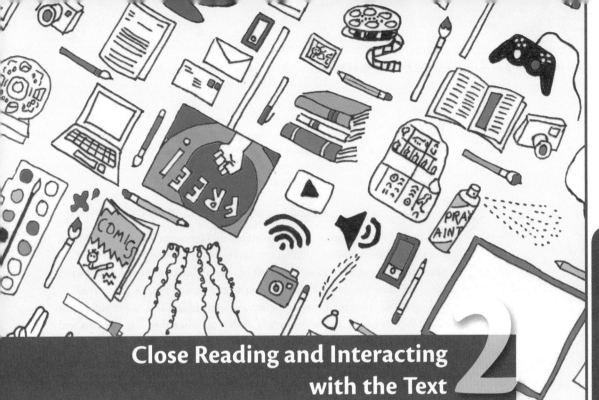

Close Reading and Interacting with the Text

2.1   Close Reading: An Overview

2.2   Annotation and Close Reading for Fiction

2.3   Annotation and Close Reading for Poetry

2.4   Annotation to Understand and Respond to an Argument

2.5   Reviewing for Analysis

2.1 Close Reading: An Overview

We often read texts just once or scan them for relevant information. For example, you might skim the "Arts & Leisure" section of the newspaper to find film times, or you might read the Wikipedia entry about the *Mona Lisa* quickly for the information you are most interested in. You might also scan a chapter in a biology textbook to look for important terms that will be on your next exam. Such one-time reading for information, however, is insufficient for many of the tasks you will perform in your courses, including the work for your first-year writing classes. In addition to reading a text for information, you will need to read texts with a particular purpose in mind.

When you practice **close reading**, you focus your attention on the aspects of the text that seem most important to your purpose. One common way to think about the strategies you use when you read is to divide the process into three phases: **the first occurs before reading, the second during active reading, and the third when reviewing your notes and the text.** The strategies that follow in this chapter can be applied to many reading experiences. For example, you can annotate a scholarly article, a blog post, or even a music video, and you can be an active reader when conducting research or reviewing a course syllabus. Whatever your purpose might be, practicing to become a more efficient and critical reader will help you in your first-year writing classes and your other courses here at the University of Arizona.

Why Annotate?

> Making annotations in the text not only helps me get a deeper understanding of what I'm reading, it allows me to think from perspectives I wouldn't have if I was simply reading the book without a pen in hand.

—UA Student Michael Cox

Annotation is the process of writing notes and comments about a text. When you write in the margins, highlight or underline important passages, and take notes on the pages, you make the most of your ability to understand and write about the text. You can also annotate texts on a separate paper if you are borrowing books from the library or analyzing something like a music video. Just remember to keep track of the details of the text—like the page numbers and lines from the text you are annotating or the timestamp from the music video—so you can return to it later.

Annotation makes thinking deeply about the text you are reading much easier. Maybe you realize that you circled a certain word more than once—why? Maybe there was something that confused you at the beginning but that makes more sense after reading the whole text. Maybe you noticed certain kinds of images popping up more than once or elements of the writer's language that create a certain feeling or response. Or, like Michael, perhaps you start to notice something from a different perspective.

If you are actively reading and processing the text as you go, writing down ideas as they come to you and marking sections to refer back to and ponder, you are starting to take apart the text to see how it works, which is the basic process of analysis.

Phase One: Pre-Reading

Before you start reading, take time to scan the text and consider the general questions below. It's important to first establish the **genre** because different genres carry their own expectations for how one might "read" them. For example, alliteration or line spacing might be more significant in poetry than in an academic article. Familiarizing yourself with elements such as the title, genre, medium, organization, and any introductory materials will help you begin to anticipate what you will encounter as you engage with the text.

Things to look for:

- What is the genre? What is the usual purpose of that genre? What expectations might you (and other readers) bring to this particular genre?

- Are there any chapters or sections with designated headings? Is there another indication of structure? What might this structure suggest?

- What information does the title offer?

- Are there any visuals, such as graphs or pictures? How do they influence what you expect from the text?

- Do you expect the language to be literal or figurative? Should we expect to find many symbols, metaphors, and similes?

- Can you expect a story arc, an argument, a collection of images?

- If the text contains sound, what kinds of sounds do you expect to hear?

- Are there many printed words or just a few? How does that impact how much attention you should pay to each word?

- Do you know anything about the author or artist?

Phase Two: Active Reading

Observations, Questions, and First Interpretations

Now that you have scanned the text, you are ready to take a closer look at its content. Your first reading is like the first day of class. You become familiar with features of the course like the teacher, the structure, the theme, and the basic requirements. However, you will have to attend again, multiple times, before you have mastered the goals of the course and answered all of your questions.

When you practice close reading, you might think of yourself as an active participant engaging with the material rather than as a passive observer. Reading actively will make it easier for you to remember what you have read and will enable you to respond effectively when writing about the text. As an active reader, you have two goals during your first reading:

Goal 1: Read and take notes. Record your initial reactions and impressions while also trying to understand the text. Your focus should be on what is happening in the text on a literal or basic level. Don't skip on observing the obvious. If you are reading a short story, for instance, talk back to that story by annotating and writing in your journal or notebook, recording your thoughts about the narrative, the characters, and the plot. If you are reading an academic article, your responses might be focused more on the writer's ideas, use of evidence, or connections to other arguments.

Your responses should reflect what you are noticing about the text and what you find interesting. You may want to begin by identifying the who, what, where, and when of a text. The following is a limited sample of the questions readers might answer in their observations throughout their first reading:

- Is there a narrator, voice, or speaker? How would you describe it?

- Who/what are the subjects or characters (if any)? How would you describe them?

- What verb tenses are used? Are they active or passive? Who is doing the actions?

See the Tips & Strategies Box on page 19 and Chapters 8 and 9 for specific tips on visual analysis and reading photographs.

2.1

- What happens in the text? Does anything in the text seem figurative or symbolic?

- Is there anything that confuses you? Does anything surprise you? Why?

- What images, ideas, or words are repeated? Do some of them seem more important than others?

- Does the text indicate any suggestion of place or location?

- Where in the text are main ideas presented? What else do you notice about the organization of the text?

- How are you interpreting the text? What are its main ideas and purpose?

- Does the mood seem to change in different places? Try tracing how the text makes you feel at various points. Does the speaker or narrator seem to contradict your own feelings? Do you think the author shares the same feelings as the narrator/speaker?

Goal 2: Ask questions. You want to start locating places in the texts that you don't understand or have questions about. Making note of the questions that arise as you read is another way to actively engage with a text. Take note of your inquiries in the margins of the text or in a writing journal. This way, you can return to your questions and read the text again with these questions in mind to help you see the text differently. You might also use these questions as discussion starters to start a dialogue with others who have read the text. Below are a few examples of Goal 2 annotations, but your own questions will vary according to your purpose and understanding. You can find other samples of questions within the annotations of sections 2.2, 2.3, and 2.4.

- What does this word mean?

- What is important about this detail?

- What is the motive for this action?

As you read, you will start to make some inferences about your observations and questions. During your first reading, try not to think of inferences or claims about the text as "finding the right answer" to the text, but rather as one possible interpretation. A second reading might produce other observations, questions, interpretations, or reactions.

Phase Three: Directed Reading

Inferences, Answers, Nuanced Meaning, Evidence

During Phase 2, you were taking notes on the who, what, when, and where of the text. In Phase 3, you are looking at the how and why. Revisit your initial annotations, observations, and questions. Use these observations and questions to guide your second reading. Try to understand how different elements of the text function and why certain aspects of the text seem confusing, important, or intriguing. In this phase, you will address your questions and look for patterns that might relate to possible themes, ideas, complications, and interpretations.

While your first reading mostly produces observations and questions, the second reading allows you to start analyzing the ideas of the text and how they are produced. This is also the time to identify potential symbolic or figurative meanings and alternative interpretations.

Phase 3 Annotations:

- Try to start answering some of the questions from your first reading.

- Review everything that seemed strange or didn't seem to fit. Do these places relate to something now that you have a better understanding of the text?

- Return to your initial observations and annotations. Do any of them seem particularly striking now that you've read the text again? Why did you make note of certain details? Do you notice any patterns in your annotations?

- Look for contradictions and changes in the ideas or form. What are the purposes of these conflicts in meaning, tone, characterization, interpretation, connotation, etc.?

- Locate connections between repeated words, images, and ideas.

- Write down any ideas that are called to mind when you read certain phrases or think of particular images. Is there evidence for a symbolic or figurative reading in addition to the literal reading?

Close Reading Strategies for Multimodal Texts

Close reading is important for reading any kind of text. Think about observing a painting. You often have to look at it multiple times, or for an extended period of time, to understand much of what is going on. You can apply the same close reading process explained in section 2.1 to a music video, a website, or even a space on campus like the Arizona Stadium. Understanding any text is dependent upon careful observation and inferences.

As a class or with a partner, take a look at one of the multimodal texts located in this book and think about how the reading process is similar and different. Review the process outlined in section 2.1 and select questions that are applicable to a multimodal text. Try to generate new questions specific to your medium.

Sample texts:

- Photographs (Chapters 7, 8)
- A space on campus (Chapter 7)
- Film (Chapter 7)
- Cultural artifact (Chapter 8)
- Advertisement (Chapter 9)
- Graphic Art/Comics (Chapter 9)
- Video (Chapter 11)
- Website (Chapter 11)

Once you have finished your second reading, you should try to organize your notes and look for some general conclusions and initial claims. Organizing your ideas now will help you to be better prepared to write and talk about the text since you will have narrowed your observations down to some main ideas. The following are examples of annotated close readings of a short story, a poem, and a newspaper opinion article. See section 2.5 in this chapter for specific techniques to review and reorganize your annotated notes after reading.

See section 5a in *Rules for Writers* for advice and examples of annotations.

2.2 Annotation and Close Reading for Fiction

You read a short story differently than you read an academic article or poetry because short stories serve a different purpose and utilize different techniques and conventions. For example, pieces of fiction typically contain characters, setting, and a plot. Though sometimes the "point" of a story seems quite obvious, you should remain open to any symbolic interpretations. When close reading a work of fiction, the phases from section 2.1 can help guide your annotations and interpretations.

The following is an annotation of Stephen Crane's short story "The Snake." Annotations in italics were made during the Phase 3 reading.

What does wend mean? Same as winding? *To meander, go in an indirect route.*

Why wended, winding, curly all together? *Refers to the action of snakes or the shape of snakes.*

Figurative language. What is the effect? *Sets up a mythical feeling; you know something strange is going to happen.*

> Where the path wended across the ridge, the bushes of huckleberry and sweet fern swarmed at it in two curling waves until it was a mere winding line traced through a tangle. There was no interference by clouds, and as the rays of the sun fell full upon the ridge, they called into voice innumerable insects which chanted the heat of the summer day in steady, throbbing, unending chorus.

Characters: Man and Dog. Also, narrator seems to not be a character in the story, but uses lots of description so far.

Why use "brawled"? *Makes me think of fighting or violence. Foreshadows violence with snake.*

Dog is white and yellow. What does man look like? *Never find out. Could be any man or all men? Animals and nature are detailed but not man.*

> A man and a dog came from the laurel thickets of the valley where the white brook brawled with the rocks. They followed the deep line of the path across the ridges. The dog—a large lemon and white setter—walked, tranquilly meditative, at his master's heels.

"Suddenly"—quick action.

Rattle? Like the Snake from the title. Dry makes me think of the desert or peeled snake skin.

What is smote? *Past tense of smite: to strike firmly. Why such a strange way to say the man froze? Maybe emphasizes terror, violence.*

Death has fingers: personification. Why? *Makes death seem like a real thing, a threat that is physically there.*

> Suddenly from some unknown and yet near place in advance there came a dry, shrill whistling rattle that smote motion instantly from the limbs of the man and the dog. Like the fingers of a sudden death, this sound seemed to touch the man at the nape of the neck, at the top of the spine, and change him, as swift as thought, to a statue of listening horror, surprise, rage. The dog, too—the same icy hand was laid upon him, and he stood crouched and quivering, his jaw dropping, the froth of terror upon his lips, the light of hatred in his eyes.

> Slowly the man moved his hands toward the bushes, but his glance did not turn from the place made sinister by the warning rattle. His fingers, unguided, sought for a stick of weight and strength. Presently they closed about one that seemed adequate, and holding this weapon poised before him the man moved slowly forward, glaring. The dog with his nervous nostrils fairly fluttering moved warily, one foot at a time, after his master.

Narrowing in on hands. Makes it seem like they are acting independently.

Both man and dog are frozen in terror. *Cold images from death contrast hot setting.*

Why not just go away? Why does he want to go after it? *Like his ancestors from later in text. Hatred of snakes is in his blood, an instinct.*

But when the man came upon the snake, his body underwent a shock as if from a revelation, as if after all he had been ambushed. With a blanched face, he sprang forward and his breath came in strained gasps, his chest heaving as if he were in the performance of an extraordinary muscular trial. His arm with the stick made a spasmodic, defensive gesture.

The snake had apparently been crossing the path in some mystic travel when to his sense there came the knowledge of the coming of his foes. The dull vibration perhaps informed him, and he flung his body to face the danger. He had no knowledge of paths; he had no wit to tell him to slink noiselessly into the bushes. He knew that his implacable enemies were approaching; no doubt they were seeking him, hunting him. And so he cried his cry, an incredibly swift jangle of tiny bells, as burdened with pathos as the hammering upon quaint cymbals by the Chinese at war—for, indeed, it was usually his death-music.

"Beware! Beware! Beware!

The man and the snake confronted each other. In the man's eyes were hatred and fear. In the snake's eyes were hatred and fear. These enemies maneuvered, each preparing to kill. It was to be a battle without mercy. Neither knew of mercy for such a situation. In the man was all the wild strength of the terror of his ancestors, of his race, of his kind. A deadly repulsion had been handed from man to man through long dim centuries. This was another detail of a war that had begun evidently when first there were men and snakes. Individuals who do not participate in this strife incur the investigations of scientists. Once there was a man and a snake who were friends, and at the end, the man lay dead with the marks of the snake's caress just over his East Indian heart. In the formation of devices, hideous and horrible, Nature reached her supreme point in the making of the snake, so that priests who really paint hell well fill it with snakes instead of fire. The curving forms, these scintillant coloring create at once, upon sight, more relentless animosities than do shake barbaric tribes. To be born a snake is to be thrust into a place a-swarm with formidable foes. To gain an appreciation of it, view hell as pictured by priests who are really skillful.

As for this snake in the pathway, there was a double curve some inches back of its head, which, merely by the potency of its lines, made the man feel with tenfold eloquence the touch of the death-fingers at the nape of his neck. The reptile's head was waving slowly from side to side and its hot eyes flashed like little murder-lights. Always in the air was the dry, shrill whistling of the rattles.

"Beware! Beware! Beware!"

The man made a preliminary feint with his stick. Instantly the snake's heavy head and neck were bended back on the double curve and instantly the snake's body shot forward in a low, strait, hard spring. The man jumped with a convulsive chatter and swung his stick. The blind,

---

Margin annotations:

Man and snake share same emotions. Repetition of words "hatred" and "fear." Why? *Man and Snake are alike.*

Once: like a fable.

Body receives shock. Why not say he? Shock from what? *Maybe another reference to instinct.*

Ambush—Like snake had tricked him into bush? *Text keeps shifting blame and sympathies.*

Strained, heaving: he is having a hard time physically.

The snake is mystical? *Like the figurative language in setting.*

Foes? Sounds like some epic battle/fantasy. *Again, back to myth or fable setting idea.*

No wit, but he knew? *Relationship between animal instinct/knowledge and human ways of knowing.*

Hunting and "cry" makes us feel bad for snake, like he is the victim. Cry is shaking of rattle.

What? "Burdened with pathos": like pity for man? Or emotion? What does this have to do with Chinese at war? *Even though it seems to have a Southwest setting, pulls in different ethnicities. Maybe to help make the setting seems mythical, exotic?*

Inherited fear of snake? From ages ago? *Again, like a myth. Also, seems to suggest it is instinctual for human too, not just rational.*

Caress: like a romantic relationship gone wrong? Creepy.

Hell is snakes? *Contradicts with pity for snake felt earlier, maybe because this is man's view and not snake's view.*

Scintillant: sparkling.

Hot eyes? Like a glare. They are having a standoff.

Man attacks first. Seem to trade blows.

Repeat of beware/rattle.

2.2

Despairing—Snake is losing. Effect of despair? *Another instance of pitying him.*

Gallant like a knight? *Like a noble death in epic battle.*

Lone chief? Why this image? *Relates to Southwest setting, also makes him seem like the last defender, the good guy, tied to nature.*

Mutilated and torn—really graphic, violent. Snake can't recover. Still fights, so nature fights to the end. Epic battle.

Stick becomes the enemy. Why? *Moves blame to stick so that we empathize with both man and snake.*

Man wins the battle. Watches it die.

Last war cry, funeral hymn: like the dying echoes. *Makes me think of the "lone chief"—pity, loss.*

Almost cartoony dog name, same with Mr. Snake. Why so out of place? *With snake dead, no mythical presence, back to ordinary, country life.*

Wants to show daughter and wife (?) the corpse of snake, like a war trophy.

Dog goes back to behavior in beginning. *A return to normalcy.*

sweeping blow fell upon the snake's head and hurled him so that steel-colored plates were for a moment uppermost. But he rallied swiftly, agilely, and again the head and neck bended back to the double curve, and the steaming, wide-open mouth made its desperate effort to reach its enemy. This attack, it could be seen, was despairing, but it was nevertheless impetuous, gallant, ferocious, of the same quality as the charge of the lone chief when the walls of white faces close upon him in the mountains. The stick swung unerringly again, and the snake, mutilated, torn, whirled himself into the last coil.

And now the man went sheer raving mad from the emotions of his forefathers and from his own. He came to close quarters. He gripped the stick with his two hands and made it speed like a flail. The snake, tumbling in the anguish of final despair, fought, bit, flung itself upon this stick which was taking his life.

At the end, the man clutched his stick and stood watching in silence. The dog came slowly and with infinite caution stretched his nose forward, sniffing. The hair upon his neck and back moved and ruffled as if a sharp wind was blowing, the last muscular quivers of the snake were causing the rattles to still sound their treble cry, the shrill, ringing war chant and hymn of the grave of the thing that faces foes at once countless, implacable, and superior.

"Well, Rover," said the man, turning to the dog with a grin of victory, "We'll carry Mr. Snake home to show the girls."

His hands still trembled from the strain of the encounter, but he pried with his stick under the body of the snake and hoisted the limp thing upon it. He resumed his march along the path, and the dog walked tranquilly meditative, at his master's heels.

After annotating this story, you may already see some patterns. You can probably identify the tone and perhaps begin to make an argument about what this story might signify or suggest. Based on the annotations above, you might want to explore themes and ideas like the struggle between humans and nature, the motif of an epic battle, or what the snake represents about nature or instinct.

2.3 Annotation and Close Reading for Poetry

Reading and understanding poetry can be a very different experience than reading and understanding prose. One poem might be highly symbolic or abstract and may be difficult to understand. Another poem might have such a specific focus on details that you are not sure of its purpose. Different reactions to poetry are due, in part, to the fact that the genre is incredibly diverse. This can become challenging as what we know about one type of poem may not be true of another.

In most cases, poems are easy to identify because of their use of form and other poetic patterns, including rhythm, rhyme, meter, repetition, line breaks, stanza breaks, spatial organization on the page, and so forth. Sometimes a specific pattern, form, or technique will produce as much meaning as the actual words. When you read a poem, you should consider how both form and language affect meaning and interpretation.

Practice Annotating
Try it for yourself:

In this annotation box, write down three or more of your annotations from a text you have been assigned to read and then try to make connections between your ideas and reactions and the details in the text.

Your annotations from the text

What are some connections among the ideas or impressions you noted?

What do these connections help you notice about the text?

2.3

Craft Box: INVENTION

When reading a poem, you can use the strategies found in section 2.1. You may also want to consider these additional questions:

1. What are the patterns—and what does not make sense or seem to fit with those patterns?

2. What techniques are used to make the patterns?

3. How do these techniques and patterns affect how you read the poem?

4. How do these effects support or challenge your interpretation of the poem's meaning?

Annotations in italics were made during the Phase 3 reading.

Libertad! Igualdad! Fraternidad!

By William Carlos Williams

You sullen pig of a man
you force me into the mud
with your stinking ash-cart!

Brother!
    —if we were rich
we'd stick our chests out
and hold our heads high!

It is dreams that have destroyed us.

There is no more pride
in horses or in rein holding.
We sit hunched together brooding
our fate.

    Well—
all things turn bitter in the end
whether you choose the right or
the left way
        and—
dreams are not a bad thing.

Looking at these annotations, you can notice how both form and language work to produce ideas and meaning. For example, a reader might notice the pattern of disconnected lines to conclude that the poem represents a conversation. Another reader might use differences in tone and word choice to come to a similar conclusion. Based on the above annotations, other analyses might focus on power dynamics, wealth disparity, the need for revolution, a sense of fraternity, or other possible interpretations.

Left margin annotations:

What language is this? *Spanish.* What do these words mean? *Liberty, Equality, Fraternity (brotherhood). Also, this is the slogan of the French Revolution.* Why is it in a different language than the poem? *Maybe he is calling for "Revolution" for a Spanish-speaking population, immigrant workers, etc.*

Who is you? *Maybe some rich guy.*

"Sullen pig" is very insulting.

Force: violent. *So sullen pig man has power over speaker.*

Is he talking to someone? *Maybe it's a conversation.* A real brother? *Reference to "Fraternidad"—all humans are "brothers."*

Rich—*power difference seems to be about money.*

Why is this line on its own? *Maybe part of a conversation. If so, who is saying this?* How can dreams destroy someone? This is surprising because usually dreams seem like a positive thing.

Really pessimistic.

Why line break between right and left? *Line break emphasizes difference between two paths.* Right as in "good" or as in the direction? *Maybe both.*

Why use "left" instead of wrong? *"All things turn bitter," so there is no right and wrong way, all directions lead to same "bitter" end.*

Right margin annotations:

Why this detail? *Increases the idea of power difference, lowest people thrown into the mud by the "sullen pig of a man," seems extra-insulting.*

What does "stinking ash-cart" signify? Type of job?

Pride, confidence. *They don't do this because they are not rich.*

The "no more" seems to hint that there used to be pride in the past, but now there isn't.

Do horses/rein holding mean a particular job? *Seems to be no longer respected or valued. Perhaps the laborers hold the horses for rich people to mount. It could also mean holding something back or "waiting," like waiting for something better to happen.*

Using "we" and "together," sense of "fraternidad."

An expression? Why formatted like this? *Could be evidence for conversation, an interjection.*

"Not a bad thing" contradicts earlier line about dreams destroying us. Are there two speakers?

2.4 Annotation to Understand and Respond to an Argument

In addition to being useful for understanding literary meanings, annotation can be an extremely helpful tool in helping you figure out the argument that a particular text is making. In many of your classes, you are likely to be assigned articles that make arguments, and you will need to discuss those arguments in your writing or other coursework. These kinds of articles, however, can be dense and difficult to understand, particularly when you have to read texts for different classes at the same time.

To help you get the most meaning from a text in the most efficient way, take notes that focus on understanding the writer's main points, the evidence he or she uses to support them, and the overall logic that makes the argument cohesive. Focus on these aspects as you read the following opinion article from *The New York Times*. You can use the question and answer strategies from section 2.1, but direct your focus on the argument. You might also find this strategy useful when you are reviewing a peer's paper in order to provide feedback.

Annotations in italics were made during the Phase 3 reading.

> To assess a writer's treatment of opposing views, see section 7c in *Rules for Writers*.

2.4

When Black Feminism Faces the Music, and the Music is Rap

By Michele Wallace[1]

Like many black feminists, I look on sexism in rap as a necessary evil. In a society plagued by poverty and illiteracy, where young men are as likely to be in prison as in college, rap is a welcome articulation of the economic and social frustrations of black youth.

> She identifies herself like this right away—have an impact on the kind of argument she decides to make? *From the perspective of a black feminist.*

In response to disappointments faced by poor urban blacks negotiating their future, rap offers the release of creative expression and historical continuity: it draws on precedents as diverse as jazz, reggae, calypso, Afro-Cuban, African and heavy metal, and its lyrics include rudimentary forms of political, economic and social analysis.

> Her thesis sounds pro-rap, but the phrase "necessary evil"? *Separates sexism in rap (bad) from cultural functions of rap (good).*

But with the failure of our urban public schools, rappers have taken education into their own hands; these are oral lessons (reading and writing being low priorities). And it should come as no surprise that the end result emphasizes innovations in style and rhythm over ethics and morality. Although there are exceptions, like raps advocating world peace (the W.I.S.E. Guyz's "Time for Peace") and opposing drug use (Ice-T's "I'm Your Pusher"), rap lyrics can be brutal, raw and, where women are the subject, glaringly sexist.

> Suggests rap is: 1) a hybrid musical form and 2) can offer social critiques.

> What does she mean by this? *Education about life, not "school" education?*

> It's more important to sound cool than to be moral.

Given the genre's current crossover popularity and success in the marketplace, including television commercials, rap's impact on young people is growing. A large part of the appeal of pop culture is that it can offer symbolic resolutions to life's contradictions. But when it comes to gender, rap has not resolved a thing.

> More people hearing rap = more people impacted by its message, which might not be a good thing?

> Rap provides no solutions for gender problems. Why does it ignore gender? *See locker room idea.*

25

The footnote says this article was written in 1990, which explains the old examples. Are there similar examples today? *Pitbull, Rick Ross.*

She supports this point with examples from videos. The visual aspect seems to add an important element to the kind of sexism she is worried about.

Quote in its own paragraph for emphasis?

I wonder what the impacts of this kind of ban would have now that music can be shared digitally.

2.4

Women are treated as sex objects explicitly in lyrics but more often in other ways, like the visuals of the videos she mentions above.

hooks seems to suggest that sexism in rap is like collateral damage rather than an intentional attack on women.

Would people today think someone making a criticism of rap is part of "hostile white culture"? *Lots of criticism about white and black artists today.*

Misogyny? *Hostile attitude toward women.*

This paragraphs cites lots of examples of hostile responses as evidence for her point above.

This text seems to be some kind of response to the critiques listed above.

Though styles vary—from that of the X-rated Ice-T to the sybaritic Kwanee to the hyperpolitics of Public Enemy—what seems universal is how little male rappers respect sexual intimacy and how little regard they have for the humanity of the black woman. Witness the striking contrast within rap videos: for men, standard attire is baggy outsize pants; for women, spike heels and short skirts. Videos often feature the ostentatious and fetishistic display of women's bodies. In Kool Moe Dee's "How Ya Like Me Now," women gyrate in tight leather with large revealing holes. In Digital Underground's video "Doowutchyalike," set poolside at what looks like a fraternity house party, a rapper in a clown costume pretends to bite the backside of a woman in a bikini.

As Trisha Rose, a black feminist studying rap, puts it, "Rap is basically a locker room with a beat."

The recent banning of the sale of 2 Live Crew's album *As Nasty as They Wanna Be* by local governments in Florida and elsewhere has publicized rap's treatment of women as sex objects, but it also made a hit of a record that contains some of the bawdiest lyrics in rap. Though such sexual explicitness in lyrics is rare, the assumptions about women—that they manipulate men with their bodies—are typical.

In an era when the idea that women want to be raped should be obsolete, rap lyrics and videos presuppose that women always desire sex, whether they know it or not. In Bell Biv DeVoe's rap-influenced pop hit single "Poison," for instance, a beautiful girl is considered poison because she does not respond affirmatively and automatically to a sexual proposition.

bell hooks, author of *Yearning: Race, Gender, Cultural Politics* (Southend, 1990), sees the roots of rap as a youth rebellion against all attempts to control black masculinity, both in the streets and in the home. "That rap would be anti-domesticity and in the process anti-female should come as no surprise," Ms. hooks says.

At present there is only a small platform for black women to address the problems of sexism in rap and in their community. Feminist criticism, like many other forms of social analysis, is widely considered part of a hostile white culture. For a black feminist to chastise misogyny in rap publicly would be viewed as divisive and counterproductive. There is a widespread perception in the black community that public criticism of black men constitutes collaborating with a racist society.

The charge is hardly new. Such a reaction greeted Ntozake Shange's play *for Colored Girls Who Have Considered Suicide When the Rainbow Is Enuf*, my own essays, "Black Macho and the Myth of the Superwoman," and Alice Walker's novel *The Color Purple*, all of which were perceived as critical of black men. After the release of the film version of *The Color Purple*, feminists were lambasted in the press for their supposed lack of support for black men; such critical analysis by black women has all but disappeared. In its place is *A Black Man's Guide to the Black Women*, a vanity-press book by Shahrazad Ali, which has sold more than 80,000 copies by insisting that black women are neurotic, insecure and competitive with black men.

Though misogynist lyrics seem to represent the opposite of Ms. Ali's world view, these are, in fact, just two extremes on the same theme: Ms. Ali's prescription for what ails the black community is that women should not question men about their sexual philandering, and should be firmly slapped across the mouth when they do. Rap lyrics suggest just about the same: women should be silent and prone.

There are those who have wrongly advocated censorship of rap's more sexually explicit lyrics, and those who have excused the misogyny because of its basis in black oral traditions.

Rap is rooted not only in the blaxploitation films of the 60's but also in an equally sexist tradition of black comedy. In the use of four-letter words and explicit sexual references, both Richard Pryor and Eddie Murphy, who themselves drew upon earlier examples of Redd Foxx, Pigmeat Markham, and Moms Mabley, are conscious reference points for the 2 Live Crew. Black comedy, in turn, draws on an oral tradition in which black men trade "toasts," stories in which dangerous bagmen and trickster figures like Stakolee and Dolomite sexually exploit women and promote violence among men. The popular rapper Ice Cube, in the album *Amerikkka's Most Wanted*, is Stakolee come to life. In "The Nigga Ya Love to Hate," he projects an image of himself as a criminal as dangerous to women as the straight white world.

Rap remains almost completely dominated by black males and this mind-set. Although women have been involved in rap since at least the mid-80's, record companies have only recently begun to promote them. And as women rappers like Salt-n-Pepa, Monie Love, M.C. Lyte, L.A. Star and Queen Latifah slowly gain more visibility, rap's sexism may emerge as a subject for scrutiny. Indeed, the answer may lie with women, expressing in lyrics and videos the tensions between the sexes in the black community.

Today's women rappers range from a high ground that doesn't challenge male rap on its own level (Queen Latifah) to those who subscribe to the same sexual high jinks as male rappers (Oaktown's 3.5.7). M.C. Hammer launched Oaktown's 3.5.7., made the worst case scenario: their skimpy, skintight leopard costumes in the video of "Wild and Loose (We Like It)" suggest an exotic animalistic sexuality. Their clothes fall to their ankles. They take bubble baths. Clearly, their bodies are more important than rapping. And in a field in which writing one's own rap is crucial, their lyrics are written by their former boss, M.C. Hammer.

Most women rappers constitute the middle ground: they talk of romance, narcissism and parties. On the other hand, Salt-n-Pepa on "Shake Your Thang" uses the structure of the 1969 Isley Brothers song "It's Your Thang" to insert a protofeminist rap response: "Don't try to tell me how to party. It's my dance and it's my body." M.C. Lyte, in a dialogue with Positive K on "I'm Not Havin' It," comes down hard on the notion that women can't say no and criticizes the shallowness of male rap.

2.4

This is a harsh comparison. Is this criticism fair? *Maybe not, more female rappers these days but problem still exists in SOME areas of rap.*

She's against misogyny in rap lyrics but is also against censorship.

The paragraph of examples below expands this point to include comedy and then offers several examples as evidence. *She uses this pattern a lot in her argument.*

How much has this situation changed since the 1990s? *How many female rappers can I think of promoted by record companies? Nikki Minaj, Iggy Azalea, anyone else?*

Women rappers need to correct these impressions rather than waiting for men to do it.

Some women rappers are doing their own thing entirely while others are doing the same things as men with the same bad effects.

Seems to suggest that not writing lyrics means their bodies are all they add. *What about taking ownership of their bodies? Sexuality as empowerment? What is the difference between being exploited and being empowered?*

Queen Latifah introduces her video, "Ladies First," performed with English rapper Monie Love, with photographs of black political heroines like Winnie Mandela, Sojourner Truth, Harriet Tubman and Angela Davis. With a sound that resembles scat as much as rap, Queen Latifah chants "Stereotypes they got to go" against a backdrop of newsreel footage of the apartheid struggle in South Africa. The politically sophisticated Queen Latifah seems worlds apart from the adolescent, buffoonish sex orientation of most rap. In general, women rappers seem so much more grown up. Can they inspire a more beneficial attitude toward sex in rap? What won't subvert rap's sexism is the actions of men; what will is women speaking in their own voice, not just in artificial female ghettos, but with and to men.

Scat? Kind of jazz singing where the voice mimics an instrument.

She supports this point about women being "more grown up" than male rappers with lots of examples and seems hopeful that women can work to change the sexist attitudes in rap after all.

[1] Originally appeared in *The New York Times*, July 29, 1990.

Once you finish your Phase 3 reading, you can start drawing conclusions about the author's argument and where her argument succeeds and fails. As you read, you may have found yourself agreeing or disagreeing with Michele Wallace at different points. Returning to your annotations may help you identify specific strategies—like Wallace's use of examples from other forms of entertainment like comedy—that seemed to work (or not) for you as a reader. You should also be able to locate patterns in *how* she makes her argument. For more on analyzing how arguments are constructed, see Chapter 9 on Rhetorical Analysis.

In many cases, you may find yourself reading several different articles for a particular class where the authors seem to be engaging in a conversation with one another. For example, the previous selection could be excerpted in a text that offers a variety of perspectives on rap music and its impacts on society across time. Understanding an author's main points as well as his or her overarching argument will allow you to engage in the conversation as well, agreeing with some points and disagreeing or seeking more clarity on others.

2.5 Reviewing for Analysis

Once you have performed your close reading of a text, you should review your notes in order to move toward some initial claims. This section offers a few different strategies for organizing your notes during or after your initial readings.

The Observations/Inferences Chart

By Carie Schneider

The observations/inferences chart is a simple method for organizing your thoughts and annotations. It can also help you construct a thesis for a textual analysis assignment. First, look at your notes from your reading. Focus on the techniques, features, or images that you immediately notice. These should be actual observations that are physically present in the text, which no reasonable person would disagree with—things like "he uses repetition," "lots of metaphors," "there are two characters in the frame." These are observations from your Phase 2 reading. Then go back through your observations and try to figure out what each of these features could mean, signify, symbolize, or represent. These can be whatever comes to mind. They do not have to be provable; they are just whatever you infer from the features you noticed. These may come from your Phase 3 reading. List these under the "Inferences" column.

Following is an example observations/inferences chart for a visual analysis of two panels from a comic composed by Ryan Winet (the full comic can be found in Chapter 9). The first five observations in the chart relate to the first panel.

Panel One:

Panel Four:

Artwork courtesy of Ryan Winet

Observations	Inferences
Swinging door, barrel, wood construction	Swinging door reminds me of saloons in Western movies. Seems like this might be a "Western"
There are two characters facing each other with hands at their sides	If this is a Western, there will probably be a duel
Character on the left has dark hair, a crooked nose, and bandolier	These characteristics seem to imply the "bad guy"
Character on the right has lighter hair and wears a cowboy hat and cravat (neckband)	The standard cowboy outfit leads to a "good guy" association. The cravat reminds me of the Boy Scouts. Is this an American association with courage or "good"?
Text in a box highlighted by a colored background	The background of the text box means the text is not part of the scene. Is there some kind of narrator? The font is an interesting choice, too—it looks playful like Comic Sans which doesn't seem to fit a Western. Why might this be?
Crooked-nose character appears juxtaposed with the word "BANG!"; same shape coming from his gun and the cowboy's hand	It's a gunfight. The artist shows motion by using words and images
Both characters have their mouths open	There are no words printed, but it looks like they might both be screaming. One out of anger and the other from pain or fear?

For more tips on close reading and organizing your ideas, see *Rules for Writers*, section 1b.

After reading the entire cartoon and completing an observations/inferences chart, you need to organize your thoughts even further to move toward a thesis statement by grouping the techniques or features ("observations") into categories and trying to decide what the overall message or meaning of the text is.

Looking back at the sample chart, it seems that some of the main categories of features could be "composition" or "character depictions," "juxtaposition," and maybe "symbolism." These categories could be body paragraph topics, and the order of these can be changed during the writing and revision process.

Practice Observations and Inferences

Take a look at a text from *Writing as Revision* or one assigned by your instructor and fill in the observations/inferences chart below. Then, as in the example in this section, identify some main features or patterns and begin to make claims.

Observations	Inferences

Craft Box: **INVENTION**

2.5

Idea Mapping

Idea mapping, also called webbing or clustering, visually represents how the ideas in a text are related to both the main point(s) and each other. An idea map emphasizes the interconnectedness of ideas and can reveal different information than a traditional written outline. Notice that the map below shows how different parts of Crane's story relate to each other.

You can use the web or cluster to review your reading and make initial claims by following various paths represented in the map. Based on the example diagram, you could create an outline by filling in the connections between the circled ideas. Many of the words in the following paragraph are the same words that are circled in the cluster, showing one way you might incorporate these ideas into a more linear prose format:

"The Snake" is about a contest of will. The story examines the will to fight and the will to survive. The story shows how the contest of will is motivated or complicated by instinct and emotions like rage and fear, and how this contest of will is tied to human history. It also has more social or political connections like war. There is clearly a contest between humans and animals in the story, but where does the dog fit in? Rover seems more aligned with the man than the snake. What does this say about history and evolution? Everything is brought together in an act of violence when the man kills the snake.

On a separate piece of paper, try making an idea map of one of your assigned readings for this or another class.

Idea Map of Stephen Crane's "The Snake"

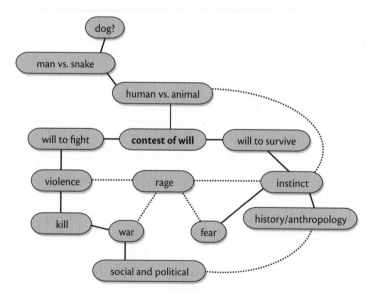

Next, you will have to figure out what the text means; you will need to interpret the overall message for the reader. Based on the notes in the sample chart, we can start to come up with some ideas. For example, one might use the inferences about the characters to argue that the Western genre relies heavily on stereotypes. Or maybe the juxtaposition of playful font and violence is suggesting something about depictions of violence in popular media.

As long as you can back up your thesis with strong evidence from the text, you have a lot of freedom in terms of what you would like to argue about this particular cartoon. See Chapter 9 for the full cartoon and further strategies for analysis.

See section 7.1 for specific strategies used in textual analysis. See Chapter 9 for examples of rhetorical strategies.

Sketching, Drawing, and Other Visualizations

There are other techniques for organizing your notes and making meaning besides writing words on a page. English professor Patricia A. Dunn suggests that the act of drawing, like writing, can help readers to make sense of texts and even find new meaning or see texts from a new perspective (138). After you annotate a text, it may be helpful to create a visual representation sketched by hand or by using the drawing function on a computer program like Microsoft Word or PowerPoint. The aesthetic value is not important, so stick figures, graphs, Venn diagrams, or any other method that works for you can be effective.

You may want to try this instead of, or in addition to, other organizational tools. Try it now by quickly sketching a representation of a reading assignment.

Some potential ideas:

- After reading an argumentative piece (as found in section 2.4), you can sketch "how it is" according to the writer, and then "how it could be."

- You might want to draw a storyboard or comic strip of a narrative (like "The Snake" in section 2.2). What plot elements or details make it to your drawings? Why might they be significant?

- When comparing multiple texts, try to show both how they are alike and how they are different.

Take time to discuss your visualizations with a classmate or in a small group. You can use your drawing as support for your explanation of the text, and you can also use the opportunity to ask for clarification about your peer's work. What are some similarities or differences in your depictions? Think about how other people's visualizations can support or complicate your impression of the text.

2.5

Section Summaries

Summaries can help you map the development of a text so you can see where it is going and how it gets there. For example, if you are writing an analysis of an academic journal article and your entire paper depends on your understanding of it, you may want to create thorough summaries of each section or paragraph that highlight the author's main points and the ways in which those points are supported. This summary would also be important when reading a short story or novel because understanding narrative structure is a crucial step to writing about literature.

A section **summary** can be as simple as a short description of each paragraph. The main advantage of section summaries is that they are quick to construct, especially if you have already annotated the text. When creating a section summary, you should accurately describe the main ideas in a portion of the text. Focus on larger themes rather than specific textual strategies and try to **paraphrase** the author in your own words.

Practice below by creating section summaries of the first three paragraphs of one of your assigned readings.

Section Summary Practice
Paragraph 1:
Paragraph 2:
Paragraph 3:

Toward Creating and Demonstrating Knowledge

In this chapter, you practiced the three phases of close reading: Pre-Reading, Active Reading, and Directed Reading. All of these phases require that you pay close attention to language, form, structure, technique, themes, arguments, and other elements that help to make meaning. You will use these close-reading skills throughout your college career and beyond when asked to read, analyze, or construct texts like films, books, music, job descriptions, lab reports, business proposals, etc. In fact, we even close read and analyze people. In the next chapter, "Writing as a Process," you will find suggestions for how to create and demonstrate the knowledge gained in close reading through your own writing.

Works Cited

Crane, Stephen. "The Snake." *The Literature Network*. Jalic, n.d. Web. 16 Mar. 2008.

Dunn, Patricia A. *Talking, Sketching, Moving: Multiple Literacies in the Teaching of Writing*. Plymouth: Boynton/Cook, 2001. Print.

Wallace, Michele. "When Black Feminism Faces the Music, and the Music is Rap." *New York Times*. The New York Times Company, 29 Jul. 1990. Web. 14 Nov. 2011.

Williams, William Carlos. "Libertad! Igualdad! Fraternidad." *Al Que Quiere!: A Book of Poems*. Boston: The Four Seas Company, 1917.

2.5

Writing as a Process

3

3.1 Writing as a Process: An Overview

Writing can be a messy process. If you are like most writers, there are times when you will feel completely in control of your work and know exactly what you want to say and how you want to say it. When this happens, the process can be exhilarating. However, sometimes the opposite will happen: you will feel as if your work is not coming together the way you imagined it would, or it is not achieving the effect you wanted.

It is important to remember that the writing process is not necessarily linear; you will not always move smoothly from planning to drafting, then to revising and submission. Instead, writing is often much more recursive, meaning that the stages discussed in this chapter (and throughout this book) do not always go in order but are flexible and tend to overlap. For example, not all of your ideas will come to you in the invention stage. Even experienced writers do not arrive at all their ideas before they write. Writers often read or write to brainstorm, then read some more, talk to other people, begin drafting, decide to refocus, read some more, freewrite, write a new thesis statement, throw out huge sections of a paper and import new material, revise the new draft heavily, and finally edit and proofread.

See *Rules for Writers*, pages 1–39, for more information about the writing process.

CHAPTER 3

If you accept that the writing process is often messy, you may be more open to new ideas as you write and revise.

In this chapter, you will:

- Discover the kind of writing habits you tend to rely on.

- Learn strategies to help you generate topic ideas.

- Find ways to assess the **rhetorical situation** before you write.

- Learn how to focus your ideas by creating an outline.

- Read about drafting, including strategies for writing introductions, thesis statements, body paragraphs, and conclusions.

- Learn the basics of the revision process (which will be covered in more detail in Chapter 4).

Every writer's process is unique; this chapter, in addition to the assignment chapters (7–12), will help you discover your own writing process, recognize where you excel, and provide you with tools to overcome your difficulties.

3.2 Discovering Your Writing Process

Different writers often have distinct habits that dictate how they write. Dr. Lisa Ede, an English professor, identifies four types of writers in her book *Work in Progress: A Guide to Writing and Revising*. Keep in mind that you might fit into more than one category, or an entirely different one altogether.

- **Heavy Planners:** These writers "generally consider their ideas and plan their writing so carefully in their heads that their first drafts are often more like other writers' second or third drafts. As a consequence they often revise less intensively and frequently than other [writers]. Many [heavy planners] have disciplined themselves so that they can think about their writing in all sorts of places—on the subway, at work, in the garden pulling weeds, or in the car driving to and from school" (32).

- **Heavy Revisers:** These writers "need to find out what they want to say through the act of writing itself….Heavy revisers often state that writing their ideas out in a sustained spurt of activity reassures them that they have something to say and helps them avoid frustration. These writers may not seem to plan because they begin drafting so early. Actually, however, their planning occurs as they draft and especially as they revise. Heavy revisers typically spend a great deal of their writing time revising their initial drafts. To do so effectively, they must be able to read their work critically and be able…to discard substantial portions of the first draft" (32–33).

- **Sequential Composers:** These writers "devote roughly equal amounts of time to planning, drafting, and revising….[S]equential composers typically rely on written notes and plans to give shape and force to their ideas. And unlike heavy revisers, sequential composers need to have greater control over form and subject matter as they draft" (33). These writers often slowly work through paragraph after paragraph, rereading and revising as they draft, working from outlines, and planning ahead.

- **Procrastinators:** Although we all occasionally procrastinate, the group Ede labels as procrastinators are people who habitually delay writing anything until they write a final draft. They might wait until the night before the paper is due to begin; therefore, they only have time to create one draft and possibly proofread it before handing it in (36). Procrastinators may justify their process by claiming that they work well under pressure, but they have rarely explored alternative approaches.

It is not important to pinpoint exactly what kind of writer you are, but rather to recognize your general tendencies and consider the advantages and disadvantages of your approach. For example, if you know you are mostly a heavy planner or a heavy reviser, you can look more carefully at the specific writing strategies suggested in those areas to expand your approach to planning or revising. In addition, you can deliberately work to develop new writing strategies. That way, if your usual method ever fails you, you will have another option to help you proceed.

Thinking about Your Own Writing Process

Use these questions to reflect on your own writing process.

- What type(s) of writer do you consider yourself to be?

- Does your writing process seem to be successful? What are the strengths and weaknesses of your approach?

- Does your writing process include several of the above approaches? If so, which ones?

- Do you think it might be beneficial for you to try a different approach? Why or why not?

3.2

Craft Box: REFLECTION

See section 1a in *Rules for Writers* for more on audience, purpose, and context.

See Chapter 9 for further discussion of the rhetorical situation.

3.3 Understanding the Rhetorical Situation

Throughout the writing process, it is important to consider the rhetorical situation of your essay. The rhetorical situation includes the **purpose**, **audience**, and **context** surrounding your work. Assessing the rhetorical situation is something you should do every time you write because having a good understanding of why you are writing and who you are writing for will help you choose the most effective language, evidence, and medium for your work. See Chapter 4 for an extended discussion of how understanding the rhetorical situation can help you with the revision process.

Defining Your Purpose for Writing

The purpose of your writing is the reason you are writing and what you hope to accomplish through writing. Your purpose might be defined by your professor, so you'll want to consider the assignment guidelines carefully. What are you trying to do, or what are you expected to do in this assignment?

Clearly defining your purpose for writing is essential because it largely determines other decisions you make in your writing process. When you have a concrete understanding of your purpose, you can better consider what to include in your draft, how you might incorporate it, and what you might want to leave out. For example, imagine that you are writing a persuasive essay arguing that medical doctors should be more open-minded about treating the common cold using alternative medicines, like herbs (Echinacea), vitamins (Vitamin C), and minerals (zinc lozenges). If you decide your purpose is to influence Western doctors who do not often rely on herbal remedies, you might write your essay as an editorial to doctors in *The New England Journal of Medicine*, using evidence that a medical audience would find most convincing such as scientific studies. On the other hand, imagine that you want to refute an opinion cited in a *New York Times* article criticizing the "guru" of alternative medicine, Dr. Andrew Weil, and his treatments of the common cold. In this case, you might choose other persuasive strategies to make your point: perhaps you tell a personal story of how Weil's treatments helped you, or you might show evidence of how effective alternative medicine can be by citing case studies and statistics about the recovery times of those who are using these treatments.

As these examples show, the purpose will influence how you approach your topic, the kinds of evidence you will use, and even the form that your argument will take.

To identify your purpose for writing, consider the following:

- What do I want to accomplish with this text?

- What do I want people to do, consider, or believe when they read my work?

- If writing for a class assignment, has my instructor already assigned a purpose for me to try to achieve? If so, what do I need to do to meet these expectations?

Identifying Your Audience

Audience plays a key role in the writing process. Even in essays you write for specific college classes, satisfying your audience is usually more complicated than simply writing to your instructor. Often, your instructor will tell you to consider a specific audience, or your instructor may ask you to identify an audience for your work. When you consider audience, you will begin to consider how complex rhetorical situations are—even down to the choice of words you use. Look at how the following sentence could be altered based on your assessment of the audience:

For an American audience: Canadian Prime Minister Stephen Harper met with Mexican President Enrique Peña Nieto last week.

For a Canadian audience: Prime Minister Harper met with Mexican President Enrique Peña Nieto last week.

For a Mexican audience in an English publication: Canadian Prime Minister Stephen Harper met with President Peña Nieto last week.

When you write, it is critical to consider carefully who your readers are and what assumptions and expectations they may have. Identify your audience and assess their needs by asking yourself:

See section 9.1 in the *Guide* for more discussion of audience, context, and purpose.

- Who am I writing for? (Remember to keep your instructor's guidelines in mind.) What are the audience's beliefs and assumptions?

- What position might they take on this issue? How will I need to respond to this position?

- What will they want to know?

- How might they react to my argument?

- How am I trying to relate to or connect with my audience?

- Are there specific words, ideas, or modes of presentation that will help me relate to them in this way?

Remember, of course, that while answering these questions is important, you want to avoid making broad generalizations about your audience as a group. This is one reason why it is helpful to narrow your audience—if you have a smaller group to analyze, it is easier to say what may or may not be important to all or most of the members of this group.

Understanding the Context

Imagine you want to ask your supervisor at work for extra hours to help pay your tuition. Now put yourself in the following two contexts:

- You have never been late to work and were recently selected as Employee of the Month.

- You have shown up late for your last three shifts and you missed two days of work last month.

3.3

In both cases, you would have to be able to explain clearly why you deserve a raise beyond simply saying, "I'd like more money." You would also want to consider the history of your relationship with your supervisor. Because the two contexts are different, the same audience (your supervisor) basically becomes two different people in each situation: a pleased supervisor in one case and an extremely irritated supervisor in the other. The way you would approach your supervisor—or even whether or not you decide to approach her or him in the first place—would be based on your assessment of the context.

When writing for class, you should also consider the context and how it can shape and guide your writing. The context of your writing includes the purpose and audience, but it also includes the immediate situation in which you are writing (writing for a class assignment, writing for a job application, writing a letter to your congress representative) and the surrounding cultural or historical situations that might impact why, how, and to whom you are writing. Imagine that you have chosen to analyze Jonathan Swift's essay "A Modest Proposal." In the class discussion of the essay, it becomes apparent that your classmates generally found his humor and sarcasm to be entertaining. While this is not an argument in itself, taking your classmates' comments as inspiration can help you formulate an essay topic. Keeping the audience and context of the class in mind, you might consider arguing for whether or not the humor and sarcasm are productive or counter-productive to Swift's argument. Compare these two thesis statements:

- "The humor and sarcasm are not only entertaining for the reader but also crucial to the persuasiveness of Swift's essay."

- "Although the humor and sarcasm in Swift's essay are entertaining, such tactics may undermine the significance of the overall argument being made."

Two different arguments are being made, and both are being shaped by the same context—in this case, the awareness that most readers generally appreciate the humor and sarcasm in Swift's essay.

The following questions can help you identify the context in which you are writing and analyze how that context might affect your writing:

- What genre are you working within? Are you writing an academic essay, creating a brochure, or filming a documentary? What genre conventions can you identify and how might they affect your writing? What does your audience expect from this genre?

- Are there any particular historical events that might impact how your audience perceives your argument or the kind of background information or evidence you need to include?

- Who else is talking about this topic? Have you heard about it in the news? On campus? In a particular academic field? How might other points of view on the topic affect how your writing functions at this time and place?

- Imagine your audience at the moment they receive your work. What factors would help make this a positive experience? Think about how you can produce that experience in your writing.

Answering these questions about context may lead you to add to or reconsider your understanding of the audience.

3.4 Invention

The process of writing begins before you type words on a page, a stage of the writing process often called invention or prewriting. Since a lot of this activity might go on in your head, pay attention to your ongoing thoughts about your topic and jot them down so that you remember them when you sit down to work on your draft.

Invention also happens as you are drafting. Sometimes a word or sentence that you create will spark a new idea. You will probably find yourself "inventing" all the way through the writing process, so don't be alarmed if your final essay or project looks much different than you originally planned.

Invention includes:

- thinking about the rhetorical situation
- exploring possible topics to write about
- choosing a topic
- generating ideas about the topic
- researching the topic
- locating evidence
- outlining or planning the essay

Depending on the type of essay you are writing and the kind of writer you are, one or more of these steps might not be part of your invention process. For example, if your instructor gives you a topic to write about, you will not need to choose the topic. If you are writing a personal, reflective essay, you might not need to do research. If you are more of a visual planner, you may want to draw an idea map or a storyboard rather than writing an outline.

Generating Ideas about Your Topic

After a preliminary assessment of the rhetorical situation, you need to start generating ideas about your topic, purpose, audience, and organization. Here are some strategies many experienced writers use to generate ideas:

See section 1b in *Rules for Writers* for prewriting techniques.

See the chart on page 5 in *Rules for Writers* for ways to narrow a subject to a topic.

3.4

1. **Journal responses** are great for getting ideas on paper. Your instructor might assign specific journal prompts to help you find a topic or a focus for an essay. In your journals, always aim to:

   - Record your responses to assigned readings. For this purpose, you might pick passages from the readings that spark your interest, quote them, and discuss why they seem important.

   - Write down memories, observations, and passing thoughts that are relevant to your writing assignments. Many writers find that jotting down their random thoughts on a topic helps them get through this often intimidating stage in the writing process.

   If you write your thoughts in your journal throughout the semester, you can leaf through it as you search for a point of entry into an analysis of a text or use it to help you define the issues you find compelling enough to explore further in an essay.

2. **Freewriting** is designed to help you by turning off the critical editor in your head that can cause writer's block. To freewrite, set a time limit—say five to fifteen minutes—and write for that entire period.

   When you freewrite:

   - Do not worry about your spelling or grammar.

   - Do not pause—barely lift your pen from the paper or your fingers from the keyboard.

   - Do not reread until you have finished.

   Try freewriting as you develop ideas for an assignment, any time you cannot figure out what comes next, or any time you need to clarify an explanation or illustration you are having trouble getting just right. If you hit this kind of block, try freewriting on a separate piece of paper or on a new screen so that you will not feel like you need to keep what you have written.

3. **Looping** is a variation of freewriting. You review what you have produced in a freewriting exercise, circle some phrases or words that interest you, and use them as the starting point for another round of freewriting.

4. **Brainstorming** is similar to looping and freewriting, but instead of writing in complete sentences, you list any idea that comes to mind. As with freewriting and looping, you need to remain open to all possibilities as you create a list of possible topics. The main thing here is not to criticize your ideas while constructing your list. Instead, push yourself to write as many ideas as possible. As you get closer to preparing your first draft, you may find that ideas you had previously discarded seem more viable, or you may find a way to combine aspects of two or more ideas.

5. **Talking about your ideas** is a useful invention strategy. It is especially effective in helping you deal with a blank page. Often you think of an idea in your head over and over again, but you just do not know how to put it on paper. When this happens, you might want to talk about it with imagined readers or your instructor, classmates, or any friend who is willing to listen. Take notes during and after this conversation to make sure that you do not lose your ideas when it comes time to write.

6. **Clustering**—also called **idea mapping** or webbing—is a visual invention technique that involves the following steps:

   - Place a key word at the center of a piece of paper and circle it.

   - Begin to make conceptual connections by adding new words, circling them, and drawing lines between them and the original key word. As you draw visual links among related ideas, consider what idea or fact links those ideas, and write down terms or details that form those links.

   - Continue attaching words and phrases to any of the circles on the diagram.

When you are done, your page will look like a web filled with bubbles. Your webbing will represent a map of the concepts and relations that are important to your topic. This conceptual mapping can be useful if you are a visual learner who sometimes gets lost trying to find the right word for an idea. After clustering, you will have some important ideas written down and you will be able to better articulate the connections among those ideas.

> See the Craft Box on page 32 for more on idea maps.

Web that Explores Online College Classes

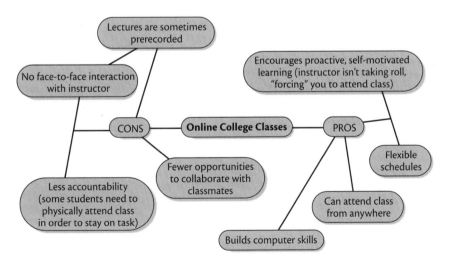

7. **Asking key questions** is a common technique that a reporter might use when investigating a story. These questions include the five Ws that enable a journalist to get the crucial details for a story: *who, what, when, where,* and *why*. A reporter may then ask a sixth question to deepen his or her sense of what happened: *how* did the event occur? Using these questions will help you consider a topic from various angles. For example, consider how the following basic questions might apply to texts such as the *Harry Potter* novels:

   a. **Who** is the author? Who are the main characters? Who are the primary and secondary audiences? Who might have influenced J.K. Rowling's writing of this series?

   b. **What** are the important plot points? What happens to the main character? What happened to the author before, during, and after writing the series?

   c. **When** did Rowling write the first novel? When does it take place? Are there historical connections with events and themes during the time the novel was written and during the time the novel is set?

   d. **Where** do the novels take place and what do we learn by comparing and contrasting the different settings? Why did the author choose these locations?

   e. **Why** does Harry take such risks against his powerful enemies? Why do some people identify with his character while others find him annoying?

   f. **How** does Rowling generate specific emotional reactions, such as fear and sympathy? How does the series reflect the cultural characteristics of the time in which the novels were written? How do the novels invite us to reflect on social issues such as inequalities of race, class, and gender?

As you can see, these questions move from basic description to analysis. You could use the same technique with topics as diverse as stem-cell research or restrictions on streetlights in Tucson.

See section 1d in *Rules for Writers* for more on formal and informal outlines.

8. **Outlining** is another strategy many writers use to bridge the ideas they have generated and the draft they are going to write. An outline will help you organize all your relevant thoughts, allowing you to reconsider some of your points and dismiss irrelevant ones even before you write a first draft. Outlines can also be helpful later in the writing process as a way to rethink the organization of your essay before revising. Traditionally, an outline looks like a book's table of contents and includes brief points that describe each part of an essay. On the next page, you will find a sample outline for an analysis essay. This is not the only way to outline an essay, but it is a good starting point if you are new to outlining or if this is the first analysis essay you have written.

EXAMPLE OF AN ANALYSIS ESSAY OUTLINE

Introduction

- Draw readers into the essay. See the "Tips for Writing Introductions" Tips & Strategies Box in this chapter for some ideas about introductions.

- Introduce the text—selectively summarize important points and explain their significance.

- State your **thesis** and forecast (what your essay will argue and how you will prove it).

Body Paragraphs

- **Point** → Your **topic sentence**. Make your first claim in one concise sentence. You might include a transition sentence that connects your first point to your overall thesis to help guide the reader through your thought process, but this is not always necessary.

- **Illustration** → Give examples (otherwise known as evidence) that show how you reached your point. You might do this by citing the primary text, bringing in secondary sources, or consulting other outside material.

- **Explanation** → Support your reading of the text by explaining how the examples you chose to include specifically address the issues from your thesis. Repeat "Illustration" and "Explanation" as many times as needed to discuss all the examples you include in each paragraph.

Repeat Body Paragraph format as many times as needed.

Conclusion

- Connect your thesis and main points to a broader analytical standpoint.

- Leave your readers thinking about your topic in an interesting or unique way.

See the "Tips for Writing Introductions" Tips & Strategies Box on page 52 in this chapter for some ideas about introductions.

See the "Tips for Writing Conclusions" Tips & Strategies Box on page 56 in this chapter for more ideas on concluding your essay.

Keep in mind that the points you outline, the organizational structure, and the content of the paper all depend on the type of assignment requirements given by your instructor. Writing instructors might have different perspectives on how you should approach the writing assignment and might emphasize different elements such as content, organization, or voice. Always keep your assignment parameters in mind as you construct your outline to ensure that you are meeting the basic goals for the assignment.

3.4

3.4

What to Do with Writer's Block

Anne Lamott, the author of a writer's guide called *Bird by Bird*, reminds us that all writers—even professional ones—have to get through the process of writing a first draft. While the blank page can be liberating for some writers, for others it is terrifying. Even if you have done excellent brainstorming and outlining, you still might come to the blank page with some anxiety and uncertainty about where to actually begin writing. What, then, can you do if you are faced with a case of the dreaded writer's block? If you are stuck, consider these time-tested suggestions for helping you rebuild your momentum:

Remove distractions. You might find that you can do your best work when you unplug the internet or turn off the television. Stopping your train of thought to check Facebook or Twitter, even just for a minute, can be particularly distracting.

Change your routine or surroundings. If you typically write at night, try writing first thing in the morning. Conversely, if you typically write in your dorm room, try visiting a local coffee shop or the library. You might be surprised at what a simple change of scenery can do for your creative energy!

Take some time to relax. If you have been working for hours, take a few minutes to give your eyes and brain a break. Go for a walk. Drink a cup of coffee. Have a snack. Call someone to chat about something else. Sometimes starting an essay is like waiting for water to boil; it feels like it takes all day if you stare at the pot, but the second you walk away everything bursts to the surface.

Lower your standards at the beginning and raise them again later. If you are worried about creating a masterpiece, let go of that thought until you start revising later on. Likewise, try not to focus on how much more you have left to write. Focus on completing the assignment one paragraph or one sentence at a time and worry about making it shine after you have got a draft on paper.

Visit your instructor's office hours. Remember, your instructor is here to help you succeed and will welcome you to his or her office hours.

Visit the Think Tank Writing Center. As writing specialists, the tutors' job is to help you work through your difficulties with writing. Schedule a session with a tutor and talk through your anxieties and concerns, and remember that it is never too early to go to the Writing Center. The tutors are happy to help at any stage of the writing process.

Take out a piece of paper, write down all of your frustrations about writing, and then tear it up and throw it away. The act of physically tossing out your frustrations can be a highly effective strategy for letting go of your worries and frustrations.

Whichever strategies you decide to try, remember that writer's block is simply a state of mind—not a real affliction. Try a number of these strategies to help get your fingers typing again. Whichever method you find best works for you, just remember: it is all about getting back to the business of writing.

3.5 Drafting

Most experienced writers know that their writing will go through multiple drafts before they can consider it "finished." Still, drafting can also feel like the most productive part of the writing process because it is the stage in which you are transforming your ideas to words on paper.

Regardless of your writing habits, remain flexible as you write because your ideas will often evolve. Give yourself time and permission to rework earlier sections if halfway through writing you discover a better approach.

Drafting a Thesis Statement

The thesis statement defines the writer's central idea in the essay. Some writers like to think of the thesis statement as a sort of contract with their readers; as a writer, you are making a promise to readers that the paper they are going to read is about what the thesis says it is about. The writer presents readers with the basic argument through the thesis.

Be open to the idea that you might change your mind about the direction of your thesis as you write and revise. You might need to narrow the thesis because you have too much information to include in the space you have available, or you might change your focus altogether. Some writers may end up writing a thesis after they have completed a draft and then use the thesis to help focus a later draft. Modifying your thesis is a normal part of writing, but you might need to discuss the change with your instructor, depending on how close you are to the final deadline. Keep in mind that if you cannot identify the main idea of your essay, it is likely that your readers will have the same difficulty.

To check the effectiveness of your thesis statement, English professors Toby Fulwiler and Alan R. Hayakawa suggest that you think about the following questions:

- **Is it interesting?** A thesis should answer a question that is worth asking and is unique to your individual interpretation of the text. For example, you might ask:

  What strategies does Axe Body Spray use to sell its products to young men? or

  In Amy Tan's essay "Mother Tongue," what does the relationship between the narrator and her mother reveal about those characters' society and environment?

- **Is it precise and specific?** You can sharpen your understanding of the thesis by stating what the issue is exactly as you see it. For instance, consider how much more effective it might be to argue that mountain bikes should have more access to specific wilderness trails rather than to argue that they should have more access to the wilderness in general. Often you can make a thesis more specific by introducing qualifications that acknowledge your readers' concerns.

See section 2a in *Rules for Writers* for more about drafting an introduction with a thesis.

See pages 142, 170, and 239 of the *Guide* for more ideas on how to draft a thesis statement.

See section 2a in *Rules for Writers* for strategies that help with revising weak thesis statements.

See the box on "Testing a working thesis" on page 19 in *Rules for Writers*.

3.5

Making Weak Thesis Statements Stronger

Use the questions from Fulwiler and Hayakawa in the "Drafting a Thesis Statement" section to evaluate the following sample thesis statements. Then decide what you could do to improve them and write a revised thesis underneath each one:

1. Hemingway's story "A Clean, Well-Lighted Place" serves as a metaphor for old age.

2. Television news presents an exaggerated view of violence in today's society.

3. "The Yellow Wallpaper," by Charlotte Perkins Gilman, challenges patriarchy.

4. These three Westerns prove that the Western movie is a genre.

5. Panda Express, one of the restaurants located in the Student Union, effectively portrays the idea that consumers want options because it openly displays its food for the public.

6. The presidential debate spurred a lively discussion across many political blogs this week.

7. Skim one of the essays in Chapter 13, identify the thesis statement, and copy it below. After carefully reviewing the essay, try answering the following questions:

    *   What does the thesis statement do well?

    *   What could you do to improve it?

    *   Revise the thesis statement so that it more clearly states the argument.

3.5

- **Is it manageable?** During the invention and prewriting stages, you probably collected more information than you can actually write about. Take this opportunity to narrow both the thesis and the paper you expect to write by narrowing the scope of your thesis statement or by adding qualifiers that specify what sorts of cases you are considering.

- **Does it adequately reflect your reading and the expected shape of your paper?** Your thesis should connect your central idea to all of the examples and evidence that you collected. Instead of ignoring facts or examples that complicate your claim, you should revise your thesis to better encompass that information.

Paragraph Development

Paragraph breaks are important because they signal to readers where one idea ends and another begins. A single body paragraph should have a single main idea. You have likely been taught that each body paragraph needs a topic sentence (one sentence that states the main point of the paragraph), solid illustrations, and compelling explanations. In your first-year writing classes, your instructors will likely refer to this structure as the PIE structure.

> See section 4a in *Rules for Writers* for a discussion of topic sentences.

PIE (Point, Illustration, Explanation) Structure: A Useful Way to Develop Paragraphs

PIE is an acronym for Point, Illustration, and Explanation. PIE is a helpful way to think about paragraph development, especially for analysis essays and persuasive arguments. The following section, created by former UA English Professor Anne-Marie Hall, discusses the important features of a PIE paragraph:

> See section 4 in *Rules for Writers* for more information on developing effective paragraphs.

PIE refers to the structure of well-written paragraphs where each individual paragraph fully covers a single point, including **illustrations** and explanation. In academic writing in particular, each paragraph should address only one point or single aspect of your argument. In some cases, it may take you more than one paragraph to fully develop a single point, but you never want to attempt to cover more than one point in a paragraph.

You may need to provide multiple illustrations or explanations to prove your point. Your paragraph structure might be more of a PIEIEIE. The PIE paragraph structure is just one type of paragraph. It happens to work well in analysis essays because it keeps ideas focused and emphasizes the importance of providing evidence and analysis in every paragraph.

3.5

Tips for Writing Introductions

By Adam Meehan

When a reader picks up your essay, the introduction is the first thing that he or she will read. It is important, then, for your introduction to make a good first impression. Of course, grabbing your reader's attention can be challenging as an introduction requires you to provide necessary context and to introduce your argument in a relatively small amount of space. As a result, your introduction needs to be intriguing, articulate, and precise.

Given that there are many different types of essays—such as analytical, argumentative, narrative, reflective—each introduction will be unique. Remember to keep your rhetorical situation in mind as you review these tips. You may find that you need to adapt your introduction for your purpose.

1. **Grab the reader's attention:**

    -   Begin your essay with a quotation that relates to your topic. A famous quote—or a quote from a famous person—may earn an important recognition from your reader and make him or her want to read further.

    -   Begin with an interesting/surprising fact or statistic. This strategy is used often in journalistic pieces; giving your readers a heavy dose of reality is a great way to get them interested.

    -   Relate a compelling anecdote. People are often drawn toward narratives. Just as a novelist or short story writer seeks to get you involved in a story, you can draw your readers into your essay by starting with an anecdote that piques their interest.

    -   Start with a rhetorical question. Opening with a question is a great way to get your readers interested in your topic. For example, asking your readers "Would you feel more or less safe if the person sitting next to you in class was carrying a concealed weapon?" is likely to make them examine their feelings on the subject, which will in turn make them want to keep reading your essay.

2. **Forecast the direction your essay will take.** While some writers choose to be more explicit with this information than others, you generally want your readers to get a sense for what your topic is, why it is important, and how you will go about discussing it.

    Here is an example of an implicit forecast:

    -   With the popularity of films like *Food, Inc.*, there is now an abundance of widely recognized evidence that the food industry in America should be reexamined. The problems that exist in the meat, agriculture, and food distribution industries suggest that, while the cost may be higher, eating organic food is ultimately better for the environment and for personal health.

    Here is an example of an explicit forecast:

    -   The popularity of films like *Food, Inc.* is evidence that many Americans are ready for major changes in the food industry. This paper will explore the problems that exist in the meat, agriculture, and food distribution industries. It will argue that, despite higher costs for consumers, eating organic food is better for the environment and for personal health.

3.5

As you can see, each example contains the same information and each provides a "road map" for the reader, which highlights the path that the essay will follow. The second example, however, is more explicit and uses phrases such as "This paper will explore" and "It will argue" to present the writer's plan for the essay.

3. **Include a thesis statement.** Every introduction should include a thesis statement that lays out your main argument. If your introduction consists of more than one paragraph, the thesis does not always have to appear in the first paragraph, but be sure it is somewhere in one of the introductory paragraphs.

4. **Avoid certain traps.** These traps may include—but are not limited to—the following:

   - *Vast Generalizations.* Bold, sweeping claims like "Since the beginning of time, humans have been searching for their place in the world" cannot be proven and do not contribute directly to your argument. While these assertions may appear to add a certain degree of importance or an "epic" quality to your paper, they are unoriginal and unsophisticated, causing readers to call into question your credibility as a writer.

   - *Introducing Evidence.* While it may sometimes be necessary to mention some component(s) of your argument—when roadmapping your argument, for example—you do not want to develop the content of your argument within the body of your introduction. One, the reader will not have the proper context to understand the evidence. Two, you will need to provide the evidence later anyway, so there's no need to repeat the same ideas in your essay.

   - *The Book Report.* Book reports tend to follow a certain formula: They introduce the writer and the text; they give a brief summary of the text; they list other interesting facts about the writer and/or text. Many students fall into the trap of using this formula in academic papers. Remember that your readers (your instructor and your classmates) have read the text in question, so an introduction that merely introduces and/or summarizes the main text or texts at hand shows a lack of audience awareness.

   - *Too Much Information.* Perhaps the most common trap is providing *too much* information. Often the anxiety over what to say in the introduction, along with the fear of not being able to meet the required page length or word count, causes students to add "fluff" or information that does not serve an important purpose. Be sure that each sentence in your introduction is *doing* something to convey a necessary piece of information. One way to determine what information is necessary is to go through each sentence in your introduction and ask yourself, "Do my readers really *need* this sentence?" and "Does this sentence actually make my essay stronger?" If the answer is "no," then consider cutting it.

3.5

Point

This is the topic sentence, and it should be among the first two or three sentences in any paragraph. It is one of the claims you have identified as supporting your essay's primary argument or thesis. Your essay should make a number of such supporting claims. Discussing this supporting claim should cover the whole paragraph—everything the paragraph does will relate to this point. Any information that does not go under this point belongs in a different paragraph. Remember: one paragraph, one point!

Illustration

This is the best evidence you have to support your paragraph's point. It is the part of the PIE that consists of necessary evidence such as another author's ideas and language, specific wording or images in a text, or your own personal experiences. You can provide such evidence in the form of direct quotations, paraphrases, summaries, observations, examples, and personal narratives, or a combination of these. You need to give your readers as much evidence as appropriate to demonstrate your point.

Explanation

This is where you explain how the illustration you have provided proves the point of your paragraph and relates to your overall argument and purpose. Without clearly discussing your reasoning, your point and illustration might feel disconnected, or your reader might interpret your point differently than you intended. You must convince readers that you understand your own point, how your illustration(s) support it, and how both relate to your essay's thesis.

Note that you can alternate between illustration and explanation several times within the same paragraph, as long as every illustration is explained. The second sample paragraph that follows demonstrates a PIEIE structure.

See Chapters 7 and 8 for more samples of PIE paragraphs.

The following excerpt is an example of how PIE works. Note how the explanations are the most substantial part of each paragraph:

> For the most part, the examples of writing by younger students are provided by Twain simply to make us laugh. **Twain reports that one student wrote, "The three departments of the government is the Present rules the world, the governor rules the State, and the mayor rules the city" (45). Another student wrote that "The first conscientious Congress met in Philadelphia" (Twain 45).** The first passage is humorous not only because it is a run-on sentence, but also because we know that the student meant to say that the president "rules" the United States, not the "world." The second passage is also worth a laugh because of a very obvious misunderstanding; the student used the word "conscientious" when he intended to use "Continental." In both cases, they are innocent errors, and Twain doesn't offer us much commentary.

A few lines down, however, Twain suggests that a mistake in a student's writing reveals some greater truth about American society. **One student writes that "The Constitution of the United States is that part of the book at the end which nobody reads" (Twain 45).** We can assume that the student was thinking of the word "index" or "appendix," but **Twain writes in response to this passage that "[t]ruth crushed to earth will rise again" (45).** Twain is suggesting that we might as well not read the Constitution because the rights granted by it are in name only, and not always a material reality. When he says that the truth will "rise again," he is perhaps arguing that society can only deceive itself for so long, that truth will eventually surface, even if it is in the most unlikely places, such as in the pages of a young student's notebook.

Remember, you must use in-text citations when referencing another author's work. Part of creating a PIE paragraph is integrating sources correctly. As you move from point to illustration, think about introducing who is speaking or what is happening in the example so that your reader can easily find your example in the original text and differentiate your ideas from the source material.

> See Chapter 5 for more on integrating sources.

Other Types of Paragraphs

Once you have practiced the PIE paragraph, your instructor may encourage you to experiment with other types of paragraphs. Other strategies you may have learned for developing paragraphs, including working through a definition, demonstrating cause and effect relationships, or discussing ideas using personal narrative, can work alongside PIE paragraphs. For example, introductions often take one of these other forms rather than a strict PIE format. The Tips & Strategies Box on pages 52–53 presents other potential formats.

Organization

The arrangement of ideas and the connections between them have a significant impact on the effectiveness of a text. Many of us are familiar with organizational methods for popular narratives: start with the introduction to characters, setting, and a problem, lead up to a climactic action, and then wind it all down to a satisfying conclusion. However, this organizational pattern does not necessarily work for all stories. You also probably won't find this format in academic texts, and it doesn't apply to most visual texts, either. So if there is no single, one-size-fits-all organizational method and your instructor does not have a specific structure in mind, how should you organize your writing?

The key to a "well-organized" text is that it is *purposeful* in its presentation of ideas and effective for the audience. You might want to think of the arrangement of your text as part of the **logos** of your argument. For example, the arrangement of the PIE paragraphs in the example above might not be effective if

3.5

the paragraphs were switched. The claim made in the first paragraph draws the reader in, and the claim in the second paragraph (the mistake reveals a "greater truth") is in direct contrast to the ideas from the first paragraph.

Tips for Writing Conclusions

One of the most important parts of your paper is the conclusion because it will contribute to the reader's final impression of your essay. You may have been taught to use the conclusion as a place to restate your thesis and introduction as a way of reminding readers of your main points. This may be appropriate in some contexts, but it also may suggest that the reader did not read the whole essay or understand the argument, which is generally not the case. A conclusion that simply repeats what the writer has already stated in the rest of the essay is not pulling its weight, so to speak, because it does little to contribute to the overall meaning of the essay. Here are some general tips for writing a conclusion, but also keep in mind that your rhetorical situation might call for a different kind of conclusion. Be mindful of your purpose, your audience, your assignment guidelines, and the context in which you are writing.

- **Answer the "So What?"**

  The conclusion can provide the larger significance of your essay, placing it in a wider context and showing how and why your argument matters in a larger sense. Some students have been cautioned against introducing new information in the conclusion, and this is certainly an important consideration. Nevertheless, it is possible to "open up" your essay at the end without including material unrelated to the rest of the essay, as long as you provide your reader with the connections between your essay's main argument and those larger issues.

- **Circle Back**

  The conclusion can return to an interesting example or story you have introduced in the essay, such as an anecdote from the introduction. If you rethink/reframe that story through the new knowledge you have offered in your essay, it brings the entire essay together.

- **Look Forward**

  Again, you generally should not start an entirely new argument in a conclusion, but it can be helpful to tell your readers what still needs to be done. For example, what new research is necessary to advance the issue you are discussing? What ideas do you have for resolving a controversy between sources? Where might the controversy be headed?

- **Paint a Picture**

  The conclusion can end with a forceful example or image that really drives your message home. Just as compelling examples can provide interesting starting points for essays, they can make for memorable conclusions that fix the point of your essay in your readers' minds.

- **Summarize Claims**

  The conclusion of an essay can simply restate your major arguments; although, if you choose this method, you will want to rephrase your main claims, rather than simply repeat them.

To construct a purposefully organized essay, consider the following questions about the placement of your sentences and paragraphs:

- Why is this idea, sentence, or paragraph in this particular position?

- How does each idea relate to the content before and after it?

- What happens to the argument or the momentum if this idea, sentence, or paragraph is moved?

- What will the audience expect to see here? Should I meet their expectations, or is there a reason for not doing so?

Notice how even the use of the word "however" in the sample PIE paragraphs signals a connection between the two paragraphs. Although we think of paragraphs as a way to present individual points, it is important to show readers how the points connect with each other. For this reason, a paragraph needs to relate to the paragraphs before and after it so that the essay moves smoothly from one idea to the next related idea. Sentences should also build upon each other and appear in a logical order. Effective transitions can help the reader understand how sentences and ideas relate to each other.

Consider these ways to create "flow" or connect ideas:

- Use transition words to connect related ideas or to shift from one topic to another. See the following Tips & Strategies Box for more on this technique.

- Forecast the content that will follow. Sometimes this might be written in the form of a concluding sentence in a paragraph that leads into the next idea.

- Use "pointing terms" such as "this" to help you move from an illustration to an explanation or from one idea to the next. For example, "this example shows" or "this idea is further complicated by…." Make sure to follow the word "this" with a noun so that your reader can clearly see your point of reference.

Sometimes your organizational options are limited by constraints such as assignment guidelines or genre conventions. For instance, in the **genre** of business letters, the audience will probably expect the body of the letter to begin with a greeting such as "Dear" or "To whom it may concern." Consider genre, your purpose, and your audience's expectations as you structure your writing.

See Chapter 11 for more on genre.

3.5

Here are some tips to evaluate the effectiveness of your overall organizational method:

- Do a "reverse outline." See the Tips & Strategies Box in Chapter 7 for more on this technique.

- Cut up your essay and rearrange the pieces. This is especially helpful if you are a visual or kinesthetic learner, or you feel stuck in an organizational pattern and can't find a way out.

- Read your essay aloud. Listen for the gaps, the places where you lose interest, or the places where ideas feel random or confusing.

- Listen to someone else reading your essay out loud and position yourself as the audience. Does the reader stumble at any point? Do you lose interest as they are reading? Do you sense a "jump" in ideas?

- Draw connections between your ideas. Underline terms or ideas that are repeated to find ideas that are related.

See the "Revising with comments" boxes throughout *Rules for Writers* for more on revision. These boxes offer strategies for revising for common global and local trouble spots. See, for example, pages 30, 33, 34, 53, 67, 78, 92, 94, 468, and 472.

3.6 Revision

Revision, which you will read about in Chapter 4, is often presented as the last step in the writing process, but many writers find themselves revising throughout the drafting process. As you write, you are constantly reading what you write and testing your writing against your purpose. Systematic revision—or "re-visioning" your work—is so important that you will find the next chapter

Tips & Strategies: DRAFTING

3.6

Ways and Means of Transitions

By Devon R. Kehler

Writing is fundamentally about building communicative *relationships* for specific times, purposes, places, and people. Transitional words and phrases play a key role in the kinds of relationships writers co-create with readers.

Transitions act as connectors between thoughts. The very word *transition* is derived from a Latin word meaning to "go across." Transitions in writing are like bridges that provide readers passage across your thoughts. They link ideas across sentences, paragraphs, and pages. To determine when and where transitions are needed, writers need to repeatedly ask, "What *kinds* of connections and relationships am I trying to build?" The chart below offers common kinds of transitions:

Kinds, Purposes, and Examples of Transitional Words/Phrases					
What kind of connection are you trying to build?	**Comparison** (used for bringing different things together)	**Repetition** (used for reminding readers what's been said)	**Summary** (used for signaling a synthesis or conclusion)	**Sequence** (used for giving a sense of order or time)	**Addition** (used for explanation and support)
What words or phrases can help build this type of connection?	*Whereas* *Meanwhile* *Although* *Though* *However*	*As I have said* *As I have shown* *As noted earlier* *In brief* *Returning to*	*Consequently* *As a result* *Therefore* *In conclusion* *Finally*	*Following this* *Simultaneously* *Previously* *Subsequently* *First, second…*	*For example* *Again* *Further* *Moreover* *In addition*

Note: Many transitional words and phrases serve multiple transitional purposes.

dedicated solely to revision strategies. Revision should be about more than just "fixing" your paper after it is written—it goes much further than such local revisions as correcting spelling mistakes or comma errors. Revising is something that you will want to do at various points throughout the writing process.

Read the next chapter to further explore the process of revision.

Works Cited

Ede, Lisa. *Work in Progress: A Guide to Writing and Revising*. New York: St. Martin's, 1992. Print.

Fulwiler, Toby, and Alan R. Hayakawa. *The Blair Handbook*. Upper Saddle River: Prentice Hall, 1997. Print.

Lamott, Anne. *Bird by Bird: Some Instructions on Writing and Life*. New York: Anchor Books, 1995. Print.

Rosenwasser, David, and Jill Stephen. *Writing Analytically*. Fort Worth: Harcourt Brace, 1997. Print.

Twain, Mark. "English as She Is Taught." *The Complete Essays of Mark Twain*. Ed. Charles Neider. Cambridge: Da Capo, 1991. 36–47. Print.

3.6

3.6

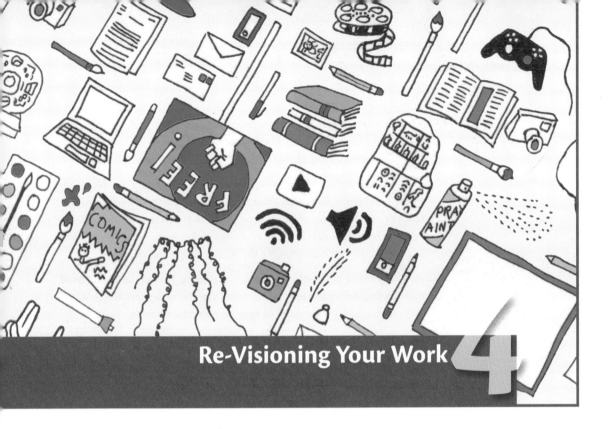

Re-Visioning Your Work 4

4.1 Feedback, Peer Review, and Revision: An Overview

4.2 Practicing Global and Local Revision

4.3 Tips for Successful Workshopping

4.4 Receiving and Making Sense of Comments

4.5 Feedback Leads to Revision

4.1 Feedback, Peer Review, and Revision: An Overview

Writing includes the recurring processes of invention, drafting, and revising. Revision is an ongoing process that is often collaborative in nature. It requires you to be open and willing to accept feedback from your instructor and peers, which can be difficult when you have already spent significant time writing.

See the "Guidelines for peer reviewers" on page 38 in *Rules for Writers* for help with giving feedback.

Your success in first-year writing as well as in future writing situations will depend, in part, on your willingness to revisit your writing and attempt to see it from the perspective of another reader. It may be difficult to see areas for improvement in your own work; therefore, seeking this feedback from your peers and instructor is an invaluable tool for identifying the strengths of your writing and potential areas for improvement. Giving and receiving feedback is important for many reasons:

- **The feedback that you give and receive will offer a fresh perspective on a draft.** Writers are often too close to their own work to imagine it taking any other shape. Because they already understand what they are trying to say, they can have trouble locating areas that need more clarification. Outside readers can offer a new perspective on what does and does not make sense to them.

CHAPTER 4

61

- **The process of giving and receiving feedback will help you understand the complexities of composition**, particularly the qualities that make a piece of writing effective for a given audience and situation.

- **The process of reviewing your own drafts, providing feedback on your peers' drafts, and evaluating the feedback you receive from other readers will help you develop your skills as a writer.** This process will help you learn how to make critical choices about the revisions you need to incorporate in order to best serve the purpose of your essay.

See section 3.2 in this book for more on discovering your writing process.

Because every writer has a unique approach to writing, part of the challenge of writing is finding a revision process that suits you. Here is some advice about the revision process from former UA first-year writing students:

- **Do Not Procrastinate:** "I think the main reason I was successful in first-year writing was that I always finished drafting my papers a few days before they were due. This helped lift all the stress off my heart. Then, I would reread my papers over and over again. Every time I reread my paper, I made changes in the text. I was not a great writer by any means, but being ahead of time helped me succeed." —*Nick Vaughn*

- **Read Aloud to Revise:** "I find it very useful to read each draft of my essay out loud before turning in the final draft. That way I can listen to certain phrases that might not make sense and paragraphs that do not flow." —*Bethany Bell*

- **Recognize that Writing Is a Process:** "I always thought writing draft after draft of a paper, and the whole revising process, was a huge waste of my time. I'd never written first drafts, second drafts, or final drafts. I would just sit down at a computer and write, and I would turn in whatever came out. This year, I was forced to go through the whole drafting process. We were required to not only turn in our first draft, second draft, and final draft; we had to do assignments that showed the research we were doing and what we thought of it. To an experienced procrastinator such as myself, this was hell. However, what resulted from this process really impressed me. All the papers I had ever written could have been so much better. This shows that revising and rewriting are not pointless efforts of teachers to make their students work hard to no end. They actually help. That is probably the most valuable lesson I have learned about writing this year." —*Katherine Byrnes*

- **Be Prepared for Peer Review:** "Peer review is an excellent tool for improving essays. However, if an adequate rough draft is not presented to reviewers, then useful feedback cannot be expected." —*Britt Burridge*

- **Give Constructive Criticism during Peer Review:** "When doing a peer response, be honest. The student will not benefit from your opinion if it is glossed over with fluffy language. And do not ditch the peer response.

It is very helpful to have someone else's opinions and/or ideas during the revising stage, especially if you are all writing on the same topic but their argument opposes yours." —*Christina Stephens*

"When writing peer edits, really dig deep into their paper. Do not just look for the obvious, because they are writing a peer edit for you as well. Think what would be useful for you." —*Rebecca Peterson*

- **Be Prepared for Instructor Conferences:** "It is very important when you go into your conference with your teacher that you have a strong thesis and a good sense of direction for your paper. It helped me very much to receive advice from my teacher because I had a good start and knew what I wanted to do, thus my teacher was able to give me good advice to refine my ideas. I know that you can fall into the trap of knowing that it is still a couple of weeks from being due, so why start it early? It really makes a difference in getting strong feedback." —*Richard Karasch*

As this advice demonstrates, revision takes many forms and can be useful in many ways. This chapter will provide you with a foundation for revision and peer review strategies.

4.2 Practicing Global and Local Revision

You might consider revision in terms of **global revisions** and **local revisions**. **Global revisions** are the significant changes you make to an essay's **argument**, organization, or **style**. Since global revisions may require you to move paragraphs around, eliminate sections of writing, or change the focus or audience, you can reduce your overall workload if you do these revisions before approaching sentence-level revisions. Otherwise, you might change the tense or sentence structure of an entire paragraph only to realize you will not use that paragraph in the final draft of the essay.

Local revisions, on the other hand, are smaller changes that occur at the sentence and paragraph level, like addressing grammar mistakes, typos, misspelled words, and awkward sentences. Another way to think about this level of revision is to see it as revising the surface layer of your paper, what we often call "editing." Local revisions are necessary and important for crafting a clear and precise essay, but they are only one part of the revision process.

Suggestions for Global Revisions

Making global revisions requires you to reread your essay with a focus on the "big picture." At this stage in the revision process, you will want to revisit the assignment guidelines provided by your instructor to make sure that your essay or project fulfills the necessary requirements. Then you might consider addressing the following:

See *Rules for Writers* pages 36–37 for more advice about and examples of global and local revision.

Why Are You Writing? Who Are You Writing For? Considering Your Rhetorical Situation as a Global Revision Strategy

See section 3.5 of the *Guide* for more on thesis statements.

When you write an academic essay, you write with a specific purpose in mind. As you read in section 3.3, in order to communicate effectively toward a specific purpose, you must keep your rhetorical situation in mind. Re-visioning your draft should include an evaluation of how well your specific choices align with your intended purpose, audience, and the context of your writing.

The following questions will be helpful as you evaluate your draft. Keep in mind that global changes based on your answer to one question may impact the rest of your essay. Rearranging paragraphs, for example, may require different transitions. For this reason, it is important to return to these questions throughout the revision process.

Reviewing Explanations

By Sylvia Chan

One way to check if you are engaging in analysis and not only summary is to review your explanations (E in PIE paragraphs). As you read in Chapter 3, the strongest explanations help the reader understand your evidence and how it relates to your claim. Strong explanations also help you connect your purpose in the paragraph to your overall thesis. Here are some tips to help you review your explanations:

- *Review the ratio of Explanations (E) to Illustrations (I).* A quotation or example from a text will require more than just one sentence to explain. As a general rule, when you look at your paragraphs, the majority of sentences should be explanation.

- *Look for evidence of inquiry, logic, or direction.* A strong explanation will guide you through the writer's thought process.

- *Identify one or more of the following components of an explanation:*

  1. *What:* Explains the evidence or quotation in your own words. Note: This step alone is not sufficient for analysis. A "what" statement should be followed by a "how" or "so what."

  2. *How:* What strategies does the author use to make his/her point, and how do they work? In other words, how does the illustration prove the point of your paragraph?

  3. *So What:* What is the ultimate goal or purpose for including this illustration? Why does it matter? How does it connect to your thesis?

Now take a look at this paragraph from Cameron Greene's analysis of the film *Babel*. First, identify the topic sentence (Point) and evidence (Illustrations). You will note they are not highlighted here.

Next, notice how each illustration is followed by multiple explanation sentences, a blend of what (blue), how (yellow), and so what (green). Consider what advice you would give to make this paragraph even stronger.

Purpose:

- What do I hope to achieve with this essay? Am I trying to persuade the reader of something? Inform them of a particular perspective? Lead them to take specific action? How might they know what my goals are?

- Am I making an argument or merely stating the obvious?

- Are my ideas properly developed? Do I progress through my argument carefully, patiently, and with enough detail? Am I supporting my ideas with appropriate evidence?

After answering these questions, you might find that you need to refocus your ideas, collect more information, rearrange sentences or paragraphs, cut unnecessary or confusing information, add more details, or make clearer transitions.

Sample "Complete" Paragraph: *Babel* allows the audience to know what it feels like to be deaf and upset, with intentional sound cuts and film shots. Chieko and her friends look to experience a night of passion and excitement. As they enter the club, the atmosphere engulfs them. Chieko is slow to warm up to the crowd of bodies bouncing around her, but soon enough, she pretends to hear the music and dances like everyone else. For a few brief seconds, all seems well, until Chieko notices her friend kissing one of the guys that they came in with (*Babel* 71:55). This is where the isolation sets in, and that reappearing emotion of loneliness turns up in her life once again. It is not merely enough for the movie to show that this is happening; the director wants the viewer to view how this is happening. To do this, there are a few movie techniques that the film began to utilize. The first thing the viewer notices is how the film will momentarily cut the diegetic sound (music and sounds found within the realm of the film) being played for the club (Szabady 154). This is done so that the audience can truly immerse themselves in the deaf life of Chieko, and feel exactly as she feels in that very moment. This way the viewer is both seeing and hearing exactly what Chieko is experiencing. Shot scale techniques are then demonstrated to further increase the immersion level. The movie shows a sequence of shots that compares the inner desires of Chieko to the reality unfolding before her. First, there is silence, and a close-up shot on Chieko's friends kissing. Without hesitation, a long shot comes in, showing Chieko standing there amongst a crowd of ecstatic people, as the sound rolls back in (*Babel* 72:15). These film techniques in this scene are used to allow the viewer to see things from Chieko's perspective and know the solitude she feels through visual engagement.

Now review your own writing while considering the tips above. Use these questions to direct your revisions:

- Does your writing have more E than I?

- Do your explanations show evidence of inquiry, logic, or direction?

- Can you identify a mix of the three components of explanations (What? How? So what?) throughout your draft?

See Chapters 3, 9, and 11 for more on audience.

Audience:

- Who, specifically, is going to be reading this essay? Who am I trying to reach with my argument? (My instructor, my classmates, members of my academic community, members of the local community, etc.)

- What are their values and expectations? Am I adequately meeting those expectations?

- How much information do I need to give my audience? How much background information or context should I provide for them without insulting their expertise?

- What kind of language is suitable for this audience?

- What **tone** should I use with my audience? Do I use this tone consistently throughout my draft?

Context:

- What are the formatting requirements of the assignment? Do I meet them?

- What are the content requirements for the assignment? Do I meet them?

- Does my draft reflect knowledge or skills gained in class in addition to my own ideas and voice?

- Have I addressed any grammatical issues that my teacher highlighted in class or in my previously-graded assignments?

Clearly identifying your audience and reviewing your draft with this audience in mind will help you with global revisions like organization and coherence of an argument. Clear identification will also help with local revisions, some of which are described in the following section.

See chapters 8–45 in *Rules for Writers* for help making informed local revisions.

Suggestions for Local Revisions

Once you feel confident in your draft, you are ready to start local revisions. Paying careful attention to issues occurring at the local level allows you to communicate effectively through your writing and enhance audience understanding. Most word processing software has a spelling and grammar check application, but you should not rely on this technology alone. These applications can be helpful for catching accidental spelling errors such as "univeristy," but they will not catch a **contextual** misspelling. For example, if you mean to say "desert," as in an arid region, instead of "dessert," such as a chocolate cake, a spell-check application cannot understand the context of your sentence to make the appropriate correction.

Also, these applications are not always reliable for locating grammatical errors. Look at the following sentence:

I ask the reader to try to dismiss any prejudices and be willing to learn.

The application will advise the writer to change the "be" to "am" because it thinks the verb should be conjugated to match the subject "I."

Therefore, even if you are going to run an automated spelling and grammar check, be prepared to go through your writing manually afterward. As you gain practice locally revising your essays, you might also start keeping a reference list of your most frequent errors and check for those first.

The following list includes stylistic elements you should consider when performing local revisions:

> See section F in *Rules for Writers* for more about academic writing at the sentence level.

- **Wordiness:** Too many words take all the energy out of a sentence. Practice expressing your ideas concisely. See how many unnecessary words you can eliminate from your writing. See pages 156–161 of *Rules for Writers* for advice on how to cut down on wordiness.

- **Tense Usage:** Be consistent with your verb tenses. While you do not need to write your entire essay in a single tense, make sure that if you do change between the present and the past or future tense, there is a logical reason to do so. See pages 243–248 of *Rules for Writers* for more on which verb tense to use in different situations.

- **Passive and Active Voice:** Pay attention to when you are using passive and active voice. In many disciplines, including the Humanities, writing in the active voice is generally favored. In your essays for first-year writing, strive to use strong, active verbs such as *achieve*, *demonstrate*, *suggest*, and *consider*, instead of their weaker, passive counterparts: *is achieved by*, *is demonstrated by*, *is suggested by*, *is considered by*. See pages 112–114 in *Rules for Writers* for more on active and passive verb constructions.

- **Pronoun Usage:** Pay attention to the pronouns (I, you, we, he, she, they) that you use in your essay. Pronouns are little words, but they carry a lot of power. For example, consider the difference between referring to a reader as "you" and referring to them in the third-person (as "one" or "he/she" or "the reader").

- **Variety:** One of the best marks of effective writing is variety. By varying the types of sentence structures, paragraph structures, vocabulary, and punctuation that you use, you can help your reader stay focused and engaged. Look for repeated sentence structures, words, punctuation, and phrases, and experiment until you have included more variety and fluidity in your writing. See pages 152–156 in *Rules for Writers* for more on adding variety to your sentences.

4.3 Tips for Successful Workshopping

By Laura Gronewold

Every writer needs a reviewer. Even the best writers send their work through multiple drafts during which the writer collaborates with other editors and writers so that a number of people contribute to the final, polished product. That is one reason authors thank so many people in the acknowledgments at the beginning of books. So think of your peers as collaborators working to produce the best essay possible. You can learn a lot about what and how to revise after several pairs of eyes have seen your work.

Discussing Your Peer's Essay during the In-Class Workshop

When you come to class, you will need to be ready to discuss your classmates' writing. Think about the ways you have talked as a class about the essays, fiction, poetry, and/or films you have read or viewed. When you talk as a class, you are not making judgments about the writer, but you are making assessments about the writing. The same goes for a workshop. Your goal is to offer "constructive criticism" or advice that serves a useful purpose. You want to keep your comments specific to the text your peer has produced so that the author will have concrete suggestions for improving and reorganizing her or his draft.

During an in-class workshop, your instructor will be present, listening and potentially participating with the group. Your instructor may help guide the workshop with questions, comments, and ideas, but the heart of any workshop's success is you and your classmates. Remember that the goal of the workshop is not just to give your classmates feedback, but to train yourself to make these same assessments of your own writing as well.

Advice for the Writer

Come to the workshop prepared to receive a critique of your work. Even if you feel that your draft is well written and has a clear argument, remember that your classmates can give you constructive criticism that will help make it even better. Bring an open mind to your workshops so that you can really listen to what ideas your classmates offer to improve your draft.

- Listen quietly to the discussion of your work when it is happening.

- Listen to the criticism you receive with a nonjudgmental attitude.

- Take notes! You should have a page of specific notes that you can refer to when you revise your paper.

- After listening, ask questions so that you are clear on the feedback your classmates have offered. At the end of the discussion, voice any additional concerns or questions about your essay.

Once you have received feedback, try to wait a few hours before revising your essay. This will give you some distance from your writing and will help you consider the comments from your workshop partners from a more objective position.

As you revise, think about the different comments from your readers. Do they all say that you need a more focused **thesis** statement? If everyone agrees, it is likely, though not certain, that this issue will remain a problem for your teacher or an intended audience. However, if only one student comments about your paragraph breaks, then you will need to assess whether or not you want to implement this revision. Remember, this is your essay, so you will need to decide which comments you will accept and reject based on your intentions and the effect you want to achieve.

Advice for the Reader

Your job as a reader is to carefully assess your classmates' drafts so that you can give them detailed feedback about their essay. Giving written (and verbal) feedback is another **genre** of writing, and it requires practice and skill, just like any other form of written or verbal communication. Even if you feel like you are not the best writer in class, your feedback during workshop is very important! If you are not clear about why a paragraph exists in another student's essay, for example, mention your confusion during peer review even if you aren't sure how to "fix" it. During the workshop, you, the author, and any other peer reviewers can collaboratively figure out how to address the issue.

As you review your peers' drafts:

- Read the writing as closely and carefully as possible.

- Consider the writer's intentions and the assignment guidelines, and provide feedback addressing particular concerns or sections of text.

- Read the essay at least twice.

- Write specific suggestions for revision on each page as you are reading.

- At the end of the essay, offer your overall reflections about the argument, the organization, the tone, and the style. Don't be afraid to state the obvious. Sometimes just restating what you think the writer is trying to do can help her know if the writing is effective.

Giving Written Feedback

Your goal when you review your workshop partners' drafts should be to write specific comments and questions that the writer can understand later, even if you are not there to explain them. Marginal comments such as "good!" or "???" are vague and will not clearly help the writer make revisions. Therefore, when you are reviewing a peer's work, consider the kind of feedback you would like to receive and strive to be constructive in your comments. See the Tips & Strategies Box that follows, "Getting the Most from Your Workshop Experience," for examples of helpful comments. If you are struggling to write meaningful and detailed comments of your own, consider using some of the sentence starters listed in the chart on the following page.

See the "Revising with comments" boxes throughout *Rules for Writers*. (See pages 30, 33, and 34 for examples.) Each has specific suggestions for revising in response to common comments.

Compliments	Constructive Criticism
• You got my attention here by…	• Here I expected…instead of …
• This example is great because…	• You need more evidence to support your claim that…
• I like the way you use…in order to…	• You might consider adding…
• I like this sentence/paragraph because…	• What about…? There are other perspectives on this **topic** including…
• This approach is effective because…	• I had to read this sentence twice because…
	• This paragraph needs more…

Getting the Most from Your Workshop Experience

In order to really benefit from a writing workshop, you will need to do several things. First, come to the workshop prepared. This means that you need to submit the draft that showcases your very best work to your peers for their feedback. Second, come to the workshop with an open mind. Instead of trying to defend your essay, listen carefully and thoughtfully to your peers when they give you feedback. Ask questions about their suggestions. Take some time to think through your options. Remember, you do not have to make all the changes your peers or instructor suggest, but you do want to give careful consideration to their feedback. Third, give helpful, specific, constructive feedback to your peers. Although it is nice to tell your peers what you like about their essays, this is only helpful if you explain your opinion in detail and let them know why you like it. Here you will see some examples of *not very helpful, somewhat helpful,* and *very helpful* workshop comments.

Not Very Helpful

"I really like this paper!"

This is friendly, but provides no concrete suggestions for the writer.

"Well, I'm just not that into poetry, so I couldn't get into your paper."

This comment is about the reader, not the paper. It does not provide any suggestions for revision.

"You use way too many commas."

Even if this critique is correct, it does not specify where commas are unnecessary. Additionally, such local suggestions are more helpful on drafts that have already been revised for global concerns.

Somewhat Helpful

"I really like your first body paragraph, but after that you kind of lose me."

This comment identifies strong and weak areas but does not tell the writer what makes them strong or weak.

Questions to Consider When Giving Feedback

Please note: The following questions are in order of how likely they are to appear in a Textual Analysis paper. Other assignments and writing situations may not utilize each of these elements or may not include them in this order. Use your understanding of the assignment prompt to determine how much weight to place on each element.

1. **Introduction:** As the reader, your job is to make suggestions for how the writer can make her or his introductory paragraph specific and interesting. Does the introductory paragraph establish the theme or idea of the essay? Is the introduction focused, or does it jump around and confuse the reader? Does the introduction offer the basic facts about the topic (short **summary** of a text, brief overview of a political issue, etc.) to help orient the reader? Think about how you might help the writer restrict the summary to the points in the text that are most relevant to the central argument. See the "Tips for Writing Introductions" Tips & Strategies Box in Chapter 3 for specific advice.

"You assume that I already know what this poem is about and that I think it is a great poem. Since I do not know anything about the poem, I feel lost when I read this paper."

This honest reaction identifies the assumptions made in the draft. It might also identify an opportunity for global revision, if the assignment requires the writer to assume that the reader is unfamiliar with the poem.

"In this sentence, the commas actually make it harder to understand. Maybe you should take them out."

This local editing comment might be appropriate at a later stage of workshopping. It effectively identifies a problem sentence, it connects the idea (or the content) to the form, and it provides a specific suggestion.

Very Helpful

"I really like this paragraph because you choose an interesting example from the text and in the last sentence you show how this paragraph supports the thesis. Maybe you could do this more in your other body paragraphs."

This comment identifies what makes the paragraph strong and gives the writer specific suggestions for improving the weaker paragraphs.

"If you gave a little bit of summary and background at the beginning of the paper, it would really help me to understand what's going on, because I've never read the poem before. You could also connect your argument about racism in this poem to a recent event, which would help people who do not know much about poetry to be more interested in your overall argument."

This comment expands the "Somewhat Helpful" comment by providing specific suggestions for revision.

"In this sentence, the commas actually make it harder to understand. You could take them out. In the next sentence, you have an unnecessary comma again, but the sentence is also a run-on. Try making this into two separate sentences, which would make it easier to understand and would give the paragraph more variety."

Again, this is a local revision suggestion, but it identifies specific problems, provides specific suggestions, and addresses both clarity and style.

2. **Thesis Statement:** Does the author have a precise thesis statement (or central claim) that includes a specific opinion or argument about a topic? Your job is to provide suggestions to the writer that could help make the topic more focused and include a supportable, debatable opinion. If the thesis statement already includes an opinion, is it phrased in a way that makes you as a reader interested in reading the rest of the essay? See the "Making Weak Thesis Statements Stronger" Craft Box in Chapter 3. There are also discussions of thesis statements in Chapters 7–11.

See the Tips & Strategies Box on page 64 for examples on how to review analysis and explanations.

3. **Summary and Analysis:** Does the author have too much summary of the text or too much vague information about a research topic? How can the writer add **quotations** or other specific evidence from the text? How can the writer move beyond offering only a summary of the text(s) they have read? Mark places where the writer is doing a great job making specific claims and using supporting evidence, but also make note of where analysis can be strengthened.

4. **Use of Evidence:** Does the writer support claims with evidence? Does the kind of evidence—quotes, anecdotes, summary, outside research, personal experience, etc.—match the expectations of the assignment? Point out where the evidence is especially effective, where you think more evidence is needed, or where a different kind of evidence might better support the claim.

Tips & Strategies: REVISION

Approaching Instructor Feedback
From The University of Arizona Writing Instructors to Our Students

As part of the ongoing revision process, you will receive feedback from your instructors, sometimes during conferences, and most often after you submit your final draft for a grade. The following statement aims to help you make sense of how instructors generate written responses to your writing and how they hope you will use these responses. Though there is often a relationship between the instructor's comments and the letter grade you will ultimately earn in the class, this message encourages you to use both the grades and the comments as tools for improving your writing throughout the semester and beyond.

1. We would like you to understand that our comments are part of the teaching and learning process. We write comments not just to evaluate your essay, but to help you see how the lessons about writing from class emerge in your writing. One way to better understand the purpose of our comments is to participate actively in class and carefully read the assignment sheet, rubric, and any other assignment materials your instructor distributes. These are the ways we communicate with you ahead of time about what we are looking for in your writing.

5. **Use of Sources:** Does the writer integrate sources appropriately in the essay? Does the writer make it clear to the reader when another text is being quoted? Do you ever have any questions about the original source for a quotation or an idea (especially if it is an idea that is **paraphrased**)? Your job is to help the writer establish credibility and ensure that all of the sources are utilized effectively. See Chapter 5 for specific strategies for integrating sources.

See pages 43–44 in *Rules for Writers* for more examples of helpful peer comments.

6. **Organization:** Does the organization of the essay support the purpose? Should any paragraphs be moved around, expanded, or deleted? See the "Reverse Outlining" Tips & Strategies Box in section 7.3 for strategies to test the effectiveness of organization.

7. **Transitions:** Does the author have smooth transition phrases between the paragraphs and sentences? See the "Ways and Means of Transitions" Tips & Strategies Box in section 3.5 for more about transitions.

8. **Conclusion:** Does the conclusion leave you with a new idea or concept to consider? Does it do more than simply restate what has already been argued? See "Tips for Writing Conclusions" in Chapter 3 for some specific strategies for writing conclusions.

2. We would like you to know that we intend our comments to be constructive. We value your ideas and want to learn from you and hope that you will use our comments to learn from us as well.

3. We would like you to approach each essay not as an independent unit, but as a brief moment in your overall development as a writer. Our comments are meant to be useful to you in this assignment and your future writing.

4. We would like you to accept responsibility for using our comments in the revision process. We also expect you to share your strengths as a writer in commenting on your peers' papers.

5. We would like you to understand that comments are both descriptive and evaluative. Writing a letter grade is perhaps the least interesting thing we do as writing instructors. Take the time to reread the entire essay alongside our comments to understand the grade in context. We invite you to use our comments as an opportunity to talk further about your writing.

Written by UA instructors Roseanne Carlo, Anne-Marie Hall, Faith Kurtyka, Rachel Lewis, Jessica Shumake, and Cassie Wright in collaboration with Professor Nancy Sommers, former director of Harvard University's Expository Writing Program.

4.4 Receiving and Making Sense of Comments

Once you receive written and oral comments from your peers and instructor, how do you decide what to use? What do you pay attention to first? What if there is too much for you to take in all at once? Here is some advice:

- **Read through all the comments** from all the reviewers before making any decisions.

- **Watch for patterns** in the responses you receive. If three out of four readers suggest you expand a certain point, chances are good that future readers would want you to say more about it, too.

- **Look for global issues** such as focus and organization that need attention before you attend to local problems such as grammar and word choice. You will waste your time if you fix sentences that you decide to delete later on, but it may be useful to note errors that you make repeatedly.

- Always **keep an open mind** as you read comments. Try to see it from the reviewer's point of view. Did you leave out important information or explanation that would solve the problem?

- If you really think a comment is questionable, **ask other readers what they think**. Sometimes you will decide not to take action on a suggestion or comment.

- If you have a specific concern that is not included in the feedback you get from your readers or you want more feedback in general, **do not be afraid to ask people for specific advice**. A workshop is a partnership, and it is your responsibility to ask the questions that you would like answered.

- **Think critically about all comments** and then make the revisions you think are most important for the purpose and scope of your work. You are the writer and you make the final decisions.

4.5 Feedback Leads to Revision

By Jen Heckler and Kristen Haven

In the following sample rough draft of a Textual Analysis, a student explores her interpretation of Raymond Carver's short story "So Much Water So Close to Home." What you see here is the draft marked up with instructor comments. As you read, consider the following:

- Reflect on these comments—can you break them down into local and global?

- How would you rewrite your paper based on these responses? (Remember that it makes sense to consider global feedback first.)

- Which comments would you take into consideration?

A Draft with Instructor Comments

Draft of essay one

"So Much Water so Close to Home"

Suspicious behavior and over done violence are all scary tell tale signs of a criminal. People that are often involved in dangerous and unfortunate situations usually have obvious characteristics that seem to comply with their behavior. In the short story, "So Much Water So Close to Home" a housewife Claire is terrified of her shady husband. Claire hears about a murdered girl close by to the place her husband and his friends were fishing and camping. Claire is immediately very aware of his actions and is investing him and facts about the murder for fear that it was in fact of her husband. Whether or not Claire's husband is really guilty, he gives many signs that could cause someone to believe, in this situation Claire, that he did murder the young girl.

Author name?

Use first or third person instead of second.

Many people would expect that when something traumatic and mysterious happens to you on a trip, one of the first things you would do when you got home was to tell your family about it so that would understand the severity of the situation and be sure their family members had nothing to do with such a bad situation. The exact opposite happens to Claire and her husband. Claire's husband sees a girl dead in the water when he is camping, but he and his friends decide to just leave her there overnight and deal with it in the morning. Claire's husband comes home and goes to sleep and doesn't say anything to Claire about it until later the next day. "'Why didn't you tell me last night?' I asked. 'I just…didn't. What do you mean?' he said" (280). Rightly so Claire found it wierd that she woke up to hear her husband screaming cusses in to a telephone and then he saying to her "I have to tell you something" (280). The situation is awkward, one would think that if you dragged a body to police in the morning and were wanted for murder you might want to first tell your wife about it. This is one of the many odd behaviors that Claire's husband displayed.

Sp. weird. Actually, "strange" or "startling" might work better here.

Comma splice.

Stay in present tense.

Another sign that there might be a problem is a person's violence and overall behavioral tone. Throughout the short story, Claire's husband is increasingly moody and violent. At different points, Claire's husband snaps out at her and even acts in a violent manner. "Suit yourself then. I could give a fuck less what you do" (285).

Clarify what you mean by this phrase.

Dropped quotation. Integrate.

Slang—"curses" or "obscenities" would be better.

Give your paper an original title as you continue revising.

You have a broad introduction, which successfully eases readers into your discussion; however, there are a few places where being more specific will help readers understand your purpose. For example, what is "over done violence"?; "dangerous and unfortunate situations"?; "shady"? These are interesting descriptive words, but they are broad and general; consequently, readers will not know what you are talking about. How does all of this relate to the story?

This sentence sounds like it contradicts itself. First you mention that she is "aware of his actions" (what actions? Fishing?), and then I hear mention of murder. What's the connection?

Redundant—"situation" used twice. This is broad for a topic sentence. Perhaps letting readers know what you are trying to prove will help guide them. Your thesis seems to say that her husband (What is his name?) killed someone. Is that what you are trying to show in this paragraph?

Use more precise vocabulary here—how is it bad?

I thought you said he killed the girl in your thesis…

Run-on—needs punctuation. Great quotation, but it's dropped into the text without integration. Introduce it, and explain how it illustrates your point.

He was harsh, so she suspected him of murder? I think this is making a huge leap here. What else made Claire suspect Stuart? Was it his reaction to the subject of the discussion?

How does this paragraph relate to your thesis? It seems like it is contradicting what you are trying to prove.

Wordy. Try using "is." "Common" already tells us the same thing as "can often be."

Again, a general topic sentence. Think about making a claim about the text here.

Use a quotation from the story to back up these claims.

"Struggles" would read more smoothly.

I'm hearing that it doesn't matter if he's guilty or not guilty; his actions prove he is guilty. Doesn't this seem repetitive? This is also a rather general final sentence. Keep the story in mind.

Stuart, Claire's husband, starts to really scare Claire with his overzealous behavior and temper. Claire does not understand why Stuart needs to really act like this, and this causes her to question his behavior and the murder situation. If Stuart had been normal and not lashed out at her in specific situations, she would less likely want to question, but since he acted in such a harsh way it caused her to question his motives.

A common characteristic of a criminal can often be substance abuse. Many criminals have problems that root from an alcohol addiction or other drug problem. Yet because one decides to partake in these activities does not necessarily mean they are out to kill someone. In the short story, Stuart is constantly drinking and smoking, even around his child. When Claire mentions she wants to go to the store, alcohol is the first thing Stuart asks to get. When Stuart seems upset or wanting to do something, smoking or alcohol is seemingly the first thing he turns to.

Throughout the short story, "So Much Water So Close to Home" Claire is afraid that her husband is involved in the murder of a young girl. Stuart's actions start to become very mysterious and shady to Claire, and she is struggling with believing her husband. There are many different things Stuart does that would make many people believe he is guilty. The point is that whether or not he is guilty his actions prove otherwise. A person's actions can have a great impact on the people around them and cause them to be more and more questionable.

Instructor comments: 1. Are you trying to illustrate that Stuart is capable of killing someone or are you trying to prove that there is a "problem"? Or are you trying to prove something else that I missed? Your thesis sounds like you are trying to prove that Stuart's behavior indicates that he has the potential to kill someone, but that is not what your **topic sentence** says here.... Perhaps you should mention Stuart's name before this paragraph? 2. Does Claire suspect Stuart of murdering the girl? 3. What is the overzealous behavior like?

Revisions in Action

After receiving her instructor's feedback, the student reworked her draft. Highlighted in **orange** is new text, and highlighted in **blue** are revised words/phrases from the original. Compare the two versions. Then consider:

- Would you have integrated the instructor's feedback in ways other than this student did?

- What additional changes would you have made?

- Do you see more local or global revisions at work here?

- How does the student define the writing situation? How can you tell?

- Considering that this is still a rough draft, how would you revise this paper again both globally and locally? List three suggestions for each.

Revised Draft

A Criminal Mind in Carver's "So Much Water So Close to Home"

Suspicious behavior and violence are all seemingly obvious telltale signs of a criminal. People that are often involved in dangerous situations usually have obvious characteristics that seem to comply with their behavior. What things do many consider traits of a criminal? Does one have to be shady or over violent? What about if a person is just displaying suspicious behavior or acting in a dangerous manner? In Raymond Carver's short story, "So Much Water So Close to Home" a housewife Claire becomes terrified of her shady husband, Stuart. Claire hears about a murdered girl close by to the place her husband and his friends were fishing and camping. Claire begins to become more and more nervous that her husband was involved with the death of the girl, and starts to analyze her husband Stuart's actions. Whether or not Stuart is really guilty, he gives many signs that would cause any person to believe that he is guilty. A person's actions are key in determining a crime situation and Stuart does not seem to be innocent.

Carver's portrait of guilty behavior hinges on Stuart's lack of communication with Claire surrounding the discovery of the dead girl. Truth and honesty, two devices that hold a relationship together, are two devices that Stuart fails to uphold. His initial silence regarding the discovery of the dead girl in the water near a campsite he is vacationing at with friends, and his ensuing reticence and verbal abuse lead the reader (and Claire) to suspect his capacity for serious, even murderous, violence.

One of the actions that causes Claire to question her husband is his late mentioning of the dead body he encountered on the trip. Many people would expect that when something traumatic and mysterious happens to them on a trip, one of the first things they would do when they got home was tell their family about it so they would understand the severity of the situation and be sure their family members had nothing to do with such an awful situation. The exact opposite happens to Claire and her husband. Claire's husband sees the body in the water, but he and his friends decide to just leave her there over night and deal with it in the morning. Claire's husband comes home and goes to sleep and doesn't say anything to Claire about it until later the next day. Claire is deeply troubled by this lack of communication. "Why didn't you tell me last night? I asked. "I just...didn't. What do you mean? he said" (280).

Rightly so Claire finds it unsettling that she wakes up to hear her husband screaming obscenities into a telephone and *then* saying to her "I have to tell you something" (280). Claire questions her husband because she finds it odd that he would not tell her when he got home that he saw a dead body on his camping trip. If Stuart helped get the body to authorities in the morning he would have to know the police are going to call and question him about it. What did he think his wife would feel if we were getting police calls? It doesn't make sense that he did not tell her quickly that there had been some problems on his fishing trip. The situation is awkward; one would think that if you dragged a body to police in the morning and were wanted for murder you might want to first tell your wife about it. This is one of the many odd behaviors that Claire's husband displayed.

Stuart's violence and overall behavioral tone are indicative of his dangerous potential. Throughout the short story, Claire's husband is increasingly moody and violent. At different points Claire's husband verbally lashes out at her and eventually abuses her physically. When Claire tells him she wants to spend the night alone, he snaps, "Suit yourself then. I could give a fuck less what you do" (285). Stuart starts to really scare Claire with his overzealous behavior and temper, and particularly with the way he responds to her confusion and questions with sexual advances rather than answers. Claire does not understand why Stuart acts like this; the effect is only to alienate her further from him. I think this makes Claire more likely to believe that Stuart was involved in the assault and murder of the girl. If Stuart had been normal and not lashed out at her in specific situations, she would less likely want to question, but since he spoke so violently and rash it caused her to question his motives.

A common characteristic of a criminal can often be substance abuse, and Stuart fits this description. Many criminals have problems that root from an alcohol addiction or other drug problem. In the short story, Stuart is constantly drinking and smoking, even around his child. When Claire mentions she wants to go to the store, alcohol is the first thing Stuart asks her to get. When Stuart seems upset or wanting to do something, smoking or alcohol is seemingly the first thing he turns to.

Throughout "So Much Water So Close to Home" Claire is afraid that her husband has been involved in the murder of a young girl. Stuart's actions become increasingly confounding and distancing to Claire and she struggles with believing him and eventually with even being near him. Indeed, Stuart's behavior would make many people believe he is guilty. Carver convey's the way that a person's actions in the face of trauma can have a great impact on the people around them, and in Claire and Stuart's situation, can expose and widen the fractures already present in a relationship.

Works Cited

Babel. Dir. Alejandro González Iñárritu. Perf. Brad Pitt, Cate Blanchett. Paramount, 2006. Web.

Carver, Raymond. "So Much Water So Close to Home." *Writing as Revision*. 3rd ed. Ed. Beth Alvarado and Barbara Cully. Boston: Pearson, 2010. 354–67. Print.

Szabady, Gina, Kristin Mock, and Stephen Pallas. *A Student's Guide to First-Year Writing*. 34th ed. Plymouth, MI: Hayden-McNeil. Print.

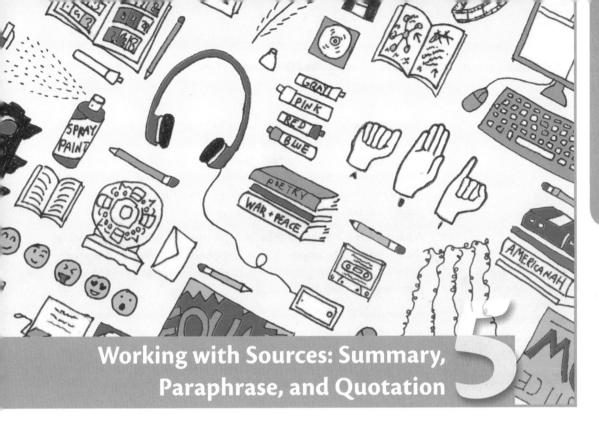

Working with Sources: Summary, Paraphrase, and Quotation

5.1 Working with Sources: An Overview

During your time at the University of Arizona, you will be asked to engage with the ideas of other writers. Whether you are writing an analysis, a research paper, a marketing plan, or even designing an infographic for a biology class, you will often draw upon other writers' ideas or research and integrate them into your own writing. Effectively incorporating outside sources can help strengthen the argument you are making, whether you are providing evidence for a claim or placing your own ideas in conversation with other arguments. In any writing situation, incorporating outside sources can demonstrate active engagement with a text, an issue, or an idea.

See pages 480–490 in *Rules for Writers* for advice about how to cite sources in MLA style.

Key Terms

There are three major techniques you can use to integrate sources in your work in your first-year writing courses: **summary**, **paraphrase**, and **quotation**. Remember that regardless of whether you are summarizing, paraphrasing, or quoting, when you use the ideas of others, you must cite the source so that your readers know where the material is coming from.

- A **summary** is an abbreviated version of a longer text. It should highlight the most important points of the text and strive to be an accurate and un-biased representation of the text's ideas. A summary will vary in length depending on the length of the original text, your purpose as a writer, and your writing situation. Generally speaking, a summary will be shorter than the original text.

- A **paraphrase** is a rephrasing of a source in your own words while retaining the meaning of the original source. Paraphrases are often used to clarify technical language or complex ideas, to emphasize a point, or to add variety if you are also using direct quotations.

See sections 57 and 58 in *Rules for Writers* for help with integrating quotations, summa-ries, and paraphrases into your writing.

- A **quotation** is the exact words found in the original source placed inside quotation marks. Sometimes you will need to change words in the quota-tion to make your sentence grammatically correct. You will place brackets around any changed words. You may quote an entire sentence or a part of a sentence, depending on what is most useful for your purpose.

Using Sources in Context

Summarizing, paraphrasing, and quoting are not analysis in and of themselves. If you simply include a quotation in the middle of a paragraph without sufficient context, your reader will likely have trouble understanding what the idea means, or how it relates to your overall argument. Providing context is key when ref-erencing sources to avoid confusing your readers. It should be clear to readers which ideas are from external sources and which are your own.

To maintain a high level of academic integrity, you must understand how to responsibly incorporate source material. In addition to providing context and proper citations, you will want to provide an accurate representation of an au-thor's ideas. If you take quotations out of context or twist a paraphrase to suit your needs, you could misrepresent an author's claims, weaken your argument, or even commit plagiarism. While it is true that readers will interpret texts in different ways, there is a significant difference between reading a text in a unique way and misrepresenting its meaning altogether.

The guidelines in this chapter will help you integrate sources with integrity and enable you to work with texts in ways that are appropriate for academic audi-ences. Specifically, this chapter will help you:

- Represent the ideas of your sources fairly and accurately by using effective summary, paraphrase, and quotation.

- Demonstrate clear distinctions between your own ideas and the ideas of the sources you use.

- Name the text's author and appropriate pages that were consulted (in-text citation).

5.2 Summary: Main Ideas

Providing summaries in your writing can help you point out the most important parts of a text to your readers and highlight how that text or idea connects to the point you are making. By using summary, you can convey large amounts of information in fewer words and place the information in language that matches your purpose and your audience's needs.

See section 5c in *Rules for Writers* for guidelines on writing a summary.

The length of a summary varies depending on the length of the text and your purpose for summarizing. A summary can be as short as one or two sentences or as long as a paragraph. A summary of the major plot points in Stephen Crane's "The Snake" might look something like this:

> In his short story "The Snake," Stephen Crane describes a man who encounters a rattlesnake while walking with his dog. As the man and the snake face each other, both are filled with rage and a desire to kill the other that resembles the experience of war and instinctual violence.

See Chapter 2 to find a full version of Stephen Crane's "The Snake."

Writing with Integrity: Intentional vs. Unintentional Plagiarism

Plagiarism involves taking credit for someone else's work or ideas without giving proper credit. Although plagiarism is not always intentional, the consequences for committing plagiarism are the same regardless of intention. The UA Code of Academic Integrity strictly prohibits any form of cheating, plagiarism, or fabrication.

Unfortunately, many students make honest mistakes and plagiarize without intending to because they do not understand the conventions of academic citation or fail to see that their actions are academically unethical. The chart below outlines some common forms of plagiarism—some of which might seem surprising. Admittedly, it is sometimes hard to know when to cite a source in your paper and when you do not need to. The general rule is: if you had to look it up somewhere, you should cite it. For example, you may want to mention in your paper that about a half million people live in Tucson. You know that fact because it is an approximate figure that people just happen to know. It is common knowledge, and, in this case, there is no need to cite a source. However, if you are writing a paper on the fluctuating population of Tucson and you use statistics from the U.S. Census Bureau or the City of Tucson's website to offer precise figures for the population between 2001 and 2010, you should cite the source that provided the information.

For more information on avoiding plagiarism and writing with integrity, refer to section 55 in *Rules for Writers*.

Intentional Plagiarism ← → **Unintentional Plagiarism**

Using someone else's work (or essay examples from websites) as your own

Submitting the same work for multiple classes without instructor consent

Writing a paraphrase too similar to the original text

Paying someone else to write your paper for you

Quoting without using quotation marks

Assuming borrowed information is "common knowledge"

Incorporating sources without proper citations

Tips & Strategies: DRAFTING

On the other hand, if you were writing a textual analysis of "The Snake" that focused on how Crane emphasizes conflicts between humans and nature, you might write a longer and more detailed summary of Crane's story that mentions several of the most important ecological moments in the text. This kind of summary might spend a good deal of time considering specific moments in the text rather than just summarizing the overall plot.

See Chapter 2 in this book for advice on how to write section summaries.

Strategies for Effective Use of Summary

- **Start by writing smaller summaries in the margins of the text you wish to use in your writing.** Distilling large sections of text into manageable pieces will help you focus on the major claims of the text and provide you with a sense of the arrangement of ideas in the original text. Keep in mind that merely restating the main ideas of a text in the same order does not make a good summary; instead, you must determine which points are most critical to your analysis and include only those points in your writing.

- **Introduce the author before or early in the summary.** This contextual information will help your reader distinguish the summary from your own ideas. If it is the first time a source is mentioned, make sure to include all necessary contextual information (author's name, title, type of work, etc.) with a strong **signal phrase**, such as "As [author] writes," or "In [author's] story," or "According to [author],". There are more examples of ways to effectively contextualize your summaries throughout this chapter.

- **Integrate a summary smoothly into your own writing.** You can integrate a summary into a larger paragraph or section of your writing in order to orient your reader, to introduce a quotation, to emphasize certain arguments made by your source, or to initiate a discussion. Remember to make it clear to the reader which materials are drawn from a source and which ideas are your own contribution to the discussion. Review the sample student essays included in Chapter 13 to see how and why writers integrate summaries with their own ideas.

5.3 Paraphrase: Specific Ideas

A paraphrase is more specific than a summary but less precise than a quotation because it does not quote the author's actual words. While a paraphrase does not have to retain all of the content from the original, the meaning and intent of the original passage should not be changed. When you paraphrase, you borrow from the ideas in a text, but you must use language that is different from the original source. For example, you might paraphrase the introduction to Crane's "The Snake" as follows:

5.3

Original Text:

A man and a dog came from the laurel thickets of the valley where the white brook brawled with the rocks. They followed the deep line of the path across the ridges. The dog—a large lemon and white setter—walked, tranquilly meditative, at his master's heels (Crane 1).

Paraphrase:

"The Snake" opens with a man walking through the mountains, his dog following closely as they pass over a stream.

See page 476 in *Rules for Writers* to see another example of an effective paraphrase.

This paraphrase retains much of the specific detail of Crane's original story, but it does not use any of Crane's original language.

Summary Practice

With a partner or as a class, select one of the sample essays in Chapter 13.

Step One: By yourself, start by writing paragraph summaries in the margins of the essay you have selected following the advice in section 5.2. After summarizing each paragraph/section, what do you see as the main claims and supporting evidence in the essay? Make a list here:

Step Two: Now choose the most important points from your list and, using just a few sentences, describe the essay in terms of these points. Remember to include the main claim and the most important supporting evidence in your summary. Write your brief summary here:

Step Three: Revise your summary for clarity/conciseness. Consider the following questions: Were you able to include all necessary information? Did you include too much information? At this point you may need to add another sentence or two, revise, or delete information.

Step Four: Now compare your summary with a peer. How are your summaries of the same sample essay similar or different? Did you both identify the same main claim? Did you identify the same supporting evidence? If not, can you identify why that might be? Discuss when this type of summary might be useful in your writing.

Craft Box: DRAFTING

See section 58b in *Rules for Writers* for more examples of signal phrases and advice on how to integrate quotations.

5.3

The following guidelines will help you paraphrase effectively and avoid plagiarism.

- **Always include a signal phrase**, making sure to identify the original speaker and making it clear that you are borrowing from someone else's ideas.

- **Change the language** so that it no longer matches the original.

- **Change the word order and sentence structure** so that it no longer resembles the original.

- **Cite the source** using in-text citation so that readers know where the original material comes from.

Craft Box: DRAFTING

Paraphrase Practice

1. **Read the following passage from Michele Wallace's "When Black Feminism Faces the Music, and the Music is Rap" (you can find a full version of this essay in Chapter 2):**

Queen Latifah introduces her video, "Ladies First," performed with English rapper Monie Love, with photographs of black political heroines like Winnie Mandela, Sojourner Truth, Harriet Tubman, and Angela Davis. With a sound that resembles scat as much as rap, Queen Latifah chants "Stereotypes they got to go" against a backdrop of newsreel footage of the apartheid struggle in South Africa. The politically sophisticated Queen Latifah seems worlds apart from the adolescent, buffoonish sex orientation of most rap. In general, women rappers seem so much more grown up. Can they inspire a more beneficial attitude toward sex in rap? What won't subvert rap's sexism is the actions of men; what will is women speaking in their own voice, not just in artificial female ghettos, but with and to men (Wallace).

A one-sentence summary of the above paragraph might read as follows: "Wallace argues that female rappers hold the power to change the dominant sexist attitudes presented in rap music." This sentence summarizes Wallace's paragraph well because it captures the main idea of the paragraph. It is not, however, a *paraphrase* because it is not a specific reference to a particular detail or context. Nothing is mentioned about Queen Latifah, "political sophistication," "voice," or female rappers as more "grown up," for example.

Now try to put the passage into your own words while maintaining the tone and the text's meaning. Practice your own paraphrase here:

_____

_____

_____

_____

_____

_____

_____

_____

2. **Read the following attempt at paraphrase. Does it effectively paraphrase the passage without plagiarizing the language?**

5.4 Quotation: The Source's Words

Writers use quotations for a variety of reasons. Quotations can demonstrate a key point using the source's exact words; they can set up the writer's analysis or close reading of a source; they can begin or conclude an essay with a provocative, exact statement from an author; and they can honor the particular language or style of a particularly well-stated phrase. Using quotations effectively can be difficult because it is sometimes hard to determine how and when you should insert a quotation into your writing. You do not want to over-quote, where the voices of others take over your essay. However, you also do not want to under-quote, as that makes it difficult to provide specific details from the text to support your analytical claims. The following are some guidelines for deciding when to use a quotation in your writing.

See section 58a in *Rules for Writers* for more on limiting your use of direct quotations.

Queen Latifah's video for "Ladies First" is a good example of how women rappers seem so much more grown up than their male counterparts. The only way to change rap's sexism is if more women can leave the label of "female rapper" and speak in their own voice with and to men.

The above example has serious problems, enough that the writer could be accused of plagiarizing Wallace's passage. Why? Although some words are changed and some of the word order appears to be different, too much of the original passage's language and sentence structure remains intact. These are the hallmarks of an incorrect paraphrase. Also, notice that the passage is not cited, giving no indication that the material actually comes from an outside source. Did you make any of these same mistakes in your paraphrase?

3. **Here is a more effective paraphrase:**

While male rappers talk about sex like they are stuck in the teenage mindset, Wallace writes that female rappers tend to be more mature. Using Queen Latifah's socially conscious video for "Ladies First" as an example, she suggests that mainstream female rappers have the power to challenge and change attitudes about sex in rap music (Wallace).

Notice that this successful paraphrase features very different sentence structures and word choices. The writer also uses a signal phrase to name Wallace in the first sentence of the paraphrase and includes an in-text citation at the end of the second sentence. Paraphrasing is especially useful when there is no compelling reason to use the exact words of your source in order to further the discussion. However, when the author's language seems especially effective or unique, or you want to analyze it in more depth, you should use a quotation.

4. **Return to your original paraphrase above to see if it can be revised more effectively.**

Revise your paraphrase here:

_____

_____

_____

_____

_____

_____

_____

When to Quote

- When the wording of the source is especially effective or unique, or when a writer expresses a point so precisely that you cannot restate it without altering the meaning or effect.

- When you wish to highlight an author's stylistic choices, such as his or her particular words or sentence structures.

- When the words of reliable and respected authorities, scholars, or authors support your point.

- When you wish to emphasize an author's opinion as distinct from your own.

- When you wish to cite an author whose opinions challenge or vary greatly from those of other experts.

Integrating Quotations Successfully

See section 58b in *Rules for Writers* for more examples of signal phrases and advice on how to integrate quotations.

Use the following suggestions to help you include quotations in a way that does not disrupt the fluidity of your writing:

- **Always frame your quotations with signal phrases.**

  As with paraphrases, you should alert your reader that you are about to use somebody else's language by providing a signal phrase that names the author before you start. Here are some commonly used signal phrases. You could replace "X" with the name of the author(s) you are quoting, or you could insert the title of text you are referencing in place of X.

As X writes,	X explains that	X states
X argues	In the words of X,	X suggests
X shows	X interrogates	According to X,

  It is also a good idea to introduce your source by including the author's credentials—relevant details about the author that explain why he or she is worth quoting. For example:

  In a paper talking about the style of a specific poem:

  As 2012 U.S. Poet Laureate Natasha Trethewey writes, …

  In a paper weighing the benefits of recycling:

  Davis Guggenheim, director and producer of the documentary *An Inconvenient Truth*, suggests that…

- **Always explain the quotation.**

  There are two ways to explain a quotation. The first method is just what it sounds like: explain what the quotation means. Sometimes, though, the meaning of a quotation is self-explanatory. In these cases, you should explain how the quotation relates to what you are saying in your essay. You can also choose to include both types of explanation—what the quotation means and how it relates to your thesis—in your discussion of a quotation.

Composition scholars Gerald Graff and Cathy Birkenstein call quotes that have no signal phrase and no explanation "hit-and-run quotations" because dropping a quotation into a paragraph without explaining who was responsible for it is similar to bumping into a car in a parking lot and then driving away without leaving a note (41–44). Following is an example of a classic hit-and-run quotation:

> Some point out that female rappers offer the potential to challenge sexist attitudes. "The politically sophisticated Queen Latifah seems worlds apart from the adolescent, buffoonish sex orientation of most rap. In general, women rappers seem so much more grown up" **(Wallace).**

While the above example accurately cites the quotation, it does not include any kind of signal phrase to explain where the quote came from or why the quote is important. This can confuse readers, interrupt the flow of your writing, or make it sound like your sources are speaking for you rather than supporting your ideas. A revision of the hit-and-run quote might look like this:

> Some point out that female rappers offer the potential to challenge sexist attitudes. **As Michele Wallace argues in** *The New York Times,* "The politically sophisticated Queen Latifah seems worlds apart from the adolescent, buffoonish sex orientation of most rap. In general, women rappers seem so much more grown up." **The political content of Queen Latifah's music demonstrates a maturity not found in much of the sexually-charged songs of her male peers and shows the potential for female rappers to challenge sexism.** This observation helps to counter the common arguments that frame rap as a wholly negative influence on youth.

In the previous example, the writer uses a clear **signal phrase** and **explains** the meaning of the quote. However, the author goes beyond a simple explanation of the quotation's meaning by connecting the quotation to the topic of the paper, which in this case is rap music's cultural influence. Notice that because the author is cited in the signal phrase and there is no page number, the citation is correct according to MLA style. By including all of these elements when you use a quotation, you can ensure your purpose for including the quotation is clear to your readers.

See sections 58a–58b in *Rules for Writers* for advice about including quotations correctly and effectively.

Drawing Ideas from a Quotation in PIE Paragraphs

By Jessica Lee

Part of writing a successful analysis requires the ability to draw evidence from a text to support your main points in each paragraph, which in turn will support your **thesis**. One way to use a quotation is to connect that quote to the main point of your paragraph, explaining how the quotation illustrates your main point. This is one part of the "E" (Explanation) in **PIE** (Point, Illustration, Explanation). In addition to describing how the quotation illustrates your main point in the paragraph, you can also explain how your main point supports your thesis. Using the best quotations to support your assertions, however, is not always as easy as it sounds. This exercise is designed to help you strengthen your ability to use quotations strategically, making sure that the conclusions you draw from your quotations are logical.

Instructions:

1. Fold a piece of paper so that you have four rows.

2. Write your thesis in the first row.

3. Write one of the main points that support your thesis in the second row.

4. Write down an illustration, or quotation, that you plan to use to support that main point in your third row.

5. In the fourth row, write an explanation of the quotation that:

   a. Explains what the quotation is saying or demonstrating.

   b. Makes a point that follows logically from the quotation.

   c. Effectively explains how the quotation advances the thesis.

Read the rows from top to bottom. Does your explanation follow logically from the quotation? Does your explanation clarify how the quotation supports your main point? Does your explanation describe how your main point supports your thesis? How can your explanation be improved? You can repeat this exercise for all of the main points of your paper. The following is an example of a textual analysis of Stephen Crane's "The Snake."

Example:

Thesis	Stephen Crane's short story, "The Snake," uses symbolic objects, vivid descriptions, and historical **allusions** in order to express the ways human survival instincts and nature conflict with each other.
Point	Crane's use of symbolism illustrates how human actions can disrupt certain features of nature.
Illustration	"Where the path wended across the ridge, the bushes of huckleberry and sweet fern swarmed at it in two curling waves until it was a mere winding line traced through a tangle."
Explanation	Crane uses symbolism to show how nature is disrupted by human actions. Because nature is disrupted by human actions, man and nature conflict with each other.

Craft Box: DRAFTING

Analyzing the Example:

1. **Does the explanation logically follow from the quotation?**

   - Somewhat, but the explanation doesn't explain the quotation very specifically.

2. **Does the explanation clarify how the quotation supports the main point?**

   - Not really. The explanation seems to be just repeating the main point.

3. **Does the explanation describe how the main point supports the thesis?**

   - Not exactly. The explanation seems to be just repeating the thesis in addition to repeating the main point.

4. **How can the explanation be improved?**

   - The explanation needs to explain the ways Crane uses symbolism specifically in this quotation. How do these symbols "show how nature is disrupted by human actions"?

Revised Example:

Thesis	Stephen Crane's short story, "The Snake," uses symbolism, vivid description, and historical allusion to express the ways human survival instincts and nature conflict with each other.
Point	Crane uses symbolism to illustrate how instinctual human actions disrupt certain features of nature.
Illustration	"Where the path wended across the ridge, the bushes of huckleberry and sweet fern swarmed at it in two curling waves until it was a mere winding line traced through a tangle."
Explanation	Opening the story with this sentence makes the symbolism contained within it particularly significant. One interpretation might read "the path" to be a symbolic representation of "man" in that it is "man-made" and "the bushes of huckleberry and sweet fern" to be a symbolic representation of nature. According to Crane, putting the path together with the bushes, or, putting man together with nature, results in the path becoming a "mere winding line" and the bushes becoming a "tangle." The human action of creating the path disrupts nature as represented by the bushes. By symbolizing man with the path and nature with the bushes, Crane effectively demonstrates how the combination of man and nature results in conflict.

Analyzing the Revised Example:

1. **Does the explanation logically follow from the quotation?**

   - Yes; this is seen in the ways the explanation draws directly from the quotation.

2. **Does the explanation clarify how the quotation supports the main point?**

   - Yes; this is seen when the main point is repeated in the sentence: "In other words, the human nature of creating the path disrupts nature as symbolized by the bushes."

3. **Does the explanation describe how the main point supports the thesis?**

   - Yes; this is seen when the thesis is repeated in the sentence: "By symbolizing man with the path and nature with the bushes, Crane effectively demonstrates how the combination of man and nature results in conflict."

4. **How can the explanation be improved?**

   - Can creating a path really be seen as a "survival instinct"? Might need more explanation equating the two in order to make this point support my thesis.

- **Consider pairing quotation with summary or paraphrase.**

  Pairing quotations with summary or paraphrase is a more in-depth way of framing and explaining quotations. Summarizing or paraphrasing what an author is saying before a quotation can help your readers understand the context of the quotation. Consider this example of how to use paraphrasing to lead into a quotation:

  > **Wallace begins her argument by noting the potential for rap music to raise complicated social issues.** She writes, "In a society plagued by poverty and illiteracy, where young men are as likely to be in prison as in college, rap is a welcome articulation of the economic and social frustration of black youth."

  Notice how the writer frames the quotation with a **paraphrase** of Wallace's text followed by the full quotation. While readers may have an idea of what is meant by "complicated social issues," the full quotation from the original source gives us a much clearer picture of the type of "issues" involved in this discussion, including race, poverty, education, and inequality. Furthermore, offering the paraphrase before the quotation helps readers understand how the quotation fits into the larger picture of Wallace's argument.

  Remember: Always cite every quotation. This includes putting opening and closing quotation marks (" ") at the start and end of the borrowed language as well as the correct in-text citation information, usually the author's name and page number, for each quotation you use.

See section H in *Rules for Writers* for a discussion of the underlying logic of different citation systems.

5.5 The Mechanics of Quoting: In-Text Citation Guide

Following are some of the most common types of in-text citation you will use in first-year writing. These examples use MLA style, the most common system for formatting papers and citing sources in the liberal arts and humanities.

As you review the following examples and practice integrating quotations in your own writing, keep these guidelines in mind:

- Quotations can go at the beginning, middle, or end of any sentence, as long as you follow some basic rules for grammar and punctuation.

- It is important to always set off quotations using quotation marks.

- The parenthetical citation, or the part where you cite the author and page number, usually goes at the end of a sentence.

Parts of a Quotation

Anzaldúa suggests that some people can "see in surface phenomena the meaning of deeper realities" (60).

- Signal phrase/frame for quote
- Quotation mark
- Quoted text
- End punctuation
- Parenthetical

Basic in-text citation styles:

Quote without a signal phrase: Frame the quotation and follow with the "quoted text" (Author Page#).

Example: Some people can "see in surface phenomena the meaning of deeper realities" (Anzaldúa 60).

Quote with a signal phrase: Follow the signal phrase with the "quoted text" (Page#).

Example: Anzaldúa suggests that some people can "see in surface phenomena the meaning of deeper realities" (60).

Beginning with a quotation: Set quotation off with a comma and place the parenthetical at the end of sentence.

Example: "When Gregor Samsa woke up one morning from unsettling dreams he found himself changed in his bed into a monstrous vermin," begins Franz Kafka's famous story of transformation and realization, *The Metamorphosis* (3).

Ending with a quotation: The parenthetical goes directly after quotation but before end punctuation mark.

Example: In *Borderlands/La Frontera*, Gloria Anzaldúa describes the experiences that lead one to develop *la facultad*, or "the capacity to see in surface phenomena the meaning of deeper realities" (60).

Quoting in the middle followed by an analytical statement: Be sure to mark clearly where the quotation begins and ends. Parenthetical goes immediately after the quotation to distinguish the source text from your own ideas.

Example: Stevenson shows that Mr. Hyde's acquaintances describe him very differently, but they all perceive his "haunting sense of unexpressed deformity" (64), which suggests that Hyde possesses an abstract yet observable abnormality.

Dividing with your words: If you need to interrupt a quote with necessary information, such as the name of the writer(s), use commas or other appropriate punctuation between the quotation. Parenthetical goes at the end of sentence.

Example: "Enlightenment's program," Horkheimer and Adorno write, "was the disenchantment of the world" (1).

In-Text Citation Troubleshooting

The following chart represents the most common types of in-text citation that you are likely to encounter in your first-year writing class. You can find a more complete guide to citation in *Rules for Writers* starting on page 457.

Citing What?	What to Do	Example In-Text Citation
Prose (includes essays, short stories, novels, and scholarly articles)	Cite the author and the page number. Don't use the word "page" or "pg."	(Anzaldúa 122)
Poems	Use line numbers for your citation—the first time, use the word "line" or "lines"—after that just use the line number(s). *Note: Line breaks in poetry quotes of three lines or less should be represented with a "/."*	*First Use*: (Donne line 11) *Subsequent Uses*: (Donne 12–13)
Plays	Provide act, scene, and line numbers.	(Shakespeare 4.2.145–7)
Websites	Cite author, title of article, or title of website. You do not need page numbers unless you are looking at an electronic document with stable page numbers, like a PDF of a print text.	(Ewing) ←Best option: if author is known. ("Euro Zone Strain") ←Second best option (*NYTimes.com*) ←Third best option
Multiple texts by same author	Include author name, part of the title of text, and page number.	*Quote from first story*: (O'Brien, "Things" 19) *Quote from book by same author*: (O'Brien, *Cacciato* 124)
Multiple authors	For 1–3 authors, list all authors in the same order they appear in the publication. For 4+ authors, name the first author followed by "et al.," the Latin abbreviation for "and others."	*1–3 Authors*: (Bolter and Grusin 227) *4+ Authors*: (Miller et al. 116)
Quote from a source that is not its original source (source-within-a-source)	Cite name of person you are quoting, then write "qtd. in" followed by the name of the source where you found the quotation. **or** Provide name of person you are quoting as a signal phrase, and start citation with "qtd. in." **or** To avoid this type of quotation, find the original source.	"All wisdom is rooted in learning to call things by the right name" (Kung-fu Tze qtd. in Hamill 548). **or** According to Kung-fu Tze, "All wisdom is rooted in learning to call things by the right name" (qtd. in Hamill 548).

Citing What?	What to Do	Example In-Text Citation
Long quotations (quotations of more than four lines of prose or more than three lines of poetry in MLA)	Use "block quote form." Set the quotation off on a new line with 1" indentations on the left side. Don't use quotation marks. End the quotation with a period and put the citation after the period. *Note: Block quotations should be used sparingly and deliberately, so you don't let the voices of others take over your essay.*	After all, imperialism has led us to see only how we are different from one another: No one today is purely one thing. Labels like Indian, or woman, or Muslim, or American are not more than starting-points. (Said 336)
Two quotations from different sources in one sentence	Place the parenthetical for the first quote directly after the quotation, then put the parenthetical for the second quotation at the end of the sentence.	Stevenson and Kafka both discuss deformity, but Stevenson's comes in the form of "unexpressed deformity" (64), while Kafka transforms his protagonist into a type of "monstrous vermin" that his family refuses to acknowledge (3). *Note that both of these quotations use signal phrases. If you don't have a signal phrase, include the author in the parenthetical citation as well.*

Changing the Quotation

- **If the quotation has an error**, copy it as-is and add the notation *sic* in brackets:

    The citizen wrote, "I felt vindicated by out [sic] actions and rules" (Archive).

- **When you omit words**, use ellipsis marks in place of the missing words. Use three dots to indicate that you have left words out.

    Rackin observes the "liberatory potential of Shakespeare's...cross-dressed heroines" (74).

- **To insert your own material** into a quotation, use brackets. You should only insert material to clarify or to change the tense so it makes sense within the grammar of your own work:

    "[This group] is a quasi-historical community" (Sartre 145).

    Most prisoners of Soviet gulags believed that "the struggle of man against power [was] the struggle of memory against forgetting" (Kundera 4).

See pages 470–71 in *Rules for Writers* for more on using brackets.

Remember to leave time for your Works Cited page. See section 59 in *Rules for Writers* for MLA formatting, and section 64 for APA. Note that the entries are alphabetical in all formats.

Works Cited

Anzaldúa, Gloria. *Borderlands/La Frontera: The New Mestiza*. 2nd ed. San Francisco: Aunt Lute, 1999. Print.

Crane, Stephen. "The Snake." *The Literature Network*, n.d. Web. 16 March 2008.

Graff, Gerald and Cathy Birkenstein. *They Say, I Say: The Moves that Matter in Academic Writing*. New York: Norton, 2006. Print.

Hamill, Sam. "The Necessity to Speak." *Writing as Revision*. Ed. Beth Alvarado and Barbara Cully. Boston: Pearson, 2011. 465–73. Print.

Horkheimer, Max and Theodor W. Adorno. *Dialectic of Enlightenment: Philosophical Fragments*. Trans. Edmund Jephcott. Palo Alto: Stanford UP, 2002. Print.

Kafka, Franz. *The Metamorphosis*. New York: Bantam, 2004. Print.

Kundera, Milan. *The Book of Laughter and Forgetting*. New York: HarperCollins, 1994. 1–5. Print.

Lamberton, Ken. "Sacred Regrets." *Wilderness and Razor Wire*. San Francisco: Mercury House, 2000. 33–44. Print.

Newman, Louise M. Rev. of *Woman Suffrage and Women's Rights*, by Ellen Carol DuBois. *The Journal of American History* 88.1 (2001): 215–16. *JSTOR*. Web. 9 May 2009.

Rackin, Phyllis. *Shakespeare and Women*. New York: Oxford UP, 2005. Print.

Said, Edward. *Culture and Imperialism*. New York: Vintage, 1993. Print.

Sartre, Jean-Paul. *Anti-Semite and Jew*. New York: Schocken, 1995. Print.

The September 11 Digital Archive. Center for History and New Media and American Social History Project/Center for Media and Learning. 2007. Web. 30 June 2008.

Stevenson, Robert Louis. *Dr. Jekyll and Mr. Hyde*. New York: Signet, 2003. Print.

Wallace, Michele. "When Black Feminism Faces the Music, and the Music is Rap." *New York Times*. The New York Times Company, 29 Jul. 1990. Web. 14 Nov. 2011.

Research as Part of the Writing Process

CHAPTER 6

6

6.1   Research: An Overview

6.2   Developing a Research Topic

6.3   Narrowing Your Research Topic

6.4   Evaluating Sources

6.5   Engaging with and Keeping Track of Sources

6.6   The Annotated Bibliography

6.1 Research: An Overview

See page 420 in *Rules for Writers* to view a sample calendar for a research project.

This chapter provides an introduction to the important role research plays in first-year writing at the University of Arizona. It will give you a foundation for doing research in your future classes by going through the process of developing a research topic and question, evaluating and keeping track of sources, and eventually writing an **annotated bibliography**.

Your instructor will help you learn how to conduct research within a given context, including how to tailor your research and writing to a specific course, assignment, audience, and topic. You can also learn a great deal by going to the Main Library and asking for help at the Information Commons Reference Desk or by consulting with a librarian via the "Ask Us" function on the UA library website. You might also schedule an appointment to meet with a specific member of the library staff in person. The library staff is specially trained in finding and evaluating information and will serve as a valuable asset to you throughout your college career. As you explore the research process, you might also work through the set of research tutorials developed by the University of Arizona libraries, which you can find by visiting http://libguides.library.arizona.edu/engl102-108.

Visit the UA Library in person or visit online at <http://www.library.arizona.edu>.

95

You can also access the library tutorials using the following directions:

1. Go to the University Libraries homepage (http://www.library.arizona.edu).

2. Navigate over to the "Search and Find" tab.

3. Hover over "Search and Find" until you see "Research and Writing Help."

4. Click on "Course Guides." Then click on your course.

5. The tutorials you see there will help you learn to use your local resources more effectively.

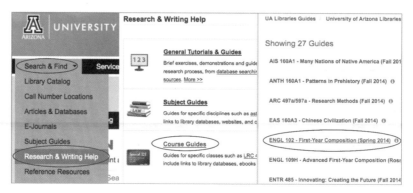

As you begin your own research project, remember that all well-researched ideas build on existing conversations. Learning how to choose appropriate sources, engage them in analysis, and incorporate them properly into a paper will help you enter these conversations in first-year writing and beyond.

6.2 Developing a Research Topic

See section 53a, "Pose questions worth exploring," in *Rules for Writers*.

Sometimes discovering what you want to write about and finding an appropriate focus are the hardest parts of writing a research paper. Some students are accustomed to working with assigned topics and may find it difficult to choose one that they find sufficiently interesting to research. Others are interested in so many ideas that they find it difficult to select just one topic. However you come to your topic, keep in mind that you will spend a great deal of time thinking, reading, talking, and writing about your research, so be sure that the topic is one you are committed to exploring. Your instructor can help you decide if your topic is appropriate for the assignment, but you should begin by thinking of several possible research topics from which to choose.

See Chapter 7 in *Writing Public Lives* for more on choosing a research topic.

Most first-year writing classes will include assignments that ask you to find a topic that has multiple viewpoints; this is typically called a **debatable topic**. Debatable topics must fulfill two criteria. First, they have to stimulate some sort of argument or disagreement, meaning they go beyond reporting undisputed facts. Second, others will have written enough about a debatable topic for you to be able to locate multiple perspectives to inform your understanding of the issues involved.

Here are some strategies you might employ to find a research topic for any paper you are asked to write:

Identify a topic or issue introduced in one of your classes: A good place to begin exploring topics is to reflect on the discussions and readings in your classes. If you are taking a history class, for example, you might research a contested historical event and decide which of several interpretations seems most compelling. Or, you may simply want to further explore a subject that was discussed in a class. Many first-year writing courses are organized around particular themes that will provide a way or ways to approach your research topic.

See Chapter 10 for more on generating topics for a research essay.

Research an issue in your chosen major: Each academic discipline contains its own hot topics or controversial issues. If you are interested in a particular field of study or career, you may find it helpful to discover what topics are currently debated in that discipline. For example, a pharmacy student may want to consider the merits of current laws that require medications containing pseudoephedrine to be dispensed only from behind the counter because of the use of that substance in manufacturing methamphetamine. An aspiring teacher may choose to explore the efficacy of current testing methodologies in evaluating student learning and teacher performances or the effectiveness of teachers' unions in promoting a better quality of life for teachers and better outcomes for students.

6.2

Investigate an extracurricular interest: Your instructor may ask you to identify some non-academic interests as a way of discovering issues to write about. For example, students who are passionate about fishing might investigate the environmental issues surrounding the stocking of trout at Rose Canyon Lake on Mount Lemmon, while students who enjoy reading might investigate changing **literacy** practices in relation to technological developments.

See *Rules for Writers*, pages 26–29 for more on writing an effective thesis for an argument.

No matter what approach you take when choosing a topic, it is important to maintain an appropriate authorial voice for the project. Balancing careful research with your own claims and perspectives can be tricky. Keep in mind that the research you present should achieve several goals: it should show that you are informed about the topic; you are aware of the complexities of the debate you are entering; and you have considered the various definitions, contexts, counterarguments, and assumptions underlying your argument. Focusing on these goals will demonstrate attention to the ongoing conversation and strengthen your argument for your readers.

The Research Checklist

The following checklist can help you keep track of all the stages in the research process and assess your progress. Keep this list handy and check off items as you complete them.

☐ Check the assignment sheet to find the due date for the initial and final drafts of your essay as well as any other assignment to be turned in along the way, such as an annotated bibliography. Write down relevant due dates here:

Rough Draft(s):

Final Draft:

Other Requirements:

☐ Brainstorm topics and write down a few ideas below:

☐ Browse a site like *CQ Researcher* or Course Guides on the library's website to gather ideas about topics.

☐ Narrow down your list of possible topics to one or two ideas and jot them down here:

☐ Get more details and sources on your topic or topics using keyword searches in the Library Catalog and databases like *Academic Search Complete*. Remember, you can also find other good sources from the references cited in the books and articles you find.

☐ Record promising sources: email lists of links to full-text articles, call numbers, and other information to yourself and/or print out reference pages and full-text articles. Keep notes about print sources in a well-organized notebook or folder or make photocopies you can write on. You may also want to use a service like RefWorks or Zotero to keep track of your sources.

☐ Explore the library's book collection. When you find a relevant book for your topic, browse the shelves around this book.

☐ Formulate focused research questions and write a few of them here:

☐ Read through your sources. Take notes and summarize your best sources.

☐ Schedule an interview with an expert on the issue you are interested in. Prepare questions ahead of time.

☐ Meet with a librarian, either at a reference desk or by appointment.

☐ Double-check that you have all of the sources you need. Check that you've written down all information needed for your own Works Cited list.

☐ Consider writing an annotated bibliography to help keep track of your sources and their primary arguments in relation to your paper.

☐ Begin writing your first draft!

6.3 Narrowing Your Research Topic

Sometimes a research idea that seems like a good topic for a class project turns out to be so broad that sifting through all the available research will be overwhelming. It is crucial to find a topic large enough that others have published information about it but also narrow enough for you to identify the most important sources and arguments within a limited time frame. Here are a few tips for narrowing your research topic:

Brainstorm sub-topics: After you have found a topic that interests you, try making it even more specific by breaking it down further or investigating specific arguments within the broader context of your topic. Preliminary research can help you identify sub-topics. The UA research librarians recommend checking out what has been written about your topic in *CQ Researcher* or another UA library **database** to begin narrowing your topic.

> *Broad topic:* Alternative energy sources
>
> > *Possible sub-topics found through preliminary research:* Biofuels, electric cars, solar power, environmental activism efforts in Tucson

Through your research, you might find that even a sub-topic can be narrowed further.

> *New topic:* Solar power
>
> > *Possible sub-topics:* solar-powered high-speed trains, solar ovens, solar panels on electric cars

Pair your topic with a related issue: Sometimes pairing one topic with a second one helps to provide a more specific and defined lens for your research. As you do preliminary research on your topic, keep an eye out for an angle that you might bring to your research idea.

> *Research topic:* Solar ovens
>
> > *Possible pairings:* Solar ovens in disaster zones, solar ovens in developing countries, solar ovens and elementary education

Ground your research in something you know: Approaching a research topic that you already know something about may help you develop a personal stake in your findings. Similarly, it helps to narrow any abstract ideas into more concrete subjects. Mechanical engineering majors might narrow "alternative energy sources" to solar-powered cars, for example, whereas an environmental science major might be more interested in studying environmental activism in Tucson. Ask yourself: "What do I have to say about this topic?"

See pages 5 and 422 in *Rules for Writers* for more on narrowing research topics.

6.3

See Chapter 9 in *Writing Public Lives* for more on researching a local issue.

Write a pointed research question: A clear, focused research question helps you narrow your topic and stay focused throughout the research process. Remember that if you are not interested in learning the answer to your question, your audience will probably not be very interested in the answer either. Focus your research on a question you are interested in answering and that others might find interesting as well.

> *Research topic:* Solar ovens
>
> > *Research Question 1:* How have solar ovens been used recently in disaster zones, and what were the positive and negative effects of this use?
> >
> > *Research Question 2:* What environmental factors influence the effectiveness of solar ovens, and does this make them better suited for use in certain geographic regions?
> >
> > *Research Question 3:* How are solar ovens built, and what impact does the selection of a particular building material have on the cooking effectiveness of the finished oven?

Strong research questions share a few qualities:

- **They are clearly significant; they carry an answer to the "so what?" question.** For example, Research Question 2 above sets the writer up for an argument about why solar ovens should only be used in certain parts of the world.

- **They can be answered in the space you have available.** It would be nearly impossible to find a definitive answer to the world's reliance on oil in the space of a five-page paper, for example. However, it might be manageable to examine the political reasons for and economic impacts of raising fuel standards for vehicles made during the 2011 model year.

- **They have not already been answered by somebody else.** For instance, asking, "What is climate change?" is not an original research question, although it might be a question you have to answer in your essay to make your own researched argument.

Having a strong research question will be key to finding sources and evaluating their effectiveness.

See Chapter 8 in *Writing Public Lives* for help with formulating a strong research question.

6.4 | 6.4

6.4 Evaluating Sources

See page 401 in *Rules for Writers* for more advice on determining if a source is scholarly.

When conducting research in an academic setting, your job as a student and critical thinker is to sift through the many claims and competing opinions and decide which are the most credible and reliable. Begin evaluating your sources by focusing on how the information is portrayed to its primary audience. Be aware that information is often portrayed differently in scholarly and popular sources. Both types of sources can help you gain a more thorough understanding of the way different publics view and understand your topic. Always check your assignment to see if your instructor requires certain kinds of sources.

- A **scholarly source** is a text written by and for researchers and scholars with specialized knowledge about a particular subject. Sometimes scholarly sources are also referred to as "academic sources," meaning they are written by and for academics, peer reviewed, and published in academic journals or books.

- A **popular source** is written for a broader audience and seeks to engage in a public debate or conversation. Popular sources include magazines and newspapers as well as videos, websites, blogs, and other media. They can be written by professional writers, journalists, or anyone with publishing capabilities.

See the box below to compare the major distinctions between scholarly and popular sources.

Scholarly vs. Popular Sources: A Quick Reference Guide

Characteristic	Scholarly Source	Popular Source
What does it look like?	• Usually includes many citations referencing other scholarly sources using an established citation system (MLA, APA, etc.). • Front covers are often plain with few pictures. • Usually takes the form of extended written texts that sometimes include charts, graphs, or related images.	• Includes few end citations. Sources cited using signal phrases, reference to credentials, or other means. • Front covers and inside pages are often full of photographs and short snippets of text. • Tends to be shorter and less formal, and may include images, graphics, or video.
What is its purpose?	• Seeks to contribute to an ongoing academic debate or a discussion in a specific field.	• Seeks to engage in a public debate or conversation.

6.4

Characteristic	Scholarly Source	Popular Source
How and where is it published?	• Published through a process called "peer review," which means that before being accepted for publication, the article is read by experts in the field who assess its reliability, relevance, and the quality of its research and writing. • Generally found in academic books and academic journals.	• If it is edited, editors are usually journalists or professional editors who may or may not be specialists in the topic the work covers. • Generally found in newspapers, magazines, books, and online sources.
What kinds of sources does it cite?	• Usually references published research to back up claims. • Almost always includes in-text citations and a bibliography of cited texts. Sources may be referenced in **quotations**, **paraphrases**, summaries, footnotes, endnotes, and bibliographies. • Quotes serve to situate the new position the author is advancing within the existing body of knowledge and to guide readers to the other credible sources of information about the topic.	• May reference sources ranging from experts to everyday people who have a stake in the conversation. • Does not always provide information on how to access sources beyond naming them. In other words, does not always include in-text citations. • Quotes usually serve as evidence for the claim the work is seeking to make.
Who is the author?	• Authors are faculty, researchers, or scholars writing for others in their field. • Many scholarly sources are written by professors at universities like the UA.	• Authors may be anyone from researchers to teen bloggers writing for a more public audience.

Characteristic	Scholarly Source	Popular Source
Who is its intended audience?	• Intended to be read by an audience with interest in the field. • Assumes readers already have some specialized knowledge.	• Written for the publication's intended audience. For instance, *Wired! Magazine* has a very different audience than *National Geographic*. • May not assume their readers have specialized knowledge.
How did I find it?	• Accessible through academic databases like *JSTOR* or *Academic Search Complete*. • Often found in academic libraries such as the UA Main Library.	• Generally accessible using popular search engines such as Google or Yahoo!, or library databases such as *LexisNexis Academic*. • Often sold at newsstands or at bookstores.
What are some examples?	• *Arizona Quarterly, Journal of Insect Science, Community Literacy Journal** *All of these journals are edited by UA faculty.	• *Time, The Wall Street Journal, Popular Science, Slate, Salon, Radiolab, NPR*

Evaluating Internet Sources

As more material becomes available on the Internet, it is increasingly important to know how to evaluate the credibility of online sources. In fact, one of the first discussions about research in your first-year writing courses will probably center on the differences between using a search engine such as Google and using a library database such as *Academic Search Complete* or *LexisNexis Academic Universe*. Generally speaking, most texts you find using library databases are either scholarly sources or popular journalism, both of which are generally considered credible resources. On the other hand, sources available through widely used search engines like Google range in terms of credibility from well-researched information published by respectable organizations to incorrect assertions published by misinformed independent authors.

Many Web pages are not subject to the review process of a peer-reviewed scholarly source or even that of a respected popular source such as *The New York Times* or *Time* magazine. Anyone with the technical skills and access to the Internet can publish a Web page on any topic, even if they do not have expertise in the subject. For instance, an angry consumer can publish a review denouncing a

See Chapter 9 for more information on rhetorical analysis.

certain product even if the consumer's dissatisfaction arose out of misuse rather than a defect of the product itself. If you were to rely only on that consumer's opinion, the research would be flawed and, at best, misleading. However, because they are not subject to review, Web pages can also provide a space for voices that are not normally heard in official publications. Unmonitored websites might also provide a more accurate, uncensored picture of what members of the public think or feel regarding a specific topic. As with any careful reading, it is important to employ the skills of **rhetorical analysis** when evaluating Internet sources. Reading critically for audience and purpose can shed light on the credibility of the source.

Online encyclopedias are commonly cited Internet resources, and they range from *Encyclopedia Britannica*, available through the university library, to *Wikipedia*, a free online resource edited by users. Your instructor may or may not allow you to use encyclopedias; if you consult these sources, you should be aware of the distinctions between them. Although *Wikipedia* may well be authoritative in certain contexts, its reliability is not monitored in the same way as an encyclopedia such as the *Encyclopedia Britannica*.

Interviews: Bringing Your Research Topic to Life

By Rachael Wendler

Having the opportunity to speak with a research source can be exciting, but effective interviewing takes thought and preparation. These steps will walk you through the process.

Step 1: Choosing an Interviewee

Consider people with different kinds of knowledge:

- Academic knowledge (a professor who studies autism)

- Professional knowledge (a staff member at a local autism advocacy organization)

- Experiential knowledge (a parent of an autistic child)

Try googling "Tucson" or "University of Arizona" and your topic to get a sense of local resources, exploring faculty profiles in relevant departments or thinking about your personal networks. You might also think about interviewing someone who disagrees with you to better understand alternate views.

Step 2: Requesting an Interview

Remember that an interview is a favor, so ask nicely! In your interview request:

- Introduce yourself (if needed), the purpose of your project, and the interview topic

- Explain why this person would be a good interviewee

- Specify how much time the interview would take, when you need it completed, and the format (in person, phone, email) and location (someplace convenient for the interviewee)

Make contact *as soon as possible*, so you have time to find someone else if your first choice is unavailable.

If your instructor does allow you to use popular sources in your research papers, it is important to evaluate their credibility. Even when a Web page looks and sounds official, you should be careful to examine its claims. In the Tips & Strategies Box on the next page, you will find a list of questions to help you evaluate the credibility of information you find online.

6.5 Engaging with and Keeping Track of Sources

As you research your topic, make a conscious effort to keep track of the sources you find. Keeping track of sources will help you stay organized and will save you time in the long run. In addition, you can begin the actual writing process as you collect your sources by taking notes and interacting with each source. This section will address both aspects of tracking sources.

> See the UA library tutorial for evaluating internet sources by visiting <http://www.library.arizona.edu/tutorials/evaluating_web_resources/>.

> See section 55b, "Keep track of source materials," in *Rules for Writers*.

6.5

Step 3: Preparing

Begin by researching your interviewee—asking for information that is available online shows a lack of consideration for your interviewee's time. Has your interviewee published something? Read it. Does she work for an organization? Check out its website. Consider what holes you have in your data and what this interviewee could offer from his or her expertise. Brainstorm questions (~8–12 for a 20-minute interview), making sure to avoid questions that could be offensive or overly intrusive. Try for open-ended questions (why/how/in what way) rather than closed questions that can be answered with a simple yes or no.

Once you have a list, put questions in an order that makes sense, such as chronologically or by topic. If there are any sensitive questions, put those at the end, after the interviewee has had time to warm up and you've had an opportunity to feel out if the question is appropriate. Finally, prioritize your questions, bolding the ones that are most important, so if time runs short, you can jump straight to the key points.

Step 4: The Interview

Bring your typed questions, a hard-backed notebook to write on, a pen, and two ways to record in case one doesn't work (hint: there are many free recording apps for smartphones). Dress professionally if you'll be interviewing in a professional context. Establish rapport through small talk first, and then ask permission to record before turning on your device and asking questions. Don't feel tied to your questions—follow your interviewee's lead if he or she brings up something interesting, and improvise follow-up questions. Pay attention to your body language (eye contact!) and your interviewee's (is a certain topic making him uncomfortable?). Don't take more time than you requested unless your interviewee invites you to talk longer, and make sure to say thanks!

Step 5: Following Up

Send a thank-you card or email, and offer to share your final paper.

Recording Crucial Information

Your research project will probably require you to identify your sources with in-text citations and a Works Cited page. It can be time-consuming and frustrating to retrace your steps later to find a publisher's name, a page number, or the database for an online article. Here are a few tips to assist your process:

> Compare the websites on pages 446 and 447 in *Rules for Writers* as you learn how to evaluate sources for reliability and relevance.

- **Keep track of your research in a research log.** To do this, record the databases and indexes you search and the keywords that you use in each database. Keep this log with the notes you take on the books and articles you are reading. This will help you keep track of where you have looked and what sources were good for your topic. Also write down sources you review that are not helpful so that you do not waste time by accidentally reviewing a source twice. See page 108 for an example.

Evaluating Internet Sources

When you find a website you think you would like to use in your research, ask the following questions to assess its credibility.

Choose a website you think you might use in your research and evaluate it using the following criteria:

- **URL:** What is the URL? Does it end with .com, .edu, .org, .gov, .biz, .name, .info, or .net? What does each of these domain names imply? Which would indicate that the source is credible?

- **Author:** Can you identify an author for the information? Can you verify the author's qualifications?

- **Last Updated:** Does the Web page provide information about when it was last updated? Is there any way of determining whether the material is out of date? What sorts of links are on the page? Where do these links lead you? Are the links still working?

- **Purpose:** What is the text trying to accomplish? Is its purpose to inform, entertain, or persuade the reader? Does it appear to be promoting a commercial product, an idea, a philosophy, or some other way of seeing something?

- **Graphics:** Are there graphics? If so, what do they illustrate and why?

- **Position on Subject:** Does the source seem biased, one-sided, incomplete, or erroneous? Who profits if viewers of the website believe its information to be true? Can you verify the information with other online or print sources?

- **Links:** Does the source suggest avenues for further inquiry such as possible readings, research, or links? Does it cite reputable sources or note the extent to which claims in the text are connected to recognized authorities in the field?

Evaluating websites carefully is an essential part of your research process, since the reliability of your own argument in an academic context will depend in large part upon the credibility of your citations and sources. Whenever you are in doubt about the suitability of a certain source, consult your instructor or the UA librarians.

- **Copy materials you cannot check out of the library for an extended period (such as journals). Print or download articles or texts that you find online.** Do not assume that you will be able to find such sources again later; they may be in use or in the process of being reshelved when you look for them again. In the case of online materials, do not assume that you can find the article again easily. It will save you time to print or download the article at the time you find it.

- **Try using RefWorks or other bibliographic software.** Another option for compiling resources is an application available through the UA libraries called RefWorks, which formats and organizes your citations and bibliographies as you work. A librarian can help you learn to use this resource.

  > You can learn more about RefWorks at <http://www.library. arizona.edu/search/ articles/dbDetail. php?shortname= refworks>.

- **Immediately write down any information that you will need** every time you copy or print materials out of a book, journal, or online database. This information will include the page numbers you read as well as all of the bibliographic information for the source. Make a habit of writing this information on the first page of anything you copy or print and record it in your research log. You can find an in-depth explanation of how to cite various types of sources on pages 490–523 in *Rules for Writers*.

- **Compile an annotated bibliography**, in which you include all the bibliographic information (in the format required for your paper) and a brief description of each text. This will help you keep track of who said what. You can easily flip through it to remind yourself of each author's main points. See the discussion of annotated bibliographies in the next section of this chapter.

- **Write the citation as soon as you use a quote, summary, or paraphrase of any source, and immediately add that source to your Works Cited page.** This way you can be certain you cited all your references, and when you revise, you won't have to look through all your materials to find the correct citation information.

- **Refer to "MLA Documentation" in *Rules for Writers*, starting on page 426.** Also view the UA libraries' MLA tutorial at <http://www.library. arizona.edu/search/reference/citation-mla.html>. Note that depending on your class, instructor, or academic discipline, you may need to use a different citation system, such as APA or Chicago style. Always make sure to check the formatting expectations before you begin integrating your sources.

6.5

Sample Research Log

Keeping a research log can help you stay organized throughout the research process. It can also help you keep track of where and how you found your sources and serve as the starting point for an annotated bibliography. In the sample below, UA student Justin Frere demonstrates how to turn a research question into search terms for an academic database. Notice how he records the database, the search string, and the articles that this search produced. This way, Justin can remember which sources he has already found and which search terms he has already used. Though this sample shows the selected results of only one attempted search, Justin will probably want to try different search strings in order to identify the best sources for his research project.

You can learn more about searching online databases—including identifying keywords and creating searches with Boolean operators (AND, OR)—by viewing the "Searching Effectively" tutorial on the University Libraries website.

Research Question: How does **student–teacher communication** in a large **lecture** setting impact **student experience**?

Keywords	Synonyms and Other Related Words
student	pupil, audience
teacher	mentor, faculty, professor, instructor
communication	interaction, contact, learning
lecture	lecture hall, auditorium, class, large, big
university	college
student experience	attitude, learning, mindset

Search #1

Database: ERIC

Search String: (student OR pupil) AND (teacher OR faculty) AND (lecture OR seminar OR auditorium) AND (communication OR interaction OR contact) AND (large OR big)—189 results

- – Title: "Student Response Systems and Facilitating the Large Lecture Basic Communication Course: Assessing Engagement and Learning"
  - o Author(s): Denker, Katherine J.
  - o Publication: *Communication Teacher*, v27 n1 p50–69 2013.

- – Title: "Digital or Didactic: Using Learning Technology to Confront the Challenge of Large Cohort Teaching"
  - o Author(s): Saunders, Fiona C.; Gale, Andrew W.
  - o Publication: *British Journal of Educational Technology*, v43 n6 p847–858 Nov 2012.

Sidebar notes:

First, highlight or underline the key terms in your research question and create a list of searchable keywords. Also consider if there are other important terms that are not in your question. In this case, Justin added "university" to his list because of the setting of his research.

Since different terms will yield different results, it is important to consider alternative words you can use to represent the key terms in your question.

Record the database and search string, so you can remember what terms you have already used. Justin used the ERIC database because his topic relates to education.

Note how Justin strategically used his keywords in combination with Boolean operators (AND, OR) to narrow his results.

Write a brief annotation for each source you open. You might also include the author's credential and a short summary. You will modify this list as you locate more sources and determine which will be most appropriate for your project. You can add information to this list to create an annotated bibliography.

6.5

- Title: "'Supersizing' the College Classroom: How One Instructor Teaches 2,670 Students"

  o Author(s): Parry, Marc
  o Publication: *Chronicle of Higher Education*, Apr 2012

- Title: "'That's It for Today': Academic Lecture Closings and the Impact of Class Size"

  o Author(s): Cheng, Stephanie W.
  o Publication: *English for Specific Purposes*, v31 n4 p234–248 Oct 2012.

- Title: "Student Engagement in Very Large Classes: The Teachers' Perspective"

  o Author(s): Exeter, Daniel J.; Ameratunga, Shanthi; Ratima, Matiu; Morton, Susan; Dickson, Martin; Hsu, Dennis; Jackson, Rod
  o Publication: *Studies in Higher Education*, v35 n7 p761–775 Nov 2010.

Engaging with Your Sources

Engaged reading requires more than just reading through a text and underlining passages. One of the best ways to engage with your sources is to take notes as you read, a practice known as **annotation**. Think about taking notes as having a conversation with the author or authors of the source and asking them the questions you might address in your paper. As you read in Chapter 2, asking questions and making comments in the margins while you read can help you remember why you took note of that section. Taking notes can also help you see patterns developing across sources, which may help you identify how you would like to enter the conversation. You may also realize that you have found sources representing only one side of an issue and need to find more sources to fill in any gaps.

Sample Research Notes

On the following page, you'll find sample research notes. This two-column strategy helps you to record the ideas you have about specific parts of a text and can save you from having to go back and hunt down specific quotations later in the writing process. These notes, taken by a UA student, were provided by UA librarian Vicki Mills. This student's research project explores how minority children in elementary school are able, or unable, to relate to the characters in the books they read.

6.5

See Chapter 2 for help with and examples of annotation.

See Chapter 2 for more information on reading critically and taking notes.

At the top of the page, record the bibliographic information.

Tolson, Nancy. "Making Books Available: The Role of Early Libraries, Librarians, and Booksellers in the Promotion of African American Children's Literature." *African American Review* 32.1 (1998): 9–16. *Academic Search Complete*. Web. 1 Oct. 2008.

In the right column, record your response to the passage on the left.

In the left column, write the page number and a quote or paraphrase that you find interesting, relevant, or even incorrect or confusing. Writing the quotation will help you consider it more fully than if you just looked at it on the page and recorded the page number.

Source Material	Notes, Questions, etc.
"African American children's books are in existence today because of the determination and dedication of African Americans who decided more than sixty years ago to remove negative depictions of servile, impoverished African Americans from library shelves. These people were able to establish criteria, petition publishers, and creatively write stories for African American children that reflected positive images at a time when few of these books could get published." (Tolson 15)	I agree with Tolson's thesis. The focus is pretty historical throughout the article though. My question is, what is happening with the depiction of minorities in children's books now? Surely they are still problematical at times. **Look for more contemporary articles on this. Also, what did these negative depictions do to children's desire to read and to their own identity? I need to look for other articles that relate the lack of books with positive minority role models to the reading ability of minority children.

Your notes should include questions or challenges you have for the text, as well as your possible responses to these questions.

Note other research you need to do, including new searches and looking up experts named in the source text.

Write yourself notes that will help you to construct your argument when you start drafting.

Source Material	Notes, Questions, etc.
"Bontemps, being both an educator and the father of six children, knew the importance of writing books that would reflect positive African American images; this meant, among other things, freeing his African American characters from the heavy dialect that most other authors had imposed upon them." (10)	This is one way I might go with this paper—the importance of parents reading to children and the problem of minority parents finding enough appropriate books to read. Like how Tolson says that the depictions in Bontemps' books meant "*freeing*... characters from the heavy dialect." The same thing happens in the depiction of other minority characters—American Indian, Hispanic, or Asian American—they are basically trapped and limited by the language and the behavior the author assigns them (particularly if that author is not from the minority group).

Don't worry about writing in full sentences; taking notes is like talking back to your sources. Being casual can make the process more comfortable and generative, and you can always dress up your language in your actual draft.

This kind of research note might very well become a central part of your paper. Keeping research notes helps to save these important insights you have as you engage with your sources.

6.5

Now that you have seen how you might take notes from a source, try it yourself. Find an article online that relates to your topic—either popular or scholarly—and create your own research notes to share in class. Make sure to keep this article handy, as you can use it again to work on an annotation for your annotated bibliography assignment in the next section.

6.6 The Annotated Bibliography

One useful way to keep track of your research is to create an annotated bibliography, a document that lists carefully formatted citations for topic-related sources. Each citation is then followed by a brief summary of the source and an evaluation of how and why you plan on using it in your research process. Annotated bibliographies are highly valued by scholars because they allow researchers to quickly review the best sources on a given topic. Even if you do not end up publishing your annotated bibliography for other researchers, it can be a useful way for you to keep track of the best sources for your research topic.

Writing an annotated bibliography for your research projects will help you gather and analyze information before you sit down to draft your project. When working with many sources, it can be very helpful to have brief summaries of each article as a quick reference. Because the annotated bibliography is primarily for you, your classmates, and your instructor, take care to write in a voice and **style** that appeals to this audience, translating technical material into your own words where you can.

Let's take a look at one annotation from UA student Stephenie Mirka. As you read, note how in this entry Stephenie considers not only what the source is about, but also how it could contribute to her research.

> Visit the *Rules for Writer's* companion website (www.hacker handbooks.com/rules) and click on "Model papers" for sample annotated bibliographies in MLA and APA styles.

Annotated Bibliography

Hardesty, Dawn Wotapka. "Long Island Landlord Group: Sex Offender Law Goes Too Far." *Long Island Business News*. The Dolan Company, 17 Nov. 2006. Web. 24 Feb. 2007.

Hardesty claims that a bill in Long Island, regarding landlords renting to sex offenders, is ridiculous. The author utilizes many quotes from people, who agree and disagree with her claim. By including both points of view in her argument, she strengthens her essay. She also explains the disadvantages of this law, and how it victimizes sexual offenders. Her purpose is to show that some sex offender laws are too extreme. This article will provide a point of view different than mine for my persuasive essay. It will give me an example of a sexual offender law that is creating problems for landlords. Hardesty provides information from the creator of the bill, which will be useful to back up my claims. I chose this source because it gave a good example of why some laws do not work against sexual offenders.

6.6

Let's see how Stephenie's annotated bibliography entry meets or does not meet the criteria in the Tips & Strategies Box below. First, Stephenie begins by stating the overall claim of Hardesty's argument: a new bill making it illegal to rent apartments to sex offenders is ridiculous. Then, she moves to a brief summary of Hardesty's methods (citing other interviews and balancing multiple points of view). Finally, she states Hardesty's main point, which is that sex offender laws are too extreme. Stephenie lets her readers know that she will be using this article to show how this proposed bill is problematic for landlords. It is also clear that this is a good resource for helping Stephenie learn about the bill, its creation, and its intended execution.

Here are a few more entries in Stephenie's Annotated Bibliography. Now that you understand the basic parts of an annotation, read to see how she relates each source to her overall argument.

Longo, Robert E. "Megan's Law Does Little to Increase Safety in US." *Community Care.* Reed Business Information Limited, 3 Aug. 2006. Web. 25 Feb. 2007.

> Longo claims that the development of Megan's Law has not been proven to decrease the number of sexual abuse cases within the United States. The author proves this by including background information, statistics, and examples. He discusses the many implications of Megan's Law, such as cost and victimization of sexual offenders. This victimization has caused many to become offenders again because

Writing the Annotation

As you begin drafting your own annotations, consider the following template. Following these guidelines can help ensure you have included all the information you need in your own work so that your audience clearly understands the major arguments in each source and how you plan to use them.

1. **Describe the purpose of the article.**

   a. Context: Contextualize the purpose in one sentence. Why was the article written?

   b. Audience: Identify the primary audience for the article.

   c. Purpose: State the overall thesis of the article in one sentence.

2. **Summarize the methods.**

   a. Mention how the study was conducted.

   b. Omit any specific details (save these for the essay).

3. **Describe the major observations/findings/results.**

   a. Provide the *key ideas* and "takeaways" but don't reflect on them.

   b. Omit any specific details (save these for the essay).

4. **Forecast future use.**

   a. Include the ways in which you plan to use the article in your essay.

they are not able to live normal lives after their release from prison. Longo's purpose is to show his readers that the only way to put an end to sexual abuse is to stop it before it occurs. Megan's Law does not aid in this since no evidence exists to prove that it has prevented reoccurrences of sexual abuse. This article will aid in my research question of deciding whether sexual offenders should be integrated back into society. It shows examples and statistics that could be used in my paper.

Miller, Kathleen. "Wyoming Fears It's Luring Sex Offenders." *Chron.com*. The Houston Chronicle, 25 Feb. 2007. Web. 25 Feb. 2007.

Miller discusses the number of sex offenders that are moving to Wyoming as a result of the harsh laws in other states. Miller uses quotes from a representative of the U.S. House of Representatives, sex offenders, a police officer, and many others. These add substance to her article, when used with background information and other facts regarding laws in Wyoming. Miller's purpose is to inform people of the lack of laws for sexual predators. She wants this to change so that more sexual predators will have to be registered, and harsher laws will be created. In my paper, this article can provide me with an opposing point of view. This will help me to draw my own conclusions about the opposing viewpoint.

Seipp, Catherine. "The Sex-Offender Lobby." *The Wall Street Journal*. Dow Jones and Company, 6 Oct. 2005. Web. 25 Feb. 2007.

Seipp states in her editorial that laws regarding sex offenders and landlords in California do not coincide well. She proves her point by explaining Megan's Law. Also, Seipp's article contains quotes from opponents and advocates of Megan's Law. By including the views of a landlord who is unable to move a sex offender out of his mobile-home park, but still needs to inform angry residents of the offender's presence, she makes her case far more understandable to the reader. The author's purpose is to let people know that lawmakers should not oppose Megan's Law. This applies to my research question by showing the opposing point of view. I can use this in my persuasive essay to show readers what others think regarding the issue of sex offenders. Seipp includes various quotes, which could be added into my paper to expand on the opposing viewpoint.

6.6

Craft Box: **DRAFTING**

6.6

Parts of an Annotation

Now use the advice from the "Writing the Annotation" Tips & Strategies Box to create an annotation for an article you plan to use in your own annotated bibliography:

1. **Purpose:**

2. **Methods:**

3. **Major Findings:**

4. **Future Use:**

Try putting all the parts together and write a full annotation. Once you have written and revised it, use this entry in your annotated bibliography!

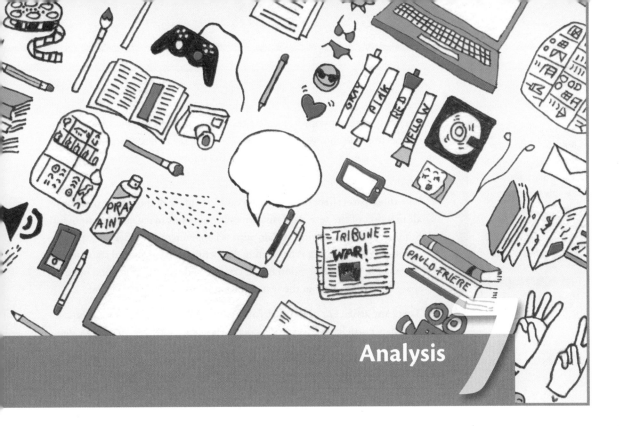

Analysis

7.1 Analysis: An Overview

All of the assignments you will complete in your first-year writing courses require **analysis**. The word analysis comes from the Greek word *analysis*, which
means "a breaking up, a loosening, a releasing" ("Analysis"). When you analyze
something, you "break it up" to examine its parts and see how it was put together
to achieve its purpose. In fact, in much of the work you do at the university, you
will be asked to analyze something and provide evidence to support your interpretation. In your first-year writing class, that "something" might be a written
text, an image, an audience, or a **literacy** event in your life. In an art history
class, you might be asked to analyze a particular social or historical **context**,
an artist's technique, or a particular medium; in a biology class, you might analyze cellular function, an ecosystem, or the life cycle of a particular organism.
Regardless of what you are analyzing, you are essentially performing the same
cognitive task: closely and carefully examining a subject in an attempt to understand or interpret it.

In your first-year writing courses, analysis requires an ability to explain how and
why a text works to make meaning. Whether you are analyzing a short story or a
literacy event in your life, you participate in creating meaning by exploring and
building an **argument** around your particular interpretation. In an analysis, you
will be challenged to think beyond the surface-level message of the texts you
read. In order to offer a complex and interesting analysis of any text, you must

See section 5d in *Rules
for Writers* for advice
on analysis as a way to
demonstrate critical
thinking.

CHAPTER 7

117

See section 5c in *Rules for Writers* for guidelines for writing a summary and for a sample summary. See also the section on page 78 in *Rules for Writers*: "Summarize less; analyze more."

read it closely, interact with it, locate sites of inquiry, and use your own lived experiences to guide your responses. Before moving into a discussion of specific types of analysis, take a moment to consider the following key terms:

- **Analysis:** Analysis is the act of breaking a text into parts and examining how those parts affect the audience's understanding of the text or the overall function of the text. Analysis moves beyond **summary** and description. Summary and description explain *what* is happening while analysis explains *how* and *why* something is happening. Remember that analytical statements reveal a careful consideration of the text beyond its main point and open a space for dialogue about the text and what it "means" to an audience.

- **Text:** Any artifact or object that you analyze. A text might refer to a book, a newspaper article, a short story, a poem, a speech, a movie, a picture, a video game, a person, an event, a space, a place, and so on.

- **Strategies:** How authors of texts present ideas to the reader. Strategies include repetition of key terms, use of extended **metaphors**, arrangement of the text, choice of color and medium, and so on.

When applying these terms in analytical writing, maintaining focus on a specific argument is essential. No single essay can say everything there is to say about a particular text or experience. If you try to take on too much in your essay, you will find that the **thesis** lacks specificity and the paragraphs make imprecise claims.

7.2 Approaches to Analysis

When you engage in **textual analysis**, you can examine something written, like a poem or short story; something visual, either a stationary visual like a photograph or a moving visual like a film or music video; something spatial, like a place you have visited or a space you use; or something experiential, like your own experience with language. In the following pages, you will find individual sections with suggestions and strategies for performing analysis on specific types of texts. In order, you will find Literary Analysis, Visual Analysis, Film Analysis, Spatial Analysis, and Analysis of a Literacy Event.

See Chapter 2 for more on close reading.

Literary Analysis of Written Texts

In order to produce an analysis of a written text, you should first review your notes from your close reading of the text. You might want to look through Chapter 2 again to remind yourself of some of the questions and strategies that can help you produce your own interpretation of a text's meaning. Consider focusing on the patterns and repeated ideas you discovered while reading, including patterns in what arguments a text is making (themes or ideas) and how it makes these arguments (literary devices and form). Below, you will find suggestions for two types of literary analysis essays: one based on thematic content and one based on the author's techniques. However, there are many other types of literary analysis essays, and you should make sure that you are following your teacher's assignment instructions and guidelines.

Thematic Literary Analysis

The goal of this type of analysis is to explain how a text engages, promotes, or challenges specific ideas or themes. The theme is a message that one interprets from the text rather than the main topic(s) of the text. A text may even place two or more ideas or themes in opposition to each other, calling for an interpretation that makes sense of a contradictory relationship.

In a thematic literary analysis, writers usually identify and support their interpretation of a text based on the author's use of details, setting, characterizations, images, descriptions, etc. To make sure you are not merely summarizing the text, consider looking at complex, ambiguous, or secondary issues within the text. Take note of your close reading annotations again and focus on phrases, images, or descriptive language that seemed particularly provoking, important, or unusual. Consider any sections with unclear purposes. If you wonder why an author used a particular detail or described a particular event, there is a good chance that they are complicating the main issues of the text in ways you have yet to consider. Remember, a text doesn't happen by accident and authors often contradict, elaborate on, or redirect what appears to be their main purpose or message.

When thinking about a topic for your essay, consider using the mind-mapping technique from Chapter 2. How many different ideas or themes are present within your text? How can you connect these ideas or group them together? Are any of the connections surprising or unusual? Does the author challenge or subvert the positive or negative values traditionally associated with these ideas or themes?

You could also consider two different themes in conversation with each other. For example, Salman Rushdie's short story "At the Auction of the Ruby Slippers" includes themes such as consumerism, violence, organized religion, nostalgia, unrequited love, and celebrity culture, among others. Consider how UA student Chloe Cho analyzes the relationship between religion and materialism in the text in order to produce a specific interpretation of Rushdie's story:

> The short story "At the Auction of the Ruby Slippers" by Salman Rushdie depicts the materialistic era and the consequential emptiness of worshiping the unachievable object. While some people consider the Ruby Slippers as just a special and glamorous object, the majority of the population idolizes the Ruby Slippers. The story mainly focuses on the narrator's point of view. He considered the Ruby Slippers as a magical object that will help him regain his romantic relationship. However, as he realizes

7.2

that his desires are unattainable, he experiences bitter feelings of empti-
ness. Since materialism functions as religion in the story, people tend to
depend on the fictional object, the Ruby Slippers, rather than acknowledging and improving their dissatisfying conditions.

Following up on student writing:

- In your own words, what is Chloe saying about the text?

- How does Chloe's thesis move her beyond summary into an analysis of
  Rushdie's story?

- How does Chloe introduce the two complex themes and her interpretation
  without being too vague or giving away too many details?

It is important to notice that Chloe's thesis does not simply state that the short
story reflects two ideas, religion and materialism, but rather that the combination of these themes produces a message within the text. Remember, like the
definition of analysis in section 7.1, it is always important to demonstrate how
your interpretations of the author's ideas (or the "parts" of the text) connect
back to a larger idea or message (or the "whole" of the text).

Literary Device-Based Analysis

In order to perform an analysis based on the techniques or literary devices used
by the author, consider the following steps:

1. Use your close reading to identify a theme, message, or purpose present in
    the text (often based on patterns or repetitions of language and form)

2. Correctly identify specific literary devices related to this theme/message/
    purpose. (See the sample list of literary devices that follows.)

3. Group examples from the text together by literary device or technique.
    For example, you might place all similes together. You might also consider
    grouping examples together based on larger categories that produce similar
    effects like sound or image. For example, symbol, simile, and metaphor can
    be grouped together as they all create mental images, while assonance and
    alliteration might be grouped together because they produce specific sound
    effects.

4. Based on your teacher's assignment, select an appropriate number of de-
    vices to analyze for your essay. You may be asked to discuss the author's use
    of a single device at length, or you might be asked to demonstrate how the
    author uses multiple devices for a single purpose. When you select devices
    and examples of where those devices are used in the text, be sure to select
    those that have a strong impact on the theme or message you wish to dis-
    cuss in your essay.

5. For each example, you should explain how the technique affects the audience's reading of the text. For instance, you might explain that the use of alliteration in a poem increases the tempo of the poem, making the audience read a specific line faster and with more urgency. You should make sure this explanation is supported with evidence from your text, using quoted words or phrasing from the text.

6. You should also explain how the specific devices, or examples of a device, impact the overall meaning of the text and the audience's understanding. In addition to the literal effect of the device on how a text is read (step 5), you should also explain how the example creates or affects the overall meaning or purpose of a text.

> Michael Lassell's poem "How to Watch Your Brother Die" can be found in *Writing as Revision.*

Consider this example of a literary device-based analysis, written by UA student Haley Gray about Michael Lassell's poem "How to Watch Your Brother Die."

Lassell utilizes enjambment when describing a phone conversation between the speaker and his wife, discussing the brother's grim fate. He includes, "Hear her say / 'Please. I don't want to know all the details'" (Lassell 481). Lassell chooses to roll over "Please. I don't want to know all the details" to put the sole emphasis on her words. He does this to pinpoint for the reader the wife's uncomfortable attitude towards the brother's homosexuality. Lassell highlights the wife's disinterest in the brother's illness solely due to his sexual preferences. He implements these line breaks to amplify a specific part of the line, to evoke emotions from the reader.

Following up on student writing:

*   How does Haley incorporate evidence from the text to support her interpretation?

*   How does Haley describe the physical or literal effect of the literary device of enjambment?

*   Where does Haley describe how the literary device impacts her interpretation of the text?

When you are writing your own textual analysis, keep in mind that you will need to move between evidence and an explanation of the evidence to prove your points. See Section 7.3, "Thinking through the Process," in this chapter for some examples of how to effectively move between evidence and explanations in your own writing.

The following strategies are defined in *The Bedford Glossary of Critical and Literary Terms.* Your instructor may introduce other terms that relate to the texts in your class.

See the sample essays in section 13.3 of the *Guide* for examples of what an analysis essay might look like.

Sample List of Textual Strategies

- **Alliteration:** the repetition of sounds in a sequence of words. Alliteration generally refers to repeated consonant sounds. For example, "Peter Piper picked a peck of pickled peppers."

- **Allusion:** an indirect reference, often to a person, event, statement, theme, or work. Allusions enrich meaning through the **connotations** they carry, or the associations that they evoke in a reader's mind. Authors may allude to a historic event by mentioning its name or to a play by Shakespeare by using the same language in their writing.

- **Assonance** is the repetition of identical or similar vowel sounds, as in "fate" and "cave."

- **Atmosphere:** the general feeling created for the reader or audience by a work at a given point. While this is sometimes referred to as **tone**, they have different meanings. Tone is an author's attitude toward the reader, audience, or subject matter, whereas atmosphere is the feeling or mood the text evokes for the reader.

- **Cliché:** an expression used so often that it has become commonplace and has lost its original impact. For example, using "under the weather" to indicate feeling ill is a cliché.

- **Figurative language:** language that employs one or more figures of speech, such as **metaphor** or **simile**. A simile compares two distinct things by using comparative terms including "like" or "as," while a metaphor associates two distinct things directly using literal language. "That child is like a cyclone" is a simile, while "that child is a mouse" is a metaphor.

- **Foreshadowing:** the technique of introducing into a narrative material that prepares the reader for future events or revelations. Examples of foreshadowing could include mentioning a gun that will later shoot someone early in the narrative or implying that a character is threatening through suggestive language before his or her actions become villainous.

- **Hyperbole:** employing deliberate, emphatic exaggeration, sometimes intended for **ironic** effect. Saying something is "the very best in the world" could be a hyperbolic statement. The opposite of this is understatement.

- **Point of view:** the vantage point from which a narrative is told. **First-person** and **third-person** are the most commonly used, while **second-person** is only occasionally encountered. First-person narratives are told by a narrator who refers to himself or herself as "I" and is often a part of the action. Third-person narrators can either be omniscient, all-knowing and reliable, or limited, restricted to a single character at a time. Second-person narrators speak directly to the reader as "you."

7.2

- **Symbolism:** the sustained use of symbols to represent or suggest associations or ideas that are not part of a thing's literal meaning. For example, you could say that an author "uses symbols of nature" to evoke a sense of freedom for the reader.

Visual Analysis

Like written texts, visual texts can lead toward a variety of potential interpretations and messages. Messages in visual texts are communicated primarily through images, illustrations, and design. As a reader, you will notice different aspects of visual texts than you would in written ones. For example, in written texts, a comparison using the words "like" or "as" signals a simile. In visual texts, where words may or may not be present, such a comparison would be made through visual cues within the text—perhaps by juxtaposing two images in an unexpected way. You would have to read the visual elements of the text closely, just as you would a written text, in order to make such an interpretation. As you investigate visuals, you want to look for aspects of the text that spark your interest. Ask yourself why those particular aspects had an effect on you. You will want to consider how certain visual strategies or techniques (design choices, areas of emphasis, symbolic representation, and so forth) work to construct meaning.

> See the model annotated visual in *Rules for Writers*, page 73, in which the writer asks questions about elements in an advertisement.

Visual Strategies

The following key terms and questions for visual analysis, from the guidelines for analyzing a photo presented by the UA Center for Creative Photography, will help you develop the language to analyze a visual text, whether it is a painting, a photograph, or a digital image. An understanding of these basic strategies can lead you to an analysis of the artist's overall message(s).

> See page 83 in *Rules for Writers* for guidelines on analyzing a visual text.

- **Angle:** From what vantage point was the photograph taken? Imagine the photograph taken from a higher or lower angle or view. How does the vantage point affect the meaning or viewer's interpretation of the photograph?

- **Framing:** Describe the edges of the view. What is included? What is not included, and why?

- **Dominance:** Close your eyes. When you open them and look at the photograph, what is the first thing you notice? Why is your attention drawn there?

- **Balance:** Is the visual weight on one side of the photograph about the same as the other—is there more to grab your attention on one side than the other?

- **Contrast:** Are there strong visual contrasts—lights and darks, shadows, textures, solids, voids, and so forth? Why would an artist choose to emphasize contrast between two parts of an image?

7.2

- **Focus:** What parts of the image are clearly in focus? Are some out of focus? Why?

- **Scale:** Discuss the size of the objects within the work. Does the scale seem natural? How does it change the way you look at a part of the image when it seems unnaturally large or small?

Depending on your assignment, you may be asked to discuss the use of a single visual element at length, or you might be asked to describe the effects of multiple strategies for a single purpose. When you select examples and devices, be sure to select those that have a strong impact on a theme or message you wish to discuss in your essay. For each example, you should explain the effect of the strategy or visual element on the audience's experience of the text. For instance, you might explain that the specific framing in a photo forces the audience to focus on the space between two figures. You also want to explain how a specific strategy or visual element impacts the overall meaning of the text. You might suggest that this framing makes an argument about the vast distance between these two figures or about their inability to connect. Use the "Analyzing a Photograph" Craft Box in this section to practice.

Film Analysis

By Amy Parziale

We tend to interpret films without acknowledging that we are thinking critically about the images we see. When asked about a film, you might answer, "I really liked that film," or "I hated it." You may not immediately be able to articulate why you had such a reaction, but, if pressed, most people will actually provide a more in-depth critique or analysis: "The dialogue was stilted and unrealistic," or "The main character wasn't fully developed, so I didn't care about her." These close readings are the beginning of film interpretation. By examining a film critically, you will be able to analyze the messages it expresses as opposed to simply summarizing the plot. As with other types of analysis, you will need to come up with a unique argument about the film and prove your claims by explaining the use of specific strategies.

Following are a list of cinematic terms and techniques commonly used when analyzing films:

- **Mise-en-scène:** literally "put on stage" in French. In films, mise-en-scène is created by four components: **lighting**, **setting/props**, **makeup/costume**, and **figure behavior**.

  o **Lighting:** the type of light used in a particular shot or sequence of shots. The most common lighting technique is **three-point lighting**, which consists of a backlight, key light, and fill light. By using these three points of light, the human face can be lit in such a way that there are no shadows on the face, thus allowing the viewer to see even minute changes in the actor's face. **Backlighting** is a technique used to illuminate the set from behind. **Key lighting** is the brightest light in three-point lighting and generally illuminates the face from the front. Because this bright light creates shadows, three-point lighting also uses a fill light, which fills in the shadows created by the key light. The fill light is generally positioned to one side of the character and near the camera to eliminate shadows. **High-key lighting** refers to a scene with a very bright key light, causing the scene to have almost no shadows. **Low-key lighting** refers to a noticeable difference between the brightness of the key and fill lights, creating deep shadows.

Analyzing a Photograph

Photo by Eli Szabady

Using the strategies listed in this section, practice analyzing this photograph of a snowy morning. You might want to start with an observation/inferences chart (see Chapter 2 for an example) before answering these questions.

1. What aspects of the picture do you find most interesting and why?

2. What do you believe the photographer wants the viewers to think about after viewing this image?

3. What specific strategies used by the photographer lead you to this interpretation?

4. What larger claim do you believe you could make about this photograph, given the information you have and the interpretation you have developed?

Craft Box: ANALYSIS

7.2

- o **Setting:** the location of the film. The setting can be on location, on a set, or created digitally.

- o **Props:** any object in the setting that has a function within the film. "Prop" is actually short for "property" and is a term borrowed from the theater. Props can act as catalysts for action, as a motif, or as foreshadowing. A famous example of a prop used as a foreshadowing motif is the use of oranges in *The Godfather* trilogy to symbolize death and betrayal.

- o **Costume and makeup:** how the characters are dressed and stylized.

- o **Figure behavior:** the movement and behavior of an actor or other element (animal, object, etc.). Figure behavior includes expression, movement, and posture, as well as acting style and degree of realism.

- **Shot:** what is captured during an uninterrupted period of time by one camera. An **establishing shot** is an initial shot that establishes the setting and orients the viewer to the world of the film. **Shot/reverse shot** is an editing technique often used between characters or actions. This technique is most often used during conversations to capture both the speaker and the reaction of the person being spoken to.

- **Cut:** the process by which two shots are joined during editing; in the finished film, cuts appear as the instantaneous transition from one shot to another. The cut is the most common technique used to transition between shots. Other transition techniques include wipes, iris open/close, dissolves, fade-in/fade-out, and fade to black or white.

- **Continuity editing** is the system by which most films' shots are combined. A **take** is the amount of time a particular camera rolls without stopping. In continuity editing, filmmakers tend not to use particularly short or long takes. Filmmakers may decide, however, to build suspense by quickly cutting between the same shot/reverse shot over and over again, or they may decide to use a **long take** in which viewers will become uncomfortable because they are not used to watching from one position for a long period of time.

- **Diegesis:** the world of the film. **On-screen space** is the space seen within the frame. **Off-screen space** is the space not seen within the frame. When a character or object is off-screen, the viewer will continue to believe in its presence unless the film gives them reason to believe otherwise.

- **Framing:** the use of the camera's spatial limits to determine what appears on screen and what does not. **Mobile framing** is framing in which the camera moves. Some common types of mobile framing include **handheld shots**, **crane shots**, **dolly** or **tracking shots**, **panning** (in which the camera moves on a vertical axis), and **tilting** (in which the camera moves on a horizontal axis).

- **Shot scale:** the distance of framing in a shot or how much is captured by the camera. There are seven generally accepted shot scales.

1. **Extreme long shot:** captures more than the human body (may show landscape, building, or crowd).

2. **Long shot:** captures the entire human body.

3. **Medium long shot:** captures the human body from the knee up.

4. **Medium shot:** captures a person from the waist up.

5. **Medium close-up:** captures a person from the chest up.

6. **Close-up:** any object shown up close so it appears quite large and fills the majority of the screen.

7. **Extreme close-up:** shows part of a larger object, part of the human body, or a very small object.

- **Shot angle:** the angle of the camera lens relative to what it is capturing. A **high angle shot** looks down at its subject from a higher angle and can evoke powerlessness. A **low angle shot** looks up at the subject from below and can evoke power and importance.

- **Sound:** There are two major types of sound in film: diegetic and non-diegetic.

  1. **Diegetic sound** is produced by something within the world of the film.

  2. **Non-diegetic sound** is produced by something outside the time and space of the film, such as voice-over narration or soundtrack.

- **Film genres:** There are many different genres and subgenres of film that have particular narrative and thematic conventions. Some examples of genres are western, horror, musical, comedy, action, mystery, and romance. Because viewers understand the conventions of each genre, filmmakers can play with audience expectations.

As with other kinds of texts, these techniques (which are manipulated by the screenwriter, producer, editor, director, and others) are used to help viewers "read" and respond to film in various ways. For instance, think about the way that *Star Wars, Episode IV: A New Hope* opens and immediately sets up the paradigm of "good" versus "evil." After the text crawl that sets the scene along with the non-diegetic soundtrack, the camera tilts down through space to show viewers a planet with two moons. A spaceship enters from the upper right portion of the screen to the center, and then another spaceship enters from the same direction. This second ship is massive compared to the one it is chasing. The ships exchange fire. This long take establishes the central conflict without ever actually telling the viewer anything at all: this is a story of the Rebels against the Empire.

As you can see in the preceding example, focusing on the non-diegetic soundtrack, the direction of the objects entering the frame, and the long take all contribute to our understanding of the film's main idea.

Make sure to read the student example of a film analysis in the "Thinking through the Process" section of this chapter to see how you might apply these terms to your own analysis of music videos, films, and other kinds of moving picture texts. Remember it is necessary to not only explain the literal effect created by the specific film techniques, but also how that effect impacts meaning and the audience's understanding.

Spatial Analysis

By Crystal Fodrey

If you are asked to conduct an analysis of a space on campus, begin by touring the grounds and buildings on the University of Arizona campus with a critical eye, looking for a location that exhibits an inequality or that has some sort of impact on its occupants. You could, for example, pick a building on campus and analyze how accessible it is for someone in a wheelchair. How difficult might it be for such an individual to get into the front door of the building without assistance and make it to a room on the second floor? What does the level of accessibility say about inclusion and exclusion? Alternatively, you could observe the outdoor green spaces on campus and analyze the different ways people use these areas. How do green spaces facilitate student interactions? How does the spatial arrangement of a lecture hall affect how students or instructors interact with other people in the room? How does the space reflect certain power dynamics?

Our campus has limitless potential for spatial analysis because any location where people have individual and/or collective experiences can be read as a text worthy of interpretation. One popular space for collective experiences at UA is Arizona Stadium. To analyze the stadium—or any other space—we can consider some of the following questions:

- What uses is the space designed to enable? How do people actually use the space?

- How does the architectural design of the space impact who uses the space and how people use the space?

- How are social relations maintained or constructed in the space?

- What elements of the space are restrictive? What elements are creative?

- Who is allowed to speak and move about in the space, and who is not?

- What does the space say about what is valued by the people who inhabit the space?

7.2

- Are the relations of power in the space made explicit?

- To what extent do the discourses and everyday practices of that space question or confirm the status quo in society?

- What is the significance of all or some of the above? The answer to this question could become your thesis.

Photo by Eli Szabady

Photo by Brad Hensley

How you analyze the space depends to some degree on your perspective:

Example one: A football player might focus more on the field and the types of interactions and power relations that the field facilitates among teammates, between players and coaches, and between players on different teams. From this perspective, the field could be analyzed as a gendered space where only referees and young men with a high level of athletic ability can gain access during the game. When someone enters the field who does not belong, teams or individuals suffer consequences in the form of personal injury or referee-imposed penalty.

Example two: A cheerleader might analyze the sideline, focusing on it as both a repressive space that restricts movement and a creative space that allows for free expression during the game.

Example three: The majority of us best know the perspective of a fan in the bleachers. From this vantage point, the stadium as a whole becomes a transformative space. People who might not otherwise interact with each other find common ground as they root for the Wildcats. They wear the same colors in support of the team, they know the same cheers, and they share the same traditions and values that are characteristic of UA football culture. Conversely, fans supporting opposing teams find themselves at odds with one another when each person believes that his or her team is superior and believes that their side will win. The energy of the space—created by shouts of praise and disgust—inspires most in attendance to act rowdier and more carefree than they would act at home, at school, or at work. Ultimately, the decisions and actions of the players on the field determine how the fans will react, which shows that the players—and the football itself—hold most of the power in this space.

This analysis of Arizona Stadium is a general one that could be developed with specifics from any given game. The focus of the analysis could even change if, for example, a game takes place during a heavy rainstorm and many fans seek shelter near the concession stands or leave the stadium to finish watching the game elsewhere. Likewise, your experience in any given space at any given time can provide you with details for an interesting spatial analysis so long as you approach the space with an open mind. Always make sure to keep track of your observations.

Analysis of a Literacy Experience: The Literacy Narrative

The Literacy Narrative assignment asks you to analyze your acquisition and use of language and writing. Sharing and reflecting on your own story is a way for you to examine how your social and cultural experiences with language and composing have influenced you as a person both inside and outside of the classroom. For this assignment, you will write a first-person narrative in which you analyze how a personal experience has influenced the ways you think, read, write, and live in the world. Al Harahap's section will help you to think about what literacy means and about your multiple literacies. The section that follows, by Sonia Arellano, Kate Chaterdon, and Katie Silvester, offers specific invention strategies and discusses some of the narrative tools that can lead to an effective literacy narrative.

What Is Literacy?

By Al Harahap

When we talk about literacy or being literate, we usually think about literacy as "the ability to read and write." We might even think that literacy is as simple as 1) being literate, or being able to read and write, or 2) being illiterate, not being able to read and write. However, this simplistic distinction does not adequately capture the range of abilities that we have when it comes to using language for various purposes. We are not divided into two distinct and separate groups of those who can and those who cannot read and write. Rather, when we think of literacy skills, we should consider how well one acquires and uses language along a continuous spectrum. Someone who is a great public speaker may be considered highly literate in the world of politics, while a successful web designer could be considered highly literate in writing for online spaces. Place these two people in the realm of creative writing, though, and they may flounder.

Identifying Your Literacies

As you begin to think about your multiple literacies, remember that literacy is not simply "the ability to read and write." Instead, think about the range of skills in regards to language or writing that you have acquired over the years and how those abilities have defined who you are as a person.

- **Think about Your Past**

  Consider the early and developmental literacy skills that you acquired growing up and continue to develop throughout your life. Have you heard any stories about your first attempts to speak or communicate with others? How did you learn to read? How did you learn to write? What languages do you speak, and in what ways did you come to learn them? "Languages" could also include informal speech patterns, regional expressions, and slang. How do you use these languages differently and in different contexts? What kinds of texts are you comfortable with reading or comprehending? What kinds of texts are you comfortable with writing or composing? These may include anything from the alphanumeric, to the visual, to the digital. Be specific—even the literacy skills used when reading newspapers and magazines, or writing emails, texting, and using social media, can be very different from one another.

- **Consider Your Literacy in Specific Communities**

  Another way to identify your repertoire of literacies is by thinking about the communities you belong to. For example, being part of a band may have allowed you to hone your skills in reading sheet music or writing poetic language for music lyrics, while being active on a social media site such as Facebook or Twitter may give you the skills to be concise and take in a lot of different information in bits and pieces. Consider the multiple communities to which you belong. What kinds of different languages do you use in these communities? Here, we are not just considering national and ethnic languages, such as Arabic or Chinese, but very specific subsets that have unique or unusual lingo and usage, such as African American Vernacular English, casual French, business Hindi, video gamer Japanese, l33t speak, and so on. How do you interact with different texts and different languages in these communities?

- **Remember Your Academic Literacy**

  Now that you have a more nuanced understanding of literacy as a multi-faceted concept in your life, consider how you will hone your academic literacy. What would you consider academic literacy? What kinds of reading, writing, and other language skills are necessary for success in college? How might you transfer certain skills you have gained from existing literacies to help you succeed in college?

Analyzing Your Literacy Experience

By Sonia Arellano, Kate Chaterdon, and Katie Silvester

In order to get started, you will want to choose an experience that has significant meaning for you, as well as one that will allow you to write an interesting narrative. Use the preceding questions and the timeline table in the following Craft Box to begin the brainstorming process.

One of the most important things to remember when writing your literacy narrative is to avoid telling your entire history with literacy in the span of your essay. Instead, try to focus on only one or two important experiences listed on your timeline, and elaborate on what those experiences mean to you and why they are significant. This will ultimately make for a much better essay.

For example, writer Sandra Cisneros explains how being the only girl in her family affected her relationship to literacy:

> "I was/am the only daughter and only a daughter. Being an only daughter in a family of six sons forced me by circumstance to spend a lot of time by myself because my brothers felt it beneath them to play with a girl in public. But that aloneness, that loneliness, was good for a would-be writer—it allowed me time to think and think, to imagine, to read and prepare myself." (89)

Cisneros explains to her reader that because she had to spend a lot of time alone, she developed the skills necessary to become a successful, published writer. Your story may not only explain how you came to be a great writer, but could also explain how your experiences have caused you to struggle with reading or writing.

After considering your lived, literate experiences, you might still be unsure how to analyze those events in order to make a claim about what literacy is and does. Developing some questions around the way literacy operates in your narrative and answering those questions in your paper will help you draw out the greater significance of your particular experience.

The following questions are designed to help you start thinking reflectively and analytically about your literacy narrative:

- How do/did others engage in literacy around you, now and when you were a child? In what ways are your approaches to literacy similar to or different from the practice of those around you?

- What inspired you to choose a particular experience for your narrative, rather than some other literacy event? Do you associate this experience with some feeling, place, special person/people, challenge, or accomplishment? Why?

- What makes your literacy experience unique or different from others? Perhaps someone close to you taught you a special technique for strumming the guitar, or you learned to draw by imitating your favorite animators. Maybe you learned to read by being read to by a parent, or perhaps you prefer expressing yourself through text messages rather than emails or letters?

- What family or community (group) literacy practices came before, during, or after the event you describe?

- In what ways did the events surrounding this experience change you? What can you see about the experience now that you could not see then?

- What could an audience, such as parents, college students, children, instructors, or aspiring writers learn from this experience?

- How has your experience affected your attitudes toward reading, writing, and communicating today? What are the implications of your attitudes toward reading and writing? In what ways might your attitudes serve you well in college? In what ways might they get in your way?

7.2

- How do you think your life experiences, cultural affiliations, race, gender, and/or religion have influenced your chosen literacy experience and your attitudes toward reading and writing? How have the following contexts influenced your experience: other languages, language or educational policies, traditions, rituals, beliefs about literacy, etc.

- In what ways is your experience similar to or different from the experiences of the published authors whose stories you have read in class? What are the reasons for these similarities and/or differences?

Craft Box: INVENTION

Timeline of Major Literacy Experiences

Before you start writing your Literacy Narrative, use the following chart to map out memories of your own literacy experiences. Refer to the questions in the "What Is Literacy?" section if you are having trouble thinking of ideas.

Timeline of Major Literacy Events

	Childhood	Young Adult	College and Beyond
Literacy at Home			
Literacy at School			
Literacy in the Community			

7.2

Strategies for Writing a Literacy Narrative

Think of the best storyteller you know. Maybe it's your aunt Nancy who used to weave yarns about the "good ol' days" while everyone sat around the dining room table, digesting their Thanksgiving meal. Maybe it's your best friend from high school, José, who used to have every one of your buddies doubled-over with laughter whenever he recounted a mishap from gym class or the lunch room. Maybe it's someone you've never met, like a famous author or director. Whoever they are, ask yourself this question: What makes them such good storytellers? Is it the way they describe the characters involved in the story? Is it the way they use humor or suspense to engage the audience? Is it the way they describe the physical setting of the story, the emotional tone of the event, the smell and taste of the food? Chances are it is a combination of these things, which we will call narrative tools. Here are some narrative tools you can use in your own literacy narrative:

- **Sensory Detail**

    Arguably, the best way to engage your audience is to write using effective sensory detail. Sensory details are words and images that help the reader to see, hear, smell, taste, and feel whatever it is the author is describing. Sensory details are important in a story because they make the reader feel as if they are actually experiencing the events; they make the reader feel as if they are "there."

    UA student Romeo Judeh effectively uses sensory detail in his literacy narrative, "Language Is My Life," when describing his move to Doha, Quatar:

    The experience began summer of 2008 after a long 16-hour flight into unfamiliar territory. I specifically remember the weather as I stepped off the plane feeling like opening an oven while in the middle of a bake. That burst of hot air burning the top layer of skin on my face, feeling like my eyebrows and peach fuzz were burning off. Then follow that with a blanket of humidity falling over my body; this is the Middle East and my new home. Just walking down the stairs from the plane, I was sweating like I just finished playing in a basketball game. The concept of green grass or trees was nonexistent as far as my eyes could see; light brown sand covered every inch of the ground, walls, and streets.

    In just a few lines, Romeo is able to convey the feeling of stepping off of the plane into the hot, desert climate of Doha for the first time. Notice his use of simile when he writes that arriving in Doha was "like opening an oven while in the middle of a bake," and "I was sweating like I just finished playing in a basketball game." The use of simile, although not the only way to illustrate sensory detail, can be an effective way to enable your reader to experience your description.

7.2

135

- **Dialogue**

  Another narrative tool that can help you to engage your audience is the use of dialogue. Dialogue, like sensory detail, has the effect of making the reader feel as if they are a "part of the moment;" it is as if dialogue helps the reader pretend that they are in the same room as the characters in the story, eavesdropping on what they are saying.

  UA student Shelby Gobert effectively uses dialogue in her literacy narrative to describe the interaction between herself and her younger siblings while in the car:

  My mom maneuvered the streets with a practiced grace, unlike the flustered, directionally challenged woman she usually exemplified. There was no school that day and my siblings and I were excited to roam around town. I listened half-heartedly as my siblings began verbally abusing each other, while I cracked open a rather worn book of mine.

Literacy Narrative as Analysis

By Stefan Vogel and Laurel Schenkoske

The Literacy Narrative is a form of textual analysis, but it follows different conventions than an analysis of a written or visual document. In this section, we'll offer suggestions for two common questions related to analysis in the Literacy Narrative. Throughout, we refer to UA student Sarah Blomquist's literacy narrative, "The Little Dinghy that Could."

1. "What will my thesis statement look like?"

As you read in Chapter 3, a thesis statement defines the writer's central idea. While the thesis is often stated toward the beginning of an academic essay, it might come across as clumsy to write something like "...and this totally changed my life" at the end of your first paragraph in a Literacy Narrative. Remember this assignment is a narrative; many stories start out opaque and general, only to reveal their message and larger significance later.

Your own purpose and organizational choices will determine when and how explicitly your thesis statement will become apparent. For example,

Sarah's thesis statement does not appear until the seventh paragraph, when she writes, "But it was not until my first job did I realize the importance and beauty of communication." This statement defines the central idea of the essay, but only after building a theme throughout her narrative. In this case, the strategy works because all of the topics throughout the text relate to the central idea and unify the essay as a whole:

- her first English class (paragraph 1)

- the move across the United States (paragraph 2)

- her reminiscence of the past (paragraph 3)

- speaking in front of others and her project presentation (paragraphs 4 and 5)

- transformation of discomfort into fear (paragraph 6)

- opening up and embracing of newfound "voice" (paragraph 7)

As you may imagine, this is not the only way to include a thesis statement in a literacy narrative. Sarah could have effectively included her thesis earlier in the essay, but she chose to build to it throughout the narrative. As you read literacy

7.2

"Scarlet likes Justin Beaver" my little brother Johnny squealed.

"No I don't!" Scarlet screeched. This went back and forth and I knew any second I was going to be pulled into this verbal war.

Shelby's combined use of dialogue and strong sensory detail paints a clear picture in the reader's mind of what this trip was like for her.

Both sensory detail and dialogue are very important parts of a narrative because they help authors to show their story to their readers, as opposed to merely telling their story to them. Imagine that both Romeo and Shelby had chosen not to use sensory detail or dialogue to write their stories and had, instead, merely chronologically listed the events that occurred. Would that have been as interesting to read? Would it have had as great an effect on the reader?

narratives and work on your own, think about how the effects of the essay might change depending upon the placement of the thesis or central idea.

Questions to consider:

- What are some positives and negatives of placing the thesis in the introduction? Somewhere else?

- Where should the thesis go in your project? Why will this placement be effective?

2. **"How can I demonstrate analysis?"**

As you read in the "Analyzing Your Literacy Experience" section in this chapter, evaluating the importance of a particular literacy experience is a form of analysis in itself. To bring your writing from summary to analysis, you should examine not only how the events made you feel but also address the larger significance of what you have learned. Conveying the story's relevance to your past, present, and future can be done in two ways, namely in terms of:

- **local evaluations**, in which you add adjectives and meta-comments judging the relative importance of a particular element of your essay. These pieces of information about the events

go beyond the techniques of summary or description and make clear your attitudes and sentiments.

- **global evaluations**, in which you address your narrative's greater significance, making clear how the event you are describing has impacted your literate life.

Here we have printed the beginning of Sarah's seventh paragraph. Notice how she begins with local evaluations—analyses of specific feelings or events, represented in *italics*—before connecting them to a larger theme, represented in **bold** lettering:

These *miserable habits* lasted up until the middle of my junior year. *I was in every sense silenced. The nerves which kept me from socializing, the tiny shouting voice in my head, was the only voice I thought existed.* **I had fully accepted the discomfort I felt among others as my reality.**

Now try to identify these components in the Literacy Narrative in section 13.4. Think about how you are using both local and global evaluations to demonstrate analysis in your draft.

7.2

- **Story Arc**

  In addition to including sensory detail and dialogue in your story, it is important to think about the overall organization of your story (i.e., the order of events) as a narrative tool that affects the way the audience reads and interprets your story. When discussing the organization of a story, people tend to think in terms of the story arc. The basic story arc for a narrative essay looks something like this:

  ### Literacy Narrative Story Arc

  Introduce your story.

  Provide some context for your literacy story: Where does your literacy experience unfold? Who is involved?

  Develop the rising action. Explain what happened. Try to show, rather than tell. Describe any conflict that results from your experience.

  Describe the crisis point/climax: Show how the events leading up to and surrounding your literacy experience change you or others.

  Consider falling action. Explain what happened afterward or what resulted from the resolution of the climax or conflict.

  Write a conclusion.

  As you can see, stories generally have an initial incident, followed by some kind of action that leads to a crisis or climax, which is then resolved in the end. In other words, most stories have a beginning, a middle, and an end. However, it is good to keep in mind that not all stories are structured chronologically. Again, think back to the best stories you have ever heard. Did they always start at the very beginning, or did they sometimes start right in the middle of the action or even at the resolution and then work backwards as a way to grab the audience's attention? Do not be afraid to play around with the structure of your story as you revise your narrative. A good rule of thumb when deciding how to organize your story is to always keep your audience (usually your instructor and the other students in your class) in mind. What kind of story arc do you think will most engage them? Will they be excited to read a story about how, at first, Jane didn't like books (beginning), but then she came across a mystery novel (rising action) that was sometimes difficult to read (climax), but eventually she made her way through the book and decided she loved reading (falling action and resolution)? Or do you think there is another way to organize this story that might be more engaging and less clichéd?

Some students initially think they have no "good" or "exciting" stories to tell about their experiences with literacy. However, many instructors will tell you that their favorite literacy narratives to read are those that are engaging because of how they are written, not necessarily what they are written about. The use of sensory detail and dialogue are two ways that you can engage your audience and help them to feel invested in your story. Planning out the action and events of your story by considering your story arc can also help to ensure that your story is structured in the most rhetorically effective way.

7.3 Thinking through the Process

Invention

Whether your instructor gives you a particular text to write about or you are able to choose your own object of analysis, you will need to engage in a close reading of the text (see Chapter 2) in order to arrive at an original interpretation. In order to do so, you might like to choose an invention method outlined in section 2.3, such as freewriting, brainstorming, mind-mapping, or creating an observations/inferences chart. While you work through this messy stage, look for main ideas and for places in the text that challenge your ideas or reinforce them, seem like integral parts of the text, confuse you, surprise you, or spark your interest. These might be good places for you to focus your analysis since there is simply not enough room to analyze all of the strategies or elements of a text in your essay.

As you begin working on your essay, remember that analysis requires more than simply summarizing. In your first-year writing courses, you will want to be careful not to confuse analysis with summary. Unlike analysis, summary is a statement of the facts about a text, not a critical examination of it. Summary functions as a way of familiarizing your readers with a given text so that they can understand your analysis.

One way to move from summary to analysis is to create a two-column table like the one below. You can use the left-hand column to write down any interesting quotes or details you found compelling in the text. Then, on the right-hand side, you can write down why those observations are important or how they contribute to your understanding of the text as a whole. As an example, let's look at how UA student Marisa Devey might have used a two-column brainstorming approach for her essay "Can Men and Women Be Friends?," a film analysis of the romantic comedy *When Harry Met Sally*.

See Chapter 13 for sample essays by UA students.

7.3

Summary	Analysis
In *When Harry Met Sally*, Harry and Sally are shown at different points in their lives as an unlikely pair of friends.	By using continuity time jumps, Director Ron Reiner is able to emphasize how complicated the relationship is between Harry and Sally as they age.
The opening scene of the film begins with a fake documentary interview.	The film relies on fake documentary footage to explore the theme of whether men and women can truly be friends by including "real voices" from ordinary people. These "real voices" make the situation more relatable and convincing for the audience.
2012 marks the 23rd anniversary of *When Harry Met Sally*.	An ever-changing outlook on traditional marriage raises questions about whether or not people of different genders might relate to each other differently today than they did in 1977.

See section 5c in *Rules for Writers* for guidelines on writing a summary and for a sample summary. Also, see the section on page 78 in *Rules for Writers*.

Notice how all of the statements in the analytical side assert something about the reader's understanding of the text by discussing how and why these points are important to an overall analysis of the film. As you generate ideas, you will want to make sure that you can use evidence to support an argument about your topic as well.

7.3

Try completing the following chart using your own text. Summarize or write descriptions of the examples you want to highlight in the "Summary" column, and make a claim related to the overall message of the text in the "Analysis" column. See the Tips & Strategies Box on pages 148–149, "From Reactions to Analysis," for further explanation.

Summary	Analysis

Drafting

In addition to focusing on the strategies employed in the text, analytical writing must also be persuasive in order to be effective. In any type of analysis, you are inviting the audience to see the text in the same way that you do. However, your goal is not to uncover the one "true" meaning that the artist/writer intended. Instead, your goal is to analyze the different strategies and messages you encounter in a text and demonstrate how they provide evidence for a particular interpretation.

7.3

Writing Analytical Thesis Statements

By Jonathan LaGuardia

Since analysis is "taking a thing apart to show how the parts work in service of the whole," an analytical thesis statement includes three main elements:

1. *The "parts"* (details in the text)

2. *"How the parts work in service of the whole"* (how the details led you to an idea)

3. *The "whole"* (how the text makes a claim about that idea)

For example, you could write a thesis that shows all of the subtle ways an advertisement tries to convince its viewers to buy body spray, but you could also write one that shows how the ad pushes its viewers into culturally specific gender roles. Both theses might use the same "parts" as evidence, but they offer very different kinds of analyses. Many first-year writing classes identify the "whole" as the claim a text makes about a specific topic area or theme, though your instructor might specify another focus for your assignment.

The exercise below will help you develop at least one working thesis statement that addresses each of these three elements. In italics, you will see examples of how a student might complete this activity based on the image used in the observations/inferences chart in section 2.5.

Making Observations

Take a close look at a part of the text—a single scene or shot from a film, a part of an image, a short passage from a written text—and observe as many details as possible. Try not to filter yourself. Write down everything you notice, obvious or insightful, meaningful or trivial:

Two characters stand, facing each other outside of what appears to be a series of Western-style buildings, one wears cowboy hat, one wears bandolier, hands at hips, different color hair, playful font

Identifying Patterns

What topic areas or themes do you see in the list of observations above? You might note that a few center on "gender roles," for example, or "economics," "violence," or even "good behavior." Write as many as you can here:

Masculinity, gender roles, power, violence, gun control, stereotypes

Making Inferences

Choose one of these topic areas or themes and place it in the blank to form a question: What does the text suggest about _____? Considering the details you observed, write some potential answers here:

What does the text suggest about masculinity?

This particular comic strip is likely playing on notions of masculinity in the Western genre, mainly by way of the setting, attire, and physical stance of the characters.

Creating Your Thesis—Answering the "So What?" Question

While any one of the answers you provided to the question above could work as a thesis, let's push a bit further to consider how the text tries to influence its audience. Try putting the topic area you chose in this blank: What does the text try to convince us to do, think, or believe as a result of its argument about _____? Write some potential answers here:

What does the text try to convince us to do, think, or believe as a result of its argument about masculinity?

The sequential comic "Somewhere in the Old West…" plays with the audience's expectations of masculinity and the Western by illustrating that what viewers expect to see—a violent duel between a hero and villain—is ingrained into boys' minds as early as childhood.

7.3

Let's take a look at the first part of Marisa's introduction to her essay to see how she moves from personal interpretation to thesis statement. To open up her essay for the reader, she reflects on her personal reactions to the romantic comedy *When Harry Met Sally*:

> The relationship between heterosexual men and women is very entangled. Some men and women claim to be the best of friends for their entire lives, while others end up happily married. But the question is whether or not men and women can remain friends or is there always that hint of something more that could potentially lead to a relationship. There is no right answer, for this question is something that is answered individually with each case.

Notice that although Marisa has situated her readers to her topic by questioning the gendered relationships between heterosexual men and women, she has not yet provided a specific analysis of the film *When Harry Met Sally*. In her thesis, which you will see below, she makes sure to tie her thesis statement back to her introduction while also introducing a more specific and arguable analysis of the film. Notice that she has remembered to mention the director, the screenwriter, and the title of the film so that her readers will know exactly which text she is analyzing.

See Chapter 3 for more information on writing an effective thesis and organizing your analysis into an essay.

Here is Marisa's thesis:

> Director Ron Reiner and screenwriter Nora Ephron evaluate the theme of whether or not men and women can be friends in the film *When Harry Met Sally* through documentary inserts, two major time jumps of five years, and the constantly changing outlook on marriage.

Following up on student writing:

- How did Marisa manage to indicate her text, her interpretation of the film, and the strategies she wants to analyze all in one thesis statement?

- Can you tell where she is headed in her essay? What might her outline look like?

Once you decide on an interpretation to discuss in your analysis, try to devise a strong, clear thesis that you can support with specific references to the text. Although different methods of analysis require writers to focus on different features, all methods of analysis are similar in that they provide a way to look closely at particular aspects of the text. Keep in mind that analysis always goes beyond mere observation. In an analysis essay, you should demonstrate your ability to develop a clear interpretation of a text based on specific evidence from the text itself.

7.3

Sample Paragraph Structure for Textual Analysis

The PIE paragraph structure is one method for writing focused, developed, and well-supported paragraphs. The acronym PIE stands for Point, Illustration, and Explanation. If you use the PIE paragraph method in a Textual Analysis essay, your paragraphs will:

- Open with a transition and topic sentence that relates a strategy or pattern to the message you will focus on (**Point**).

- Present your evidence, or examples from the text, of that strategy or pattern (**Illustration**).

- Analyze these examples by clearly connecting each to the argument about the text you are making (**Explanation**).

> See Chapters 3 and 13 for examples of PIE paragraphs used for textual analysis.

Each PIE paragraph does what your overall essay intends to do: answer both how and why. By identifying strategies, you are examining how the text is constructed and how meaning is conveyed. Then, by attaching significance to those strategies, you present one potential interpretation of the text.

In the following paragraph from Marisa's essay, note how much of the paragraph is devoted to the explanation of her ideas compared to the other two pieces of the PIE paragraph. The green text represents the topic sentence, purple represents the illustrations, and orange represents the explanations.

Thesis:

> Director Ron Reiner and screenwriter Nora Ephron evaluate the theme of whether or not men and women can be friends in the film *When Harry Met Sally* through documentary inserts, two major time jumps of five years, and the constantly changing outlook on marriage.

One body paragraph:

> In order to show the passing of time in a film, anywhere from six months to twenty years, film directors use time continuity jumps. In the film When Harry Met Sally, there are two time jumps of five years each. These time jumps allow assumptions to be made and information to be presented to us off camera. Both of these time jumps occur directly after one of the elderly couple interviews. This has extreme significance because the interviews are what make it feel like the film is somewhat of a documentary. The interviews reinstate the idea that men and women can't be friends right before we skip ahead five years. They are put there as a reminder that both Harry and Sally have a determined fate and will not be able to remain friends. The interviews are put directly before the time jumps in order to foreshadow the meeting of Harry and Sally after parting ways for five years. The transition between the interviews and the time jump is merely a fade. The camera focus is set on the couple, and then fades out into black and the next item that the audience sees is an entirely new setting when Harry and Sally are destined to meet again.

As you can see, Marisa first identifies the point she wants to make in her paragraph—that time continuity jumps are crucial to Harry and Sally's development as characters—by setting up her point with a transition about the use of this technique in the film industry in general. Then, she moves on to explaining when and where the jumps occur and why the jumps are significant.

Following up on student writing:

- How did Marisa use point, illustration, and explanation well in her paragraph? Where could she have improved?

- How will you adopt this technique in your own essay?

- Do you know of any other techniques for incorporating evidence and writing focused paragraphs?

Revision

As you learned in Chapter 4, the University of Arizona's Writing Program considers the idea of "re-visioning" a crucial part in the writing process, and revision at the university level includes both **global** and **local revisions**.

While you will most likely receive feedback from your peers and instructor on this assignment, it may also benefit you to take a few minutes to review the revision tips in Chapter 4. Then, make sure you have done the following:

Imagine you are the reader, not the writer. Putting yourself in the reader's shoes will help you be more objective as you evaluate your work. Remember, you are critiquing your work—not yourself. Read through your essay once and ask yourself: What is the most successful part of your paper so far? What needs the most improvement?

Identify your purpose. What are you really trying to say in this essay? Is the thesis communicating that? If not, you might need to revise your thesis to better reflect what you actually wrote about in your work.

Know your audience. If your audience consists of your fellow classmates and instructor, what do you need to tell them about your text? Do you need to contextualize it for them? Do you need to include publication information? Author's name? The date the text was written or created? Think about your audiences' needs and address them.

Evaluate your evidence. This can be a tough one. You will want to ask yourself if your paper actually supports your thesis in compelling and strategic ways. Do you offer enough illustrations to get your point across? If using a written text, do you include quotations? If using a visual, audio, or other multimodal text, do you offer enough detailed descriptions of what you are seeing or hearing?

7.3

Reverse Outlining

I f you are interested in determining how well your essay addresses your intended argument, you might want to consider doing a "reverse outline" of your essay. In a reverse outline, you go back through your draft and re-create an outline based on what you actually see in your writing— not on what you imagined or hoped to see. This is a very useful exercise either for working through complicated texts or for re-visioning your own essays.

To create a reverse outline of your essay, complete the following steps:

1. In the left-hand margin, write down the topic of each paragraph by using as few words as possible. If you cannot sum up the main point of your paragraph in just a few words,

   you might need to revisit the intention of the paragraph.

2. Then, in the right-hand margin, write a quick assessment of why the paragraph is necessary to enhance the argument.

3. Reconstruct your new outline and compare it to any original outlines or brainstorming work you did to see how your argument changed as you wrote your essay. Here, you can determine whether or not you need to add new information, cut redundant information, or rearrange existing information.

As an example, consider the way Marisa might have completed a reverse outline of her paper on *When Harry Met Sally*. Here is the paragraph again from page 145:

This paragraph shows how continuity jumps affect the overall argument that Harry and Sally are destined to fall in love.

In order to show the passing of time in a film, anywhere from six months to twenty years, film directors use time continuity jumps. In the film *When Harry Met Sally*, there are two time jumps of five years each. These time jumps allow assumptions to be made and information to be presented to us off camera. Both of these time jumps occur directly after one of the elderly couple interviews. This has extreme significance because the interviews are what make it feel like the film is somewhat of a documentary. The interviews reinstate the idea that men and women can't be friends right before we skip ahead five years. They are put there as a reminder that both Harry and Sally have a determined fate and will not be able to remain friends. The interviews are put directly before the time jumps in order to foreshadow the meeting of Harry and Sally after parting ways for five years. The transition between the interviews and the time jump is merely a fade. The camera focus is set on the couple, and then fades out into black and the next item that the audience sees is an entirely new setting when Harry and Sally are destined to meet again.

Necessary to provide evidence that the visual cues function as part of the film's argument.

7.3

If Marisa decided to do this for the rest of her paragraphs, she might see places where she has meandered from her topic, places where she needs to add additional evidence or subpoints.

Cut, add, and rearrange. It is often difficult to cut sentences, paragraphs, or even sections from your essay, but it may be a necessary part of the revision process. If you find that a paragraph does not quite fit with your thesis or overall analysis, you might need to remove it, alter it significantly, or put it in a different place in the essay. On the other hand, you might find that you have not offered enough evidence, summary, or explanation of something. In this case, you might need to do some additional writing to adequately express your ideas.

Tighten up the language and ideas. Some writers use their first draft to get their ideas onto paper and do not want to think about how clearly those ideas are being communicated. If you are like these writers, during the revision process you will likely notice places where you have either relied too much on

Tips & Strategies: ANALYSIS

From Reactions to Analysis

By Beth Alvarado

When you experience an emotional response to a text, particularly if a text seems to be challenging your own values and beliefs, you have a starting point for an essay. Instead of ignoring or dismissing your response, explore why you are experiencing such a strong reaction.

This approach to analysis is based on several assumptions:

- A text does not have one fixed meaning;

- Each reader, based on his or her own assumptions or experiences, will read a text differently; and

- Analyzing a text is like figuring out a puzzle: you have to go back and forth, from your reactions and inferences about the text to the pieces of text to figure out the puzzle for yourself.

When some students read Gloria Anzaldúa's essay "The Homeland, *Aztlán/El Otro Mexico*," for example, they may feel shocked or alienated by her tone; perhaps they feel unjustly accused by passages like this:

> The Gringo, locked into the fiction of white superiority, seized complete political power, stripping Indians and Mexicans of their land while their feet were still rooted in it. *Con el destierro y el exilo fuimos desuñados, destroncados, destripados*—we were jerked out by the roots, truncated, disemboweled, dispossessed, and separated from our identity and our history. (471)

Two things might bother some readers about this passage: One may be that they feel she is making sweeping generalizations about white people (or is retelling history in a biased way) and one may be that they do not understand Spanish. This gives those particular students two things to note in their re-reading of the text: where are the places they feel accused or that she is being biased? And where and how is she using Spanish? If they go back to the text and note evidence, they will see that either reaction would give them plenty to investigate. In other words, if these are their reactions, they now have a choice of two topics for a paper.

7.3

quotations, spent too much time explaining your reasoning for something, or fumbled through saying exactly what you wanted to say. Try reading your work out loud to find any confusing words, awkward phrasing, or unnecessary passages, and adjust your draft as necessary.

Improve any immediate grammar, spelling, or word choice errors. As an academic writer, you want to gain credibility with an academic audience. Careful proofreading and editing can ensure that readers focus on your ideas rather than on your grammar or spelling mistakes. Go through each sentence carefully, and make sure that you have not misspelled any words or stated something incorrectly.

Perhaps you are the essay writer and you choose the use of Spanish as your topic. In the previous passage, for instance, Anzaldúa translates the Spanish, which she does not do in other parts of the text—so that gives you two specific strategies to investigate: When does she translate the Spanish and when does she not? Then, you remember from class discussion that someone brought up the family stories, where she switched from Spanish to English, sometimes in the same sentence. Now you have at least three ways she uses Spanish or three possible patterns to investigate—where she translates, where she does not, and where she switches back and forth in the same sentence—and use as possible organizing principles for your paper. You also have a central question to guide your inquiry: Why does Anzaldúa use Spanish in these three different ways? Is there some kind of significance to the patterns? Is she trying to exclude readers?

This leads you to the issue of audience. In class, some other people said they felt excluded, and so you might conclude that she is trying to exclude some readers—non-Spanish speakers? whites?—or, perhaps, you think she is using the piece to re-create for her readers the feelings of exclusion she

has experienced. On the other hand, readers who understood Spanish said they felt included by the very same strategy that others cited as alienating. In fact, there were people in class who loved the family stories because they were reminded of the way their grandparents talked. Maybe, you think the ways Anzaldúa uses both languages illustrates something about her heritage and identity. Or about her conflicts? Or the border region?

Now you have a few possible hypotheses: "Anzaldúa uses Spanish in her essay to re-create for non-speakers the feeling of being an outsider in the hopes, perhaps, that the reader will come to understand the injustice she feels." Or: "Even though Anzaldúa risks alienating some readers by not translating from the Spanish, she is using both English and Spanish to illustrate her conflicted identity." Or: "The use of Spanish and English in the essay replicates its use in the border region." You can see how the process of inquiry can lead to different—but equally valid—interpretations of the same text. The next steps, now that you have a tentative thesis, are to go back to the text, where you can gather and arrange your evidence, test it against your hypothesis, and begin to write a draft of your paper.

7.3

7.4 Reflection

As you might remember from the Overview, the word analysis comes from the Greek word *analysis*, which means "to break into pieces" ("Analysis"). In this chapter, you practiced breaking a text into pieces in order to see the whole more critically. The strategies you practiced will help you in your future assignments in this class. In addition, applying analysis strategies might help you more clearly explain your observations and interpretations of films, text messages, and even interactions with friends or family. As you wrap up your work for this chapter, think about how you would respond to the following questions:

- How would you explain the difference between summary and analysis to a new UA student? To a family member?

- How did applying analysis strategies help you to see a text differently?

- What did you learn about writing an analytical paper?

- In what ways can you improve your analytical skills for the next assignment?

- Where else do you "do" analysis? What strategies can you take from this chapter to other classes or life experiences?

Works Cited

"Analysis." *Etymonline.com.* 2013. Web. 15 Oct. 2013.

Anzaldúa, Gloria. "The Homeland, *Aztlán/El Otro Mexico.*" *Writing as Revision.* Ed. Beth Alvarado, Barbara Cully, and Michael Robinson. 2nd ed. Boston. Pearson, 2003. 546–53. Print.

Cisneros, Sandra. "Only Daughter." *Families in Later Life: Connections and Transitions.* Ed. Alexis Walkes, Margaret Manoogian-O'Dell, Lori A. McGrew, and Diana L. G. White. Thousand Oaks, LA: Pine Forge, 2001. 89–91. Print.

Murfin, Ross, and Supryia M. Ray. *The Bedford Glossary of Critical and Literary Terms.* Boston: Bedford/St. Martin's, 2009. Print.

Text-in-Context 8

8.1   Text-in-Context: An Overview

8.2   Approaches to the Text-in-Context Assignment

8.3   Thinking through the Process

8.4   Reflection

8.1 Text-in-Context: An Overview

The **Text-in-Context** assignment, sometimes referred to as **contextual analysis**, focuses on a text and its relationship to a larger context, such as the author's biography, the historical or cultural situation surrounding the text, a particular theoretical lens, or a related text(s). To meet the goals of this assignment, you will use some of the same skills you practiced in the Textual Analysis assignment such as close reading, incorporating textual evidence, and making arguable claims.

This assignment may require you to analyze multiple texts. The following terms are often used in a Text-in-Context assignment to make distinctions between texts:

- **Primary text:** This is the text that is the main focus of your analysis. It might be a book, an article, a movie, a photograph, a painting, a place, an experience, or any of the other kinds of text as defined throughout this book.

- **Secondary text:** This text creates a context or lens that shapes your understanding and analysis of the primary text. Secondary texts complicate your understanding of the primary text by introducing historical, philosophical, theoretical, or biographical information. Secondary texts may directly address the primary text, or they might introduce a concept or other

> Contextual analysis requires you to synthesize multiple texts, seeing each in the context of the others. See section 58c in *Rules for Writers* for more on synthesis.

CHAPTER 8

information that shapes your understanding of the text even though the primary text is not discussed directly.

Secondary texts are sometimes referred to as a lens because you can use the secondary text in order to view the primary text differently.

©Hayden-McNeil, LLC

The following list includes various types of lenses and ideas for how they might impact your understanding of a primary text.

- **Historical:** What are the historical events and facts surrounding the primary text, and how do these affect how you read the text? You might consider when the text was written or composed, or you can consider the time period in which a text's narrative takes place, references to historical objects, events, people, or popular culture within the text, etc.

- **Biographical:** What were the author's beliefs, values, experiences, or influences, and how do these affect the ways that you understand the primary text? A biographical secondary text could include an interview with the author, an autobiography, a biography, or even a documentary film.

- **Critical:** What have literary, film, or art critics said or written about the primary text? In what ways do critical readings of these texts produced by others add meaning or provide information you may not have otherwise considered?

- **Theoretical:** A theory provides a framework or set of analytical tools for contemplating, understanding, or explaining a subject matter. Most disciplines have developed theories for explaining their key concepts of interest. Scientific theories, like the Big Bang Theory, develop ways of explaining natural phenomena, such as the birth of the universe. Social theories, such as Marxism or feminism, are used for questioning social phenomena, such as class, gender, race, etc. For this assignment, you might draw on the theories of a certain scholar or discipline to examine your primary text. For more on this approach, see "The Hero's Journey as a Theoretical Lens" in section 8.2.

- **Genre:** Texts are often grouped into a specific category or genre based on shared characteristics or conventions and social functions. For example, films in the horror genre commonly use creepy music; a storyline that involves suspense; a token bad character; and a familiar, but mysterious or unusual setting, such as an abandoned cabin in the woods or a dusty old mansion. To perform a Text-in-Context essay using genre as a lens, you might compare two texts of the same genre and analyze the similarities and differences between their usage of genre conventions, or you might read a more theoretical secondary text that explains some common conventions of the genre and analyze how your primary text incorporates those conventions.

Keep in mind that although your instructor might ask you to apply a type of secondary text that is not included in this list, the goal remains to analyze how ideas from the secondary text add to your understanding of the primary text.

Analyzing a text in context is much like playing with the color or filter settings on a camera: some settings will heighten certain details, like light, shadow, color, and detail, while obscuring others. As you compose the assignment for this unit, consider how the secondary text affects your understanding of the primary text. What does the addition of a secondary text highlight about the primary text? What is obscured or complicated when you add additional information or interpretations to your original reading of the primary text? The following section will introduce you to some possible approaches to this assignment. Keep in mind that your instructor may offer you a different approach.

8.2 Approaches to the Text-in-Context Assignment

Comparing Two Texts

By Jean Goodrich

To perform a comparative analysis of two texts, you might imagine that the two texts are in conversation with each other. They might be in agreement, or they might disagree. They might be similar in form and content, or they may appear entirely unrelated at the surface level.

To place two or more texts in conversation with each other, begin by tracking the obvious similarities and differences between the two texts. For example, consider the genre: are both texts poems? Is one text a short story and the second a poem? Two texts composed in the same genre are likely to have a number of characteristics in common. They may use similar patterns of language or use form in similar ways to convey meaning. Perhaps the texts you are analyzing are totally different in form but share similar points of view or attempt to describe a common experience. Finding the similarities between two texts in both form and content can provide you with evidence for a more complex analysis of one or both texts. As you track similarities among your texts, you should also take note of differences.

Here is one way to get started on your comparative analysis approach to the Text-in-Context assignment:

1. Determine your purpose for comparison. (Pay special attention to your instructor's assignment guidelines.) Is your goal to better understand one text by looking at a similar one? Are you trying to use both texts as a way of understanding some broader social issue?

2. Make a list of two columns, one for each text to be analyzed.

3. List or describe the similarities you find between the texts.

4. List or describe the differences.

5. Look for patterns or connections.

From these observations, you can begin working toward a thesis or a set of claims. Think about how or why the texts are similar or different, and consider interpretations that can be supported by your observations. A thesis that answers how or why sets up an analytical essay, rather than just a summary.

Consider the following sample analysis that presents the beginning stages of a comparative analysis of two popular children's films, Disney's classic *Cinderella* (1950) and the original *Shrek* (2001) film by DreamWorks. The purpose of this comparison was to use both films to make an argument about a common theme or social issue presented in these films. First, make a list of the similarities:

SIMILARITIES	
Cinderella	**Shrek**
animated film	animated film
primary audience is children	primary audience is children
Uses fairytale conventions of:	*Uses fairytale conventions of:*
the worthy hero on a quest (Prince Charming)	the worthy hero on a quest (Shrek)
damsel to be rescued (Cinderella)	damsel to be rescued (Princess Fiona)
damsel locked in tower room	damsel locked in tower of castle
magic (the spell to send Cinderella to the ball)	magic (that turns Fiona to an ogress)
a fairy godmother provides magic	a witch casts the spell
magic ends at midnight	magic changes at sunset and sunrise
talking animals (the mice)	talking animals (Donkey)
finding "true love"	finding "true love"
happy ending	happy ending

Next, make a list of the differences:

DIFFERENCES	
Cinderella	**Shrek**
stepmother/sisters are antagonists	Lord Farquaad is antagonist
heroine is made a servant	heroine is under an enchantment
protagonist point of view is the damsel (Cinderella)	protagonist point of view is the monster (Shrek)
story is told straightforwardly, requiring the audience to suspend disbelief	story is told self-consciously, skeptical of the unbelievable and fairytale elements
humor in the antics of the mice	humor expressed by main characters through "toilet" humor, farting, wisecracks
"true love" at first sight	"true love" is not at first sight but through interaction and getting to know the person
appearance matters: Cinderella must be dressed appropriately for the ball and is unrecognized in her daily servant clothes	appearance should not be trusted and beauty will not make you happy

The next step is to look for patterns. For instance, Cinderella's stepmother thwarts her wish to go to the ball to allow her own daughters access to the prince and the possibility of a royal marriage. She wants to use her daughters to "marry up" into wealth and privilege. Similarly, Lord Farquaad needs to marry a princess so he can be king of the perfect kingdom. For him, the title "King" is what defines perfection. As a servant (Cinderella) and an ogress (Fiona), both damsels are undesirable to most of society and the prince/lord they wish to marry. Both women have been raised on fairytale dreams and are looking for true love. These are just a few of the patterns that seem to emerge from the comparison of the two films. But how can you make these observations into a thesis statement that you can argue?

Here are two possibilities:

Possible thesis #1: *Disney's* Cinderella *and DreamWorks'* Shrek *demonstrate that marrying for love, as opposed to marrying for power, money, or beauty, is the only way to live "happily ever after."*

To support this thesis, you could argue that the stepmother and stepsisters in *Cinderella* are unsuccessful in their scheming to marry the prince. Their conniving is not rewarded. The stepmother is depicted as mean, cruel, and manipulative; the stepsisters appear silly, shallow, and quarrelsome. They are not worthy either of a prince or "true love" as their motivations to marry are based on greed and ambition. On the other hand, Cinderella is kind, hard-working, and full of dreams; she is worthy. In *Shrek*, we see Lord Farquaad as cruel when torturing the Gingerbread Man, in rounding up and evicting the fairytale creatures because they do not fit his image of perfect citizens, and in his final rejection of Princess Fiona in her ogress form. He values the appearance of perfection, as demonstrated by the sterility of Duloc (itself a satire of Disneyland), but not the deeper substance. He is also unsuccessful in marrying the princess and meets an unfortunate end. Shrek does not desire money and power, preferring to live a simple life in his swamp. By marrying him, Fiona gives up being a princess, living in luxurious comfort, and her human appearance. In both tales, love is the precondition for "happily ever after."

Possible thesis #2: *Animated films for children often teach us the values that our culture holds. While Disney's* Cinderella *portrays the fairytale ideal of "love at first sight," DreamWorks'* Shrek *demonstrates that outer appearance is not a reflection of inner worth and will not guarantee happiness.*

For Cinderella, happiness results after displaying her true beauty—perhaps inner and outer—to the prince, though it has been hidden by menial jobs, poor clothing, lack of social status, and a scheming stepfamily. Cinderella's dreams of a better future, her hope, and her endurance have made her worthy of true love. In *Shrek*, Princess Fiona faces the prospect of a loveless marriage to the "perfect" man in the "perfect kingdom." She chooses Shrek instead, despite his monstrous appearance, because of his personality and his true love for her. In the end, her choice results in her own permanent transformation to ogre-form, which she had despised all along.

Examining two texts in conversation with each other can lead to a deeper analysis of one or both texts. As demonstrated above, this analytical process can even lead to a claim about a larger social issue, such as how children's films affect or reflect a specific cultural value.

The Hero's Journey as a Theoretical Lens

By Jen Neely

See Chapter 5 in *Rules for Writers* for more on critical reading.

This section shows how one theoretical lens can shape the way you view a primary text by highlighting the development of the hero in a story. To perform a theoretical analysis, you must first understand the theory you will use as your secondary text. This example uses Joseph Campbell's theory of the Hero's Journey (also referred to as the Monomyth). Campbell's theory uses classical mythology as a basis for determining the stages of the hero's journey, beginning with the departure from home and ending with his or her successful return. The Hero's Journey creates the framework for an analysis that seeks out the particular elements of the primary text that reflect the elements of the Hero's Journey. The following diagram presents the Hero's Journey as Campbell describes it in his work *The Hero with a Thousand Faces*.

Tests
The hero goes through a series of tests to prepare for the final battle. These can be confrontations with monsters or sorcerers, puzzles or forces of nature. They frequently occur in threes, and the hero often fails one or more along the way.

Crossing the Threshold
The hero undergoes a test or ordeal in passing from the real world into the mythical world. This other world can be referred to as the underworld, or the "belly of the whale."

Supernatural Aid
This initial guide and protective figure can take a variety of forms, from a wizard to a fairy godmother, and often bestows a weapon or protective amulet.

Call to Adventure
The hero is called to adventure by an event or person. S/he may be reluctant to accept this call, but eventually they commit to the quest.

Helpers
In addition to the initial guide, who may or may not be a constant presence along the journey, the hero also encounters additional helpers to aid him or her in the journey through the underworld.

The World of Adventure

Campbell's Monomyth Cycle

The Real World

Birth
The beginning of the hero's journey establishes the hero as a person of great potential and promise.

Climax/Final Battle
In this step the hero engages in his/her ultimate battle, which may be a confrontation with a monster, wizard or warrior. The hero often does not have to win this battle, but through it will gain the Elixir.

Home
Upon returning home, the hero is now able to use the knowledge and strength gained to make his/her own world a better place.

Flight
The hero must return to the threshold in order to pass again into the real world. If s/he has gained victory by defeating all opposing forces, this may be an easy journey. On the other hand, if there is still danger it will be a swift flight.

Return
The return to the real world can take multiple forms, from an easy passage through a forest to an awakening, rebirth or resurrection. It may also take the form of a final confrontation or battle.

Elixir
This is the knowledge or artifact that the hero has gained along the journey. This may have restorative or healing properties and also serves to solidify the hero's importance within his/her own society.

The hero begins his or her journey with the Call to Adventure, Crosses the Threshold into an unknown world, passes through a series of Tests, and participates in a Final Battle before returning home with new knowledge gained along the journey. Stories from classical mythology like Homer's *The Odyssey*, or Old English tales like *Beowulf*, as well as more modern popular media, like *Star Wars* or comic book superhero stories, often fit within the Monomyth. Once you understand the theoretical secondary text, the next step is to identify how it relates to the primary text. A series of careful questions is a good way to begin the analysis.

• **What does the theoretical text ask me to understand or believe?**

It is easy to see that home is an important place within the myth. The hero both starts from and returns to a home where he or she is not only a person of importance but also contributes to the well-being of the people there, who may be family or a larger community. In this sense, the Monomyth values the family and home. The fact that the hero receives aid in the form of a spiritual or mystical guide and helpers (once he or she has passed into the unknown world) also suggests that it is important to recognize and accept help from others. However, the fact that the hero must face the final battle alone emphasizes the ideas of self-reliance and facing one's own challenges. These are a few examples of the themes that may emerge when the Hero's Journey is applied as a framework for understanding a primary text.

- **Does my primary text share in or differ from that knowledge or understanding?**

One way to begin to answer this question is to make a list of the similarities and differences of the two texts, similar to the list in the previous section. Establishing this textual relationship is important to developing a sense of how your understanding of the primary text is shaped by applying the ideas of the secondary text. The following example demonstrates how the Hero's Journey can be applied using a film as the primary text. We will use the specific steps of the Monomyth as a basis for comparison in looking at the film *The Matrix* (1999) and look for how they may be related to Keanu Reeves' character, Neo:

The Monomyth	The Matrix
The Call to Adventure	Neo receives a phone call from Morpheus and a warning from Trinity at the nightclub
Crossing the Threshold	Neo takes the red pill and is awakened from the Matrix
Climax/Final Battle	The final fight with Agent Smith
Elixir	Neo has learned how to manipulate the Matrix and now holds power over life and death

When we apply Campbell's theory of the Hero's Journey and use our comparisons to analyze the film, we come to see that Neo's journey is much like those represented by classical mythology. He must cross a threshold into a world of adventure, he goes through tests and trials, he faces a climactic battle through which he gains the elixir, and it is assumed that he will use this newfound ability to aid in the fight against the Matrix. Nevertheless, there is a major difference or point of departure from the traditional journey, and that is related to the threshold and its opposing worlds as we will demonstrate below.

- **If there are specific steps or points made in my theoretical text, are those represented in the primary text?**

An important piece of the Monomyth is the transition between the real world and the world of adventure. *The Matrix* begins in a world that looks similar to our everyday reality. Looking back to the Monomyth, this is the place within the journey that represents home and, ultimately, what the hero is fighting for. Once Neo crosses the threshold, we are introduced to a world that seems unfamiliar and alien: a world in which human beings are grown and harvested, kept in pods filled with a pink gooey fluid, and hooked into the power grid for their energy. This would seem to match with the theory of the world of adventure. However, as the story progresses, this world becomes the one associated with the idea of home and family. Unlike the traditional journey, once Neo crosses into this world, it is the original home, the Matrix, that becomes the mythical world.

Practice with the Hero's Journey

Practice using the Hero's Journey or Monomyth to analyze a text that you have looked at before. Fill out this chart with the corresponding scenes from a film or novel. If you were going to "chart" *The Matrix*, for example, you would simply write, "Neo takes the red pill" in the bubble labeled, "Crossing the Threshold."

Craft Box: ANALYSIS

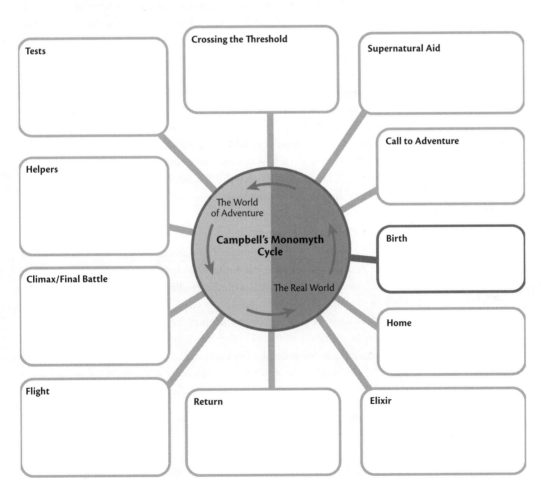

Tests

Crossing the Threshold

Supernatural Aid

Call to Adventure

Helpers

The World of Adventure

Campbell's Monomyth Cycle

Birth

The Real World

Climax/Final Battle

Home

Flight

Return

Elixir

How might we translate this into an analysis? The transformation of the meaning of "home" is a key difference between our theoretical text and the film, and examining how that change affects our understanding of what the film means will lead to a worthwhile analysis. Points of difference or conflict between your primary and secondary texts are often the place wherein you will find your thesis. While being able to identify and explain points of similarity is important, focusing on the differences will be crucial to conducting a well-developed contextual analysis.

Questions to ask as you construct your thesis include:

- On what points do the texts differ?

- Do these differences signal a change in what the text(s) value?

- How do these changes affect the text as a whole?

The Monomyth places high value and importance on the idea of home. The entire journey begins and ends there, and it is only once home that the hero uses the elixir and establishes him/herself as a figure of knowledge and power. Neo is left at the end of the film as master of both worlds (in his ability to control the Matrix and his establishment as "the One"), but the question is debatable as to whether or not the "real" world has become his home. Without a clear sense of return (note that Neo does not return across the threshold), we are left between the two worlds. With this change, what can we say the film is valuing? If it is not home and family, what is it? Beginning with these questions and identifying how specific strategies such as lighting, set design, cinematography, and others are used will help you identify what the film emphasizes and values. The answers will be your thesis for this assignment.

Texts in Cultural Contexts

Texts serve as a means of communicating culture, but they are also shaped by culture. Analyzing a primary text within the context of its surrounding culture can lead toward a more complex understanding of the culture and the text. Culture is a broad term that refers to the characteristics, beliefs, practices, creations, relations, etc., of a group of people, time period, or place. Everything from art to political systems to eating habits could be considered elements of culture that both shape the ideas in a text and an audience's perception of those ideas. In a cultural analysis, you will explore how elements of culture influence the writer's construction and/or the reader's interpretations of a text.

In a cultural analysis, you might ask yourself the following questions:

- What worldview does this text convey?

- What cultural beliefs influence the argument or content in the text?

- How does the text represent the assumptions or beliefs of a particular group of people or historical time period?

- How does the text produce culture?

- How does the text reflect culture?

The underlying assumption of cultural analysis is that "any cultural product" or, in this case, the text you are analyzing, "carries, implicitly or explicitly, ideas about how the world should be seen" (Corrigan 88). Concepts of "seeing" or "gazing" will be further explored below in Devon Kehler's and Casely Coan's analysis of "gaze" in visual texts. Alan Chu's section that follows will help you to analyze everyday objects using cultural analysis.

Remember that analyzing how a text portrays a specific view(s) of the world can be extremely difficult because culture often operates invisibly. The task of cultural analysis is to make visible those structures of culture and their effect on the text and the readers of the text. In the words of composition scholars Bonnie Stone Sunstein and Elizabeth Chiseri-Strater, when investigating culture you want to focus on "making the familiar seem strange" (10). The following two approaches will lead you through this process of making photographs or even everyday objects like a Coke bottle "seem strange" in order to illuminate their cultural influences.

The "I" of Eye: Theories of Looking

By Casely E. Coan and Devon R. Kehler

This approach to the Text-in-Context assignment uses theoretical concepts from feminist theory and cinema to analyze a primary text. Our eyes have a lot to do with the ways we experience pleasure, and they also impact the way we understand ourselves in relative positions of power with others. Eyes complexly interact with the rest of our body in the struggle to make meaning. This section explores how meaning is made not only by one's eyes and viewing experience in the moment, but also by the histories and socially situated identities and positions viewers and authors bring to a film or photograph. This section provides some key terms for how eyes *look* and *gaze* at images captured by cameras. Additionally, you are asked to examine how pleasure and power operate in visual texts by paying attention to the ways looking and gazing produce feelings, thoughts, and bodily sensations.

Laura Mulvey, a frequently cited writer on cinema, calls our attention to the "pleasure of looking." She suggests that the pleasure the eye receives from looking and being looked at is not innocent. The concept of "gaze" as explained by Jonathan Schroeder can help us explain how looking is more than just an act of seeing. Schroeder claims, "to gaze implies more than to look at—it signifies a psychological relationship of power, in which the gazer is superior to the object of the gaze" (208). In other words, gazing is embedded in power relationships and makes objects out of whatever is being seen.

When analyzing a visual text, especially those with human subjects, certain language is needed to discuss differing sorts of relationships between the looker and the looked at. Try using the following definitions and questions to analyze a family photograph or other complex visual text involving human subjects:

> See section 7.2 for more on analyzing visual texts.

Spectator's Gaze: Within this particular context, we can understand the "spectator" as equivalent to the "audience." The spectator's gaze is *your* gaze when you are viewing a film or photograph. As such, this gaze is influenced by those contexts *you* bring to the text: your identity, background, experiences, and social and cultural positions. One mode of spectatorship is termed **voyeuristic**, in which the watcher experiences power and pleasure.

- What do you feel as a viewer? Do you feel pleasure and/or power? How? Why?

- How do your own experiences or background impact your understanding of the image?

Eye of the Camera: The camera—and the person or people operating it—create certain "conditions for viewing," meaning a viewer does not get to see the whole picture, but only what was captured by a lens. Sometimes, the camera's eye places our eyes in a passive position; sometimes, the eye of the camera places us in a position of dominance.

- How does the camera position you as viewer? From what angle are you viewing the action?

- What was captured in the frame? What isn't shown? Why?

- Does the camera place viewers in a position of passivity or dominance? What about the image, the angle, the framing, the lighting, the cropping, etc., makes you feel this way?

Intra-diegetic Gaze: In film and photography involving human subjects, the characters within the text also use their gaze to create dynamics of power and pleasure. The author may employ this gaze in different ways, asking the audience to identify with either the one looking (that is, the one exercising the intra-diegetic gaze) or the one being looked at. This gaze promotes sympathy between audience and character and the experience of power or pleasure in looking or being looked at.

- Where are the characters in the image looking? What are they looking at? Why?

- How does their gaze indicate their position of power? Are they enacting power over another figure or object in the picture?

- Does their gaze indicate if/how they are taking pleasure in something?

- Who do you identify with in the photograph? Why?

Extra-diegetic Gaze: This occurs when people depicted in a visual text appear to be looking directly out of the frame at viewers. Power is primarily located with the person(s) depicted. Consider one of the most common experiences viewers have when gazing at the *Mona Lisa*: the intense sensation of being looked at or watched.

- Are any figures in the image looking directly at the camera?

- How are the figures trying to engage you as a viewer?

- Do any figures indicate a sense of pleasure in being gazed at?

Now that we have introduced some terminology that enables us to better engage how looking, power, and pleasure interact, let's apply these terms to the photo below. We'll ask questions while inviting you to engage analytical processes with the following photograph from Lauren Greenfield's *Girl Culture*.

The most popular girls at school...13 in Edina, *Girl Culture*. Photograph: Lauren Greenfield/INSTITUTE. Alli, Annie, Hannah, and Berit before the first big party of the seventh grade, Edina, Minnesota.

Eye of the Camera: This photograph is part of a larger project seeking to display everyday practices of girlhood. The camera sets these girls *outside* a suburban home, *in* a suburban neighborhood. How does this setting affect your interpretation of the photograph? What might you assume about the subjects based on this setting and their attire? What is or isn't captured in this frame? What does the arrangement of the girls in front of the camera suggest about their relationship with the photographer? With you as a viewer? Considering the purpose of this photo project, what does this particular frame ask you to see about the "everyday practices of girlhood"?

Intra-diegetic Gaze: Consider Berit on the far right. She does not engage the camera. Instead her gaze is directed towards the girls posed beside her. What does this say about the pleasure Berit experiences in being photographed? What's her relationship to the camera in comparison to the rest of the girls? How does Berit engage power dynamics by the way she gazes away from the camera and towards her friends?

Extra-diegetic Gaze: Alli, Annie, and Hannah are all looking at the photographer and, therefore, the audience. But they aren't gazing in the same way. How can we see them enacting the extra-diegetic gaze differently from one another? What do their varying postures say about the relationship between them and the camera? How does their willingness to engage the camera communicate their pleasure in being gazed at? As a viewer, how do you feel yourself responding differently to being looked at by *them*?

Spectator's Gaze: As a viewer, how does the composition of the photograph position you in the girls' world? Do you feel pleasure in looking at them? Power? How do these dynamics shift as you consider the girls looking back at you versus the girl avoiding eye contact with the camera? How do your own experiences or identity impact your understanding of the girls and situation depicted by Greenfield?

For a more nuanced analysis, return to the photograph multiple times, with greater attention to what captures your gaze on repeat viewings.

Examining Culture through Everyday Objects

By Alan Chu

Culture can be a particularly powerful lens for analyzing a text. Because it asks you to think critically about the way meaning is constructed within a particular cultural context, practicing cultural analysis has the potential to change the way you see the world. Yet, before you attempt to understand these connections, it is important to consider a crucial question: what, exactly, constitutes an appropriate text for cultural analysis?

The field of Cultural Studies has helped expand the definition of what we consider a text. For cultural critics, the empty Coke bottle in the trashcan or the University of Arizona flag above Arizona Stadium can be read as texts laden with complex cultural meaning. Considering everyday objects as meaningful texts significantly widens the scope of objects that invite analysis. For instance, consider the Coke bottle:

First, take a close look at its physical properties. What are the dimensions? Is it in a 12 oz., 16 oz., 20 oz., or 2-liter container? At first glance, the size of the container may not offer much in the way of useful cultural analysis. However, like any text, the Coke bottle is designed for a specific audience. If the bottle is located on campus, what does its size mean in relation to its audience? In other words, how would university students react if the vending machines around campus only offered 2-liter Cokes instead of 20 oz. bottles? Would it help or hinder its designed function as a product for consumption? Additionally, consider what is important to its target audience of college students. 20 oz. bottles are certainly more portable than a 2-liter container, yet it offers a greater volume of soda for consumption than a 12 oz. can. Each bottle, as opposed to a can with a tab, comes equipped with a twist-off cap, allowing for convenient storage and reuse. Finally, its size,

The Everyday Cultural Analysis

To begin a cultural analysis of an everyday object, first attempt to disassociate your prior knowledge and experience from the object, which we will refer to as an artifact. Examine how the artifact is both a product of culture and one that produces culture. By analyzing everyday objects as "unfamiliar" cultural artifacts, you can begin to answer several key questions:

1. What is the user's relationship to the artifact? Conversely, what does that relationship reveal about the user?

2. What is the economical value of the artifact? What is its value to the people for whom it was originally produced?

3. In what historical period was the artifact created? How does it reflect the customs and assumptions of that period? If the artifact has evolved over time, what does that evolution suggest about changes in the associated culture?

4. Who has access to the artifact? What factors (e.g., cost, availability, size) impact access?

5. What is the artifact's relationship to other similar objects found in the same cultural context?

6. Does the artifact reflect a particular ideology? If so, how does the artifact's ideology reproduce the culture from which it came?

7. What other factors are important to understanding the specific artifact being examined?

dimensions, and physical makeup are an indication that the bottle is a disposable item. The shape of the Coke bottle's neck prohibits future use whereas its ergonomic shape and volume suggests that its contents are a single serving—despite its designation by the FDA as containing the equivalent of 2.5 servings per bottle. Based on this brief description, one can assume that the players participating in this cultural production are the University of Arizona, Coca-Cola Corporation, American culture with its capitalist ideology, and you, the university student, its target consumer. Now, apply this critical lens to the other components that you notice on the Coke bottle: its colors, logo, and physical makeup—is it made of plastic or glass? After a bit of practice and reflection, it should become clear that each one of these properties offers an abundance of insight for cultural analysis.

The Coke bottle is but one example. Take a second look at the many objects that you are intimately familiar with and try to complicate your understanding of these artifacts. In other words, take what's familiar and make it strange. Whether at home, at a friend's apartment, outdoors, or working at a restaurant, there are innumerable artifacts that we encounter every day but give very little thought as to its connections to culture. Instead, ask yourself: what is the cultural significance of a Playstation controller? Why do some women's restrooms have couches? And what is the point of the sunglasses on that moose's head at the restaurant where you work? By conceptualizing your artifact through a cultural lens, this may very well change not only your relationship with the object, but deepen your understanding of how culture influences everything around us, from trash on the ground to flags fluttering in the sky. Use the Craft Box on the previous page to help focus your analysis.

8.3 Thinking through the Process

Invention

As you read in Chapter 3, invention begins before you start drafting. Invention involves locating the ideas or topics you will write about and potentially beginning to develop those ideas into arguments.

The following example uses a chart to organize ideas, but you could also begin by journaling, freewriting, idea mapping, or using any other strategy. Regardless of your method for invention, this assignment requires that you understand both your primary and secondary texts individually as well as in relationship to each other.

Re-reading with a Purpose

Before you consider writing your Text-in-Context assignment, it is important to review your notes and observations on the primary and secondary texts. To deepen your understanding of each of the texts, you may want to follow the "Directed Reading" phase as introduced in Chapter 2.

Applying a Lens

Once you are familiar with each of the texts you will incorporate into your analysis, determine the relationships between the primary and secondary text. You could start by either considering what you hope to explore more about your primary text or by identifying a main idea or point of interest from your secondary text. Consider using one or both of the following charts to help you start exploring relationships.

- What aspects of your primary text do you want to explore further? Are these aspects related to your secondary text in any way?

Points of Interest from Primary Text (observations, questions, interpretations)	Relationship to Secondary Text (how this text complicates, supports, answers, or challenges the points of interest from the primary text)

- What aspects of your secondary text seem most significant and related to your primary text?

Points of Interest from Secondary Text (observations, questions, arguments, key terms, interpretations)	Relationship to Primary Text (how the points of interest from the secondary text are somehow reflected in the primary text)

You may choose to explore one or more of these intersections between your primary and secondary texts as the main focus of your analysis assignment.

Drafting

As you begin drafting, keep the following tips in mind:

See Chapter 6 in *Rules for Writers* for more on making a claim and arguing with evidence.

- Articulate a specific thesis that explains how the primary and secondary texts relate to one another. For example, your texts might develop a similar theme in different ways, or the secondary text may explicitly discuss a concept that is implicitly demonstrated in the primary text. Your main claim will largely depend on the type of approach or lens you or your instructor choose(s) to use for the secondary text. The thesis may even come directly from the charts you completed in the previous section.

- Incorporate contextual evidence (e.g., evidence collected from your secondary text or texts) as well as specific evidence from the primary text in well-developed paragraphs to support your thesis.

- Examine how the secondary text creates a new context (or contexts) that contribute(s) to your understanding of the primary text.

- Explain why this new context is important and/or significant to your understanding of the primary text.

Like Textual Analyses, Text-in-Context essays are persuasive. Although your analysis will only present one of many possible interpretations, your goal is to convince the reader that your analysis is credible. Your thesis will need to demonstrate your own ideas and use secondary texts to bolster your points. Secondary texts should not be used just to structure your essay or make your arguments for you.

Drafting a Thesis Statement and Introduction for Text-in-Context

See *Rules for Writers* pp. 27–31 for strategies for revising a thesis.

Your thesis should clearly show the connection between your primary and secondary text. The information presented in your thesis statement will largely depend on the approach you are taking. For instance, a thesis statement for a paper in which you compare two texts will differ from an essay in which you apply a theoretical lens to a primary text. However, like any thesis statement, it should give your reader a clear idea of what they can expect from the rest of the essay, and in order for the thesis to be analytical, you must do more than simply summarize the main points of your primary or secondary texts. The Craft Box on pages 170–171 offers some possible formulas for crafting a Text-in-Context thesis statement, but do not feel limited by these suggestions.

Because you are now dealing with more than one text, your introduction will also need to clearly introduce both. It is up to you to decide how much summary of both texts you will need to provide for your reader to make sense of your analysis. You may want to revisit the "Summary" section in Chapter 5 as you begin.

The following example is from an essay written by UA student Nikki Javia. Notice how Nikki clearly articulates how the secondary text informed her understanding of the primary text. Even if you have not read the texts mentioned in her analysis, you can see how she structured her introduction and thesis statement to inform her audience of a particular contextual interpretation.

Approach used for the assignment: Genre/Theoretical

Primary text: The short story, "A Very Old Man with Enormous Wings," by Gabriel García Márquez

Secondary text: The book, *Ordinary Enchantments: Magical Realism and the Remystification of Narrative*, by Wendy Bush Faris

Introduction paragraph:

> Magical realism, a genre of fiction, expands the concept of the real so as to blend fantasy and magical elements with realism, thereby erasing the distinction between the two. However, unlike fantastic literature, the story is set in context of real events and scenes, and provides commentary on human nature or culture, forcing us to confront real issues. This narrative style was widely prevalent in postcolonial era, especially in Latin American literature. Gabriel García Márquez uses magical realism in his short story, "A Very Old Man with Enormous Wings", in which an angel falls on Earth due to a violent storm. The reality of the situation is never questioned, yet the angel is an astonishing manifestation. In the story, the aspects of daily life and supernatural origin work together to reveal some negative aspects of human nature. Márquez's short story, "A Very Old Man with Enormous Wings" utilizes conventions of the magical realism genre as investigated in Wendy Bush Faris' *Ordinary Enchantments: Magical Realism and the Remystification of Narrative* to mock the Catholic Church and shallowness of human nature in a realistic, yet fantastical way. Márquez achieves his purpose and his text functions adequately within Bush's vision of magical realism by using symbolic imagery and satire.

Following up on student writing:

- How did Nikki introduce the primary and secondary texts? On which text is she placing more emphasis?

- How much background information about each text did she provide in the introduction? Is it an adequate amount? Why or why not?

- Underline Nikki's thesis. Does it clearly articulate how the secondary text influenced her reading of the primary text?

- If you were to predict the rest of her paper based on this introduction, what would an outline look like?

See Chapters 10–11 for examples of how to incorporate research into your essay.

Paragraph Structure for Text-in-Context

Text-in-Context essays can still rely on the basics of **PIE** paragraphs for structure, but will need to include evidence from both primary and secondary sources. Make sure to embed proper in-text citations and signal phrases as you write so as not to confuse your reader. For more help with citations and incorporating sources, see Chapter 5.

This sample paragraph from Nikki's essay demonstrates PIE structure and incorporates both her primary and secondary texts. Notice how she does the following:

See Chapter 58 in *Rules for Writers* for advice about integrating sources smoothly and responsibly.

- Opens with a topic sentence (**Point**) that clearly relates back to the thesis.

- Incorporates textual evidence from both her primary and secondary text (**Illustration**).

- Provides analysis that explains the connection between the textual evidence in her illustration with her central claim (**Explanation**).

Drafting a Thesis Statement for Text-in-Context

Craft Box: DRAFTING

By Carie Schneider

This Craft Box presents just one possibility for constructing a Text-in-Context thesis statement. If you follow this format exactly, you will probably want to revise your **thesis** to make the structure more unique and less rigid before submitting your final draft. Remember that you can make these sentences less awkward while holding on to the essential pieces. Here are some examples of how to incorporate multiple texts in one thesis statement:

One secondary text, one primary text:

[Primary Text's Author]'s [genre], [primary text title], connects with the concept of [context/theme] as expressed in [Secondary Text's Author]'s [secondary text title] by referring to [subthemes connecting primary text and secondary text], which it accomplishes through the use of [techniques, elements, features].

Here is an example:

Ruth Kluger's biography, *Still Alive*, connects with the concept of writing as a social witness as expressed in Beth Alvarado's essay "Writing as a Social Witness" by referring to dealing with a difficult past and speaking up for the voiceless, which it accomplishes through the use of personal stories and historical references.

This is a somewhat unwieldy and repetitive sentence. Use the space below to revise the thesis for clarity and conciseness.

Sample Paragraph:

> Magical realism is often employed to serve the purpose of satire and comment on political issues since people tend to react and reflect on magical events in a more profound way and feel less offended than if the subject matter was addressed more literally. "In magical realism, reality's outrageousness is often underscored because ordinary people react to magical events in a recognizable and sometimes also in disturbing ways, a circumstance that normalizes the magical event but also defamiliarizes, underlines, or critiques extraordinary aspects of the real" (Faris 13). Marquez's "A Very Old Man with Enormous Wings" is a critique about the extent to which humans have deteriorated due to a lack of compassion and willingness to exploit fellow humans without hesitation for personal gains. Initially Pelayo and Elisenda, for example, pity the old man/angel and show concern. However, the neighbor lady who "knew everything about life and death" (Marquez 295) talks the couple out of rendering

Two (or more) primary texts, one secondary (theme/theoretical) text:

[Primary Text 1's Author]'s [genre], [primary text 1 title], and [Primary Text 2's Author]'s [genre], [primary text 2 title] relate to each other in their shared connection to the concept of [context/theme] as expressed in [Secondary Text's Author]'s [secondary text title] in their references to [subthemes connecting primary text and secondary text], which are accomplished through the use of [techniques, elements, features].

This can get completely out of hand as a single sentence, and it may be even longer if the two primary texts are using different techniques to express their shared themes. You might decide to rework this type of thesis into two sentences like in the following example:

Ruth Kluger's biography, *Still Alive*, and Ariel Dorfman's poem, "Vocabulary," relate to each other in their shared connection to the concept of writing as a social witness as expressed in Beth Alvarado's essay. Both *Still Alive* and "Vocabulary" deal with speaking for the voiceless and the need to express difficult truths, through the use of personal stories and historical references in *Still Alive* and through word choice and poetic structure in "Vocabulary."

Now write Nikki's thesis from the introduction paragraph on page 169. If you break down her thesis into a formula, what does it look like? Write the thesis and its formula below.

Now try revising Nikki's thesis in the space below. How might you rearrange the information or make it more concise?

171

8.3

assistance. Pelayo "dragged him out of the mud and locked him up with the hens in the wire chicken coop" (Marquez 295). Townspeople came to see him from far away and "even the most merciful threw stones at him, trying to get him to rise so they could see him standing. The only time they succeeded in arousing him was when they burned his side with an iron for branding steers" (Marquez, 297). The townspeople's exploitation of the angel is described with harsh details and imaginative scenarios. Why would Marquez use an angel other than to signify how people often take advantage of the innocent for personal gain? By looking at the story through the lens of Ordinary Enchantments, the use such magical events have more impact on the reader since they manage to critique and emphasize the outrageous, extraordinary aspects of the real that people often ignore or are unaware of. By making use of fantasy, through the falling of an angel and his mistreatment and exploitation, Marquez offers a satirical look into the prevalent, but often disregarded, harsh reality concerning human's tendencies to mistreat others, even the most innocent, for entertainment purposes.

> See section 13.5 for examples of what a full Text-in-Context essay may look like.

Following up on student writing:

- What kind(s) of evidence does Nikki use to support her topic sentence? Is her evidence effective?

- Does this paragraph clearly show how the secondary text informed her reading of the primary text?

- Are all quotes effectively incorporated into sentences and the paragraph as a whole (check Chapter 5 for a refresher)? How does Nikki introduce quotes or paraphrases? How does she respond to them?

- How does the author manage to include information from both the primary and secondary texts? How could she transition more smoothly between examples, or between evidence and analysis?

When incorporating secondary texts, make sure to explain the connection between the primary and secondary text clearly, and then relate this connection to your thesis. This final step is where your analysis begins to develop beyond simple summary.

Anticipating Reader Concerns

When revising your Text-in-Context essay, you might want to anticipate some of your readers' concerns. According to Donald Murray, a teacher and Pulitzer Prize-winning journalist, one way to revise an essay is to "anticipate and answer the reader's questions." Why? Because anticipating reader concerns can help you figure out what you need to add, remove, or revise in your essay.

Murray suggests that "any piece of writing is a conversation with a reader who interrupts to say":

How come?

How do you know that?

I don't get it.

What do you mean?

I'd like to know more about that.

No kidding.

Why'd she do that?

What'd he do then?

Tell me more.

Stop it. Enough already.

Get to the point.

Whoa. Back up, I don't understand.

Take a moment to read through your essay as if you are a reader approaching your essay for the first time. Where might you stop and ask one of these questions or state one of these comments? How are you, as the writer, going to respond?

Test your writing on an audience. In small classroom groups, or even with a roommate, tutor, or friend, read your paper out loud together and ask your readers to stop whenever one of these questions or comments comes to mind. Is there a section you all stumble over? Why? Is there a paragraph that loses your audience's attention? How can you get them to focus again? Are you over-summarizing, causing your reader to whine, "Get to the point"? If so, how can you slim down your summary and move into more interesting analysis?

Trying to envision your writing as a reader can help you to better anticipate the effectiveness of your communication. You might know what you want to say when writing, but does your reader understand? Do they see the importance of your analysis like you do?

Revision

Approaching revision for your Text-in-Context assignment is similar to other writing projects. You should revise for such areas as content and organization, paragraph structure, use of evidence, clarity of thought, and mechanics. However, because you are illuminating one text using another, you might be using more quotations or paraphrases in this project than you did for your Textual Analysis, Rhetorical Analysis, or Literacy Narrative. As you revise, make sure that all of your quotations are properly integrated (see Chapter 5) and that you are properly citing the authors. Additionally, see the Tips & Strategies Box on the previous page for some tips on how to address questions you imagine readers will ask in your draft.

Use the following checklist for revising your Text-in-Context essay:

✔ Underline specific evidence (quotes, paraphrases, summaries) that clearly shows how the secondary text affects your understanding of the primary text.

✔ Circle the most compelling points of analysis in your argument. Are you clearly explaining how and why the secondary text relates to the primary text and how your supporting points relate back to your main claim?

✔ Write the main point of each paragraph in the margins. Is each point focused and does it support the thesis? Does the arrangement of your paragraphs support the argument? Do the ideas build upon each other?

✔ Review your assignment guidelines and make sure your essay articulates the goals outlined by your instructor.

8.4 Reflection

Analyzing texts in context is a useful exercise in understanding how texts are not isolated acts of communication. They often speak to or about other texts, historical events, or cultural practices. You may have also noticed how your interpretation of a text changed when considered through a particular lens. What may have seemed like just an empty Coke bottle before may now seem like an object of cultural significance because of heightened contextual awareness.

As you conclude this unit, take a moment to freewrite or discuss the following reflective questions with a partner:

• How did your understanding of a text change when a particular context was introduced?

• How did you improve as a writer and critical thinker during this unit?

• In what ways can you connect this assignment to your other classes or life experiences?

Works Cited

Chandler, Daniel. "Notes on 'The Gaze'." Daniel Chandler, 2011. Web. 1 Oct. 2013.

Cinderella. Dir. Clyde Geronimi, Hamilton Luske and Wilfred Jackson. RKO Radio Pictures, 1950. DVD.

Corrigan, Timothy. *A Short Guide to Writing about Film*. 6th ed. New York: Longman, 2006. Print.

Faris, Wendy B. *Ordinary Enchantments: Magical Realism and the Remystification of Narrative*. Nashville: Vanderbilt University Press, 2004. Print.

García Márquez, Gabriel. "A Very Old Man with Enormous Wings." Ed. Janet E. Gardner. *Literature: A Portable Anthology*. Boston: Bedford/St. Martin's, 2004. Print.

Mulvey, Laura. "Visual Pleasure and Narrative Cinema." *Film Theory and Criticism: Introductory Readings*. Eds. Leo Braud and Marshall Cohen. New York: Oxford UP, 1999: 833–44. Print.

Murray, Donald. *Craft of Revision*. 3rd ed. New York: Harcourt Brace College Publishers, 1998. Print.

Shrek. Dir. Andrew Adamson and Vicky Jenson. DreamWorks Animation, 2001. DVD.

Schroeder, Jonathan E. "Consuming Representation: A Visual Approach to Consumer Research." *Representing Consumers: Voices, Views and Visions*. Ed. Barbara B Stern. London: Routledge, 1998. 193–230. Print.

Sunstein, Bonnie Stone, and Elizabeth Chiseri-Strater. *FieldWorking: Reading and Writing Research*. 3rd ed. Boston: Bedford/St. Martin's, 2007. Print.

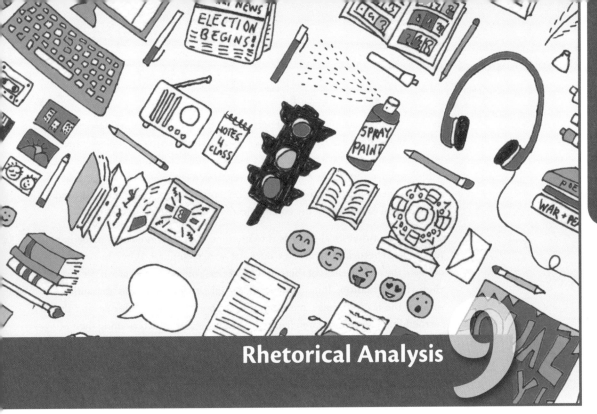

Rhetorical Analysis

9.1 Rhetorical Analysis: An Overview

We perform **rhetorical analysis** every day, even if we are unaware of it. We are constantly thinking about different forms of communication and figuring out how they affect us. For example, when arguing with your roommates about whose turn it is to take out the trash, how do you make your case? Do you use personal attacks to make them feel guilty? Do you present evidence about how you have taken the trash out for the last three weeks, making it seem only logical that it is not your turn? Do you scare them by threatening to call the landlord? Or do you offer to help so as not to cause tension? Should you bring up this issue at breakfast or wait until right before bed? Do you call a house meeting, speak privately with a roommate, or leave a note? Do you communicate face-to-face or via text message? You will probably rely on your knowledge of your roommates' personalities, your type of relationship with them, and the surrounding circumstances such as time of day, location, etc., to make these types of decisions. Evaluating decisions or strategies used to achieve a particular purpose is at the heart of rhetorical analysis.

Before discussing rhetorical analysis, let's briefly define the term **rhetoric**. You may have heard rhetoric used negatively, for example, to describe a manipulative political speech. But rhetoric's use in terms of communication is much more complex. While there are many definitions of rhetoric, for our purposes we'll draw from the Greek philosopher Aristotle, who defines rhetoric as the ability to observe "the available means of persuasion" in a given situation (Herrick 80). When we use the term rhetoric in this book, we are referring to choices writers or speakers make in order to achieve a purpose and communicate in some way with a given audience. As rhetoricians, we strive to be aware of how language works in these situations so that we can be more effective communicators and more critical evaluators of the communications we receive every day.

Your goal in a rhetorical analysis is to examine how an argument is made in a text. What **rhetorical strategies** does the writer employ? Why? In order to evaluate the effectiveness of rhetorical strategies, you must be aware of the text's **rhetorical situation**. Put simply, a rhetorical situation includes the author/speaker, the text's message and intended purpose, a specific audience, and the surrounding **context**. Before identifying strategies and/or determining their effectiveness, it is helpful to identify and analyze the rhetorical situation.

The Rhetorical Situation

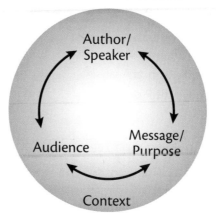

Author/Speaker

The **author/speaker** in a rhetorical situation is the person or people communicating a message to someone else. Depending on the medium, the "author" may take on different roles in the actual production of the text. For example, the author of a print text is usually the person who is actually writing the material; however, in films, the director would usually be considered the "author" for the purposes of analysis. In the roommate example at the beginning of the chapter, you are the author of whatever form of communication you choose.

In some rhetorical situations, it is easy to discover who is the author of the message. In many others, the author behind the message is less obvious. Consider a television advertisement for Welch's grape juice. While the visible speaker might be a little girl drinking a glass of grape juice, the author of the message in the advertisement is the juice company, specifically the marketing team of Welch's, who is trying to sell grape juice. Carefully consider who is responsible for the creation of the text and consider the following questions:

- Is the author immediately obvious? If not, who might be the author?

- What do you know about the author(s) of the text? Does prior knowledge about the author influence your reception of the text?

- How might another author compose the text differently?

- Do you get a sense of what the author values? How can you tell?

Audience

The **primary audience** is the person or people who the author/speaker intends to reach. Although it may be tempting to assert that an article or essay is written for a "general audience," most texts are targeted to a specific group of people. For example, when a United States President makes a primetime televised address that could be viewed by anybody with access to the speech, the primary audience is often comprised of a more specific audience of Americans and, even more specifically, voting Americans. Likewise, most material available on the internet could theoretically be read by almost anyone in the world, but bloggers, journalists for web publications, and other digital authors do not attempt to appeal to everyone in the world in their pieces; instead, they consider the people who are most likely to have an interest in their work and write with them in mind. Writers and speakers make choices based on what they know and what they assume about their intended audience.

See page 83 in *Rules for Writers* for guidelines on analyzing texts.

Keep in mind, however, that the primary audience is only one of many audiences with access to a particular text. Although an author/speaker usually intends to reach a specific audience, there is often a **secondary audience** who may also encounter the text, whether or not the writer or speaker intended for this to happen. Consider again the problem with your hypothetical roommate. If you leave a note for your roommate to take out the trash, she is your primary audience. However, your other roommates may also read this note. Perhaps it will remind them that their turn is coming up, or maybe they will think you are being too pushy.

When you analyze texts, begin by identifying the primary audience, since this is the audience the author had in mind. Then you might explore any secondary audiences to analyze how the text affects them differently. After identifying the audience(s) of your text, consider these questions:

- Who is included in the primary audience and who is excluded?

- What assumptions does the text make about the audience's values and needs?

Context

Every text reveals something about the context in which it was created. The context influences the author's rhetorical choices and the audience's reception of the text. Consider the garbage problem from the introduction of this chapter again. Perhaps this is the first time your roommate has forgotten to take out the trash, or you know they have a very understandable excuse. How you approach the situation within this context might be very different than how you deal with a roommate who consistently ignores his responsibilities. Perhaps you want to establish a routine with a new roommate or are looking for reasons to kick a disrespectful roommate out. The way you communicate your request to your audience, including format, tone, word choice, emphasis, etc., is influenced by the context. Whether you are analyzing a written, visual, spatial, or oral text, consider the following questions about context:

- What is the date of publication or delivery?

- What medium is used to deliver the message? What "rules" or conventions are typical to the medium?

- What contemporary events may have shaped the author's views and the audience's responses?

- What social and historical movements are related to the topic?

- What are the cultural and linguistic backgrounds of the primary and secondary audiences?

- What are the physical and material surroundings of the event or text (i.e., the city where a speech is delivered or the magazine in which a text is published)?

- What other texts (i.e., texts of the same genre, by the same author, written in the same time period, etc.) relate to your text? Is it a reaction to these other texts?

In order to recognize the importance of context within a text, it may help to ask how a text would be different if it was written in a different era or was presented in a different medium. For example, a job resignation announced during a toast at a company party would probably be received much differently than the same resignation written in a formal letter and handed personally to the supervisor with a verbal explanation.

Message and Purpose

You leave a note on the counter that reads, "John—you forgot to take out the trash. Again. It smells." The message in this case is self-explanatory: this is what you did, and here is the consequence. However, the purpose of the note is somewhat different. The purpose is to get your roommate to take out the trash immediately. Hopefully, John will also feel so guilty that he will be more responsible in the future. Although the message was simply a statement of fact, your purpose is to inspire your roommate to action. In other situations, the message might be a set of instructions, a moral argument, or an idea. You might think of the message as what the text is "saying." The purpose is the action or response the author hopes to achieve with their message. In other words, what is the text "doing"? It is also possible that a text might have several related messages and purposes.

Sometimes, like in the example with John, the message is fairly obvious and can usually be deciphered without too much analysis. The key to figuring out the purpose behind the message is to think about the author's specific goals. Does it appear that the author is trying to:

- express an idea or opinion?

- respond to a particular occasion or text?

- inform the reader about a topic that is often misunderstood?

- analyze, synthesize, or interpret?

- persuade an audience of something?

- reflect on a topic?

- advocate for change?

- move the readers to feel a certain way?

Of course, this list is far from complete. An author might have an entirely different purpose or try to achieve a combination of these purposes. Considering the purpose of a text is an important step in analyzing its effectiveness and/or understanding why the author used certain rhetorical strategies.

> See pages 74–75 in *Rules for Writers* for a student writer's outline of an author's message.

Rhetorical Strategies

An author makes specific choices in order to influence her audience. Rhetorical strategies might range from specific word choice to the organization of paragraphs in a written essay or from color choices to the arrangement of subjects in a painting. Aristotle grouped common rhetorical choices into three types: strategies that an author uses to establish credibility or character (**ethos**), strategies that appeal to the emotions of the audience (**pathos**), and strategies that an author uses to appeal to the audience's sense of reason or logic (**logos**). The following lists of strategies are grouped in this way. Keep in mind, however, that texts rely on multiple strategies to convey a purpose and that one strategy might affect or appeal to the audience in multiple ways.

Appeals to Credibility and Character (Ethos): An author establishes **credibility** in a variety of ways. By expressing sound logic and demonstrating knowledge about a subject, authors can convincingly establish credibility and gain trust from their audience. Credibility can also be established visually and spatially; think of the ways that a speaker's choice of clothing, grooming, and body language makes us believe that he or she is worthy of our trust, or how the design of a website or poster can lend a sense of legitimacy to the writer. Authors might also establish credibility by showing their quality of **character**. For example, an author writing a letter to parents about education reform might refer to personal experiences working as an elementary school principal and propose changes that directly impact students (such as access to technology and more counseling services on campus) in order to appear knowledgeable and personally invested in the well-being of students.

The following is a list of strategies that an author might employ to appear credible and of appropriate character:

- Personal stories

- References to credible sources

- Word choice

- Tone

- Visual arrangement

- Author's public image (i.e., reputation, physical appearance)

- Information about the author's expertise

- Acknowledgment of **counterarguments** and refutations to those arguments

See pages 109–110 in *Rules for Writers* for more on judging the fairness with which a writer handles opposing views.

- Appeals to values or beliefs shared by the audience

After identifying these strategies or other appeals to credibility and character in the text, ask yourself the following: How do these strategies affect the audience's perception of the author's credibility and character? How does the use of these strategies impact the effectiveness of the text's overall message? Are there any instances where the author's bias makes you doubt their credibility?

Appeals to Emotion (Pathos): Authors might also employ a variety of strategies that appeal to an audience's emotions. This does not always mean, however, that the author is trying to instill fear or lead his audience to tears. Even when it seems that a text lacks an emotional component, the author is making choices to that end. Consider why, for example, the writer of a lab report or a business memo might want to avoid provoking her reader.

The following is a list of strategies you might encounter that can affect the audience's emotional response to a text:

- Personal stories or other emotionally compelling narratives

- Repetition of key words

- Level of formality

- Humor

9.1

- Shocking statistics

- Images

- Color palette

- Music

- Sound effects

- Tone of voice

When identifying and analyzing these strategies, consider the following: What emotional response is the author attempting to create? Are these emotions effective or ineffective for this particular audience and rhetorical situation? How do these emotional appeals affect the credibility of the author or the argument of the text?

Appeals to Logic or Rational Decision Making (Logos): There are many ways to judge how a speaker uses logic or reason to make a convincing argument. Keep in mind as you read this section that a logical appeal does not necessarily mean an author/speaker is using sound logic; even faulty logical appeals can sometimes be persuasive if they appeal to the audience's desires or needs in a particular way.

The following is a list of strategies that an author might employ to make the message or purpose of the text appear logical to a specific audience:

See the box on page 71 in *Rules for Writers* for questions about the structure of a text.

- Historical records

- Statistics

- Interviews or expert opinions

- Effective organization of sentences, paragraphs, ideas, images, etc.

- Clear transitions between sections of text

- Arrangement of images/text for sequence

- Arrangement of images/text for emphasis/focus

- Size/color relationships between objects

When examining a text, you should also be aware of potential flaws in logic. While fallacies can be used strategically, make sure to analyze them carefully to figure out why an author/speaker has employed them.

See pages 102–110 in *Rules for Writers* for examples of logical fallacies, the points of an argument that seem reasonable but turn out to be flawed or even dishonest.

If you review the strategies outlined throughout this section, you will notice that the same strategy can serve multiple purposes. As you draft your Rhetorical Analysis, you will have to decide which strategies are the most important and why—and how—they are being employed toward an audience for a specific purpose. An informal tone, for example, can help to build a certain kind of relationship between the author and the audience (ethos), which can, in turn, help the author to connect to the audience on an emotional level (pathos). The next section will outline a few possible approaches to the Rhetorical Analysis assignment, and, in section 9.3, you will see an example of how one student approached the invention and drafting stages.

9.2 Approaches to Rhetorical Analysis

In this section, you will see a range of possibilities for rhetorical analysis and some key questions to help you identify the specific strategies used by the authors. Although all of the approaches in this chapter involve rhetorically analyzing visual texts, remember that you can conduct a rhetorical analysis on any text including pieces of literature, films, poems, speeches, etc. Please refer to *Writing Public Lives* for additional ways to approach this assignment.

Rhetorically Analyzing Advertisements

By Al Harahap

As a global, multi-billion dollar industry, advertising is a constant part of our lives. We see advertisements traveling to school or work, flipping through a magazine, watching television, and even just browsing the internet. Advertisements often use both words and images to achieve a desired effect. Unlike most other genres of communication, advertisements appear in many different media, with each medium relying on different ways of appealing to readers, listeners, or viewers. A magazine or newspaper advertisement may use words, images, or both, while a television or internet advertisement is likely to incorporate moving images and audio in the form of speech, sound effects, or music.

Advertisements are complicated texts designed by professionals to be extremely persuasive, and analyzing them can be intimidating. The following print advertisement could be found on a college campus very much like this one, and, although it may seem fairly straightforward, there is plenty here for a rhetorical analysis. When you approach an advertisement in order to perform a rhetorical analysis, you might find it helpful to move through the following steps:

Step One

Examine the advertisement and look for any outstanding images and words, but do not make any conclusions yet. You might consider making a chart of observations and inferences (see section 2.5). Also pay attention to the elements of visual rhetoric mentioned in the "Reading Visual Rhetoric" Tips & Strategies Box in this section.

See page 83 in *Rules for Writers* for additional advice and guidelines for analyzing visual texts.

Step Two

Make sure to identify and understand the advertisement's rhetorical situation. Remember that on the surface, an advertisement's message might be to sell you a product, but it might have a greater cultural influence on the audience than just convincing them to buy something. To begin building an understanding of the advertisement's context, start by answering the following questions about the rhetorical situation:

Who is the author/speaker?

The medical center's logo makes clear that the event is related to a science-oriented educational institution. Although this does not give the identity of the specific person who generated this document, it does make the organization the author is representing clear.

What is the image conveying?

The viewer is struck by a long and obviously complex equation worked out on a chalkboard. However, contrary to the viewer's expectations, the person solving the equation is not a university professor, but a young boy. Why would the advertisement play with the viewer's expectations in this way? In that moment, the advertisement has created an element of surprise, which has the effect of drawing the viewer further in.

What are the message and purpose of the text?

Looking at the largest textual element, "Learning…it's all in your mind," does not help much because it is a slogan that sounds catchy but does not necessarily give much information. However, the next largest text, "Upper Westside University Medical Center Invites You to Our Summer Open House," reveals that this ad is trying to get people to come to an open house. This flyer does not announce the date or time of the event, so it is safe to assume that the audience has some prior knowledge about the event. Perhaps this lack of specificity can help us determine the intended audience.

Who is the audience?

Given the information we have about the event, we can hypothesize that Upper Westside University Medical Center is a teaching hospital similar to the University Medical Center on the University of Arizona campus. In this context, the focus of the image and heading font, with their emphasis on education, make sense in combination with an event that appears to be promoting community health. The audience might possibly include K–12 students who are not yet in college and their parents because the message of the image advocates investing in children's education from a young age.

Step Three

Identify the rhetorical strategies employed in the advertisement and determine how they work together to help the advertiser achieve a desired effect on the intended audience. How does the author make appeals to character or credibility and/or appeal to the audience's emotions or sense of logic? You could choose to

Tips & Strategies: ANALYSIS

Reading Visual Rhetoric

By Amy Parziale

Visual rhetoric is a form of communication in which visual elements create meanings and arguments. Advertising is one form of visual rhetoric in the contemporary world, but works of art, photographs, websites, brochures, and even bumper stickers contain and create visual rhetoric. Just like textual rhetoric, the author's purpose in using visual rhetoric is to best persuade her audience of her position— whether it is which shampoo to purchase or who to vote for in an election. Thus, there are some overlaps between analyzing visual rhetoric and analyzing textual rhetoric. Like with textual rhetoric, when you analyze visual rhetoric you should consider the rhetorical situation: the author, audience, message, intended purpose, and surrounding context.

When you analyze visual rhetoric, you should also be aware of some elements worth analyzing that are not usually present in written texts. These elements include:

- The **type** of visual (text, images, clip art, photographs, etc.)

- **Color palette** (individual element's color, background, contrast, etc.)

- **Font choices** (size, color, typeface, etc.)

- **Organization** and **arrangement** of the elements in the work (foreground, background, top, bottom, etc.)

To examine a work's visual rhetoric, start by writing down everything you see.

- **Visual Composition:** What elements make up the piece? How are they arranged? How are they related? What shapes, colors, texture, lighting, shadows, and types of lines are used? What is lightest? What is darkest? Do analyze specific strategies such as the font, the placement of information, the use of the bulleted list, or even the race and gender of the subject in the photo.

The genre of advertisements might also impact how an audience receives a text's message and reacts to its purpose. How does this advertisement use the visual conventions of a modern print advertisement to make its argument? Think about its use of a logo, the combination of images and words, and the inclusion of a URL. You might also consider the types of emotional appeals commonly used in this genre. For example, in the genre of advertisements, desire is frequently an important appeal. With many advertisements that are selling physical, tangible products, the creators are appealing to their audience's material desire for something by making the product the primary focus of the advertisement. However, all advertisements are also appealing to some kind of intangible, cultural desire, such as the cultural desire to easily connect with people, made possible by the latest smartphone or social networking site. What kinds of cultural values might the medical center in this advertisement be appealing to?

After following these three steps, you will be better prepared to craft your analysis. Section 9.3 will lead you through the rest of the writing process in greater detail.

the elements complement or contrast with each other? Is a specific element repeated? Is there variety in the elements?

- **Technique:** How do you think the piece was created (photography, painting, film, computer-generated techniques, etc.)?

- **Focus:** What is in focus and what is out of focus? What size are the objects in comparison to each other? Are the objects to scale? How does your eye move around the piece? What elements draw your eye, and how is that accomplished?

- **Space:** What sense of space is created? Do objects overlap? What is in the foreground, middle ground, and background? What is in each third of the piece—top, middle, bottom, left, middle, and right?

- **Point of View:** From what vantage point is the piece created? How is the piece framed? What is included? What do you think lies beyond the edges?

- **Organization and Arrangement:** How are the people in a photograph posed? Do their movements or positions seem natural or artificially imposed? How are visual elements arranged? What is your eye drawn to first? What does the organization of elements seem to be emphasizing?

Once you have observed the many choices present in the visual text, try to infer how these choices shape, modify, or enhance the message and purpose. Understanding visual rhetoric allows us to engage with the multitude of images we are bombarded with each day on a more critical level. The next time you are driving by a billboard, strolling through a museum, or flipping through a magazine, pause and consider how the image constructs its meaning through visual rhetoric.

Advertising Analysis: Try It for Yourself

As you go about your day, be alert to advertisements and practice rhetorical analysis when you see them. Visit your local mall or places in town or browse through your favorite magazines or websites to find unique and unusual advertisements to analyze. Keep in mind that at sites you commonly frequent, you may very well be the advertisement's intended audience, so it is important that you are aware of such a subject/object position when analyzing the advertisement. Wherever you encounter ads, ask yourself the following questions and perform a mini-rhetorical analysis on the spot. When you encounter an especially interesting example, jot some notes here and practice moving beyond the ad's literal meaning to develop a more sophisticated rhetorical analysis. As you do this, you might find that some of the most interesting rhetorical situations to analyze may be in advertisements found in unexpected places.

1. What image(s) or word(s) stand out? What is your quick first impression of the image/word combination?

2. What can you identify about the rhetorical situation—i.e., about the speaker/creator, message, purpose, audience, and context?

3. What other purposes might the advertisement have beside the obvious?

4. What effect on the audience does the main image have in terms of its subjects' ages, genders, races, or other demographic variables?

5. What cultural desires is the advertisement appealing to?

Rhetorically Analyzing Graphic Art and Comics

By Joey Nardinelli and Ryan Winet

Scott McCloud, the author of *Understanding Comics*, has defined comics more specifically as sequential art made up of both visual and textual components (9). In this genre, images are linked together into a sequence based on their juxtaposition, or side-by-side proximity, to convey emotions, actions, the passage of time, and various cultural messages. One of the other keys to the creation and reception of sequential art emerges from what McCloud identifies as the gutter, or the space between panels. Comics often rely on the reader's imagination to fill in the gaps between the moments, actions, or settings from panel to panel. However, the author also has a responsibility to control the gaps, for a story with gaps too large or small could lose the reader or stall the story's momentum.

Will Eisner, a sequential art storyteller and the creator of the iconic characters Wonder Man and The Spirit, identifies **symbolism** and **genre** as some of the most important aspects of visual communication (11–16). Graphic artists can use visual metaphors or symbols to quickly convey complex ideas. Where the reader might see a character holding a gun firmly in one hand, a series of symbolic messages emerge—the character is self-assured, courageous, and most definitely trained and/or experienced. However, if an image conveys a firearm in a presumably shaking, two-handed grip of a profusely sweating figure, the audience assumes the opposite qualities likely hold true.

As for genre, sequential artists can play on the audience's expectations, stereotypes, and typical associations of literary genres such as "horror" or "Western" to succinctly convey characterizations and other values in their characters, props, and settings.

The following section will guide you through an analysis of Ryan Winet's "Somewhere in the Old West…" A portion of this comic appeared in an exercise in Chapter 2 about making observations and inferences. You might consider returning to this exercise in order to familiarize yourself with this comic and move into analysis.

9.2

Image courtesy of Ryan Winet.

Can you locate the gutters? What do you assume is happening in them? How does the juxtaposition of images, symbolism, and genre function in this comic? What other rhetorical strategies are at play? Furthermore, what do you notice about the characters in the panels?

Notice how the artist purposely keeps each character within the left and right frame of every panel, making it easier for us to keep track of who is doing what. The character on the left side seems to be a bully, possibly even evil, with a crooked nose, dark hair, and a malevolent bandolier crossing his chest, characterizing him as an outlaw. The other character is sporting a cowboy hat and cravat, making him appear as the hero according to our genre expectations and typical stereotypes of the Western. We might expect the sequence of panels to end with the death of the villain. However, the language of the characters fails to meet our expectations when our cowboy shouts, "TIMEOUT!"—it is in this moment that we notice something is amiss. The final two panels shift the focus and meaning of the comic by not delivering on our expectations—the characters, as if emerging from an afternoon playtime fantasy, now wear the guises of pained and guilty children, employing language at odds with a narrative that previously seemed fixed on typical genre expectations, uttering "GAME OVER?!" at the very end.

So what do we make of all this? Western duels are a familiar scenario in American popular culture, so by undermining our expectations, Winet offers a number of possible social commentaries.

- What might he be saying about children playing with guns or learning to play roles within certain genre expectations?

- What might he be saying about the way reality intrudes on imagination or the other way around?

- What might the disconnect—between the characters in the comic and the narrator—be suggesting?

For a rhetorical analysis of this comic, your main claim might emerge out of an answer to one of the preceding questions. How is this social commentary conveyed through specific rhetorical strategies—juxtaposition, gutters, sequence, genre expectations, character development, the connection between images and words, unexpected closure, or any other applicable strategies as outlined earlier in this chapter or in class discussions?

9.3 Thinking through the Process

Invention

When preparing to write your rhetorical analysis, consider taking the following steps:

1. Carefully read or examine your text. Practice the close-reading strategies mentioned in Chapter 2.

2. Determine the rhetorical situation. Refer back to section 9.1 for further explanation.

    - Who is the author/speaker? What do you know about this individual or group? How is the author/speaker portrayed in the text? What kind of character does this author/speaker establish?

    - Who is the intended audience? How can you tell? Is there a secondary audience as well?

    - What is the context surrounding the text? How does this affect the content and author's rhetorical choices?

    - What is the message of the text?

    - What purpose is the text attempting to achieve?

3. Identify specific rhetorical strategies employed in the text. You may identify more strategies than you can reasonably analyze in an essay. In this case, you will want to consider which strategies have the greatest effect on the audience, are used most often, or are used most effectively in achieving the author's purpose.

4. Formulate a working thesis statement using the following student example and Craft Box, "Creating a Rhetorical Analysis Thesis Statement," shown below.

Creating a Rhetorical Analysis Thesis Statement

As with any thesis statement, your rhetorical analysis thesis statement should act as a road map for your paper. If the purpose of your rhetorical analysis is to explain how an author/speaker works within a particular rhetorical situation to achieve a specific purpose, your thesis statement should help address this question. Some of the information about audience, context, the author/speaker, etc., might be embedded in your introduction, but your essay should still have an identifiable thesis statement that indicates which rhetorical strategies you will focus on in your analysis.

1. Start by listing all of the pertinent information about the rhetorical situation and rhetorical strategies found in your text.

2. Now circle the parts of the rhetorical situation and the specific rhetorical strategies that you know you want to focus on in your essay because you find them the most compelling, convincing, etc.

3. Try combining all of these underlined parts into a thesis statement. Your thesis might now be a combination of elements of the rhetorical situation and specific rhetorical strategies. A rhetorical analysis thesis is often highly complex because you are identifying many elements in the text and trying to put them all together in a statement.

4. Look at how the following thesis combines information about the author, rhetorical strategies, the audience, the message, the purpose, the context, and some of the effects on the audience. This statement could be worded in several other ways, and you may not find it necessary to mention as much information in your own thesis.

> In his 2013 inaugural address, President Obama uses repetitive phrases such as "we, the people" and an inclusive tone to convince his American audience of both his supporters and non-supporters that they must unite together to defend freedom. Although he is generally effective in evoking hope through his references to historical successes and goals for the future, his lack of specificity in regards to how his future plans will be carried out makes his message less convincing for those who did not vote for him and are perhaps skeptical of his capabilities as president.

5. After creating your thesis, make sure that it explains how the author is attempting to achieve a specific purpose. If it sounds like a summary, you need to consider how you can turn that summary into a compelling analysis.

Craft Box: DRAFTING

Connecting the rhetorical strategies an author uses to the type of action or reaction the author wishes to evoke in an audience can help you to explain the "so what" in your rhetorical analysis. Consider this example:

Theodore, a first-year composition student, decided to critique the strategies used by the "Kony 2012" video. If you are unfamiliar with this video, you can watch it here: http://invisiblechildren.com/kony/. The producers of the short film claimed that their purpose was to promote the awareness and eventual arrest of African cult and militia leader Joseph Kony. After conducting his analysis, Theodore determined that the video, which became the fastest-growing viral video at the time and yielded over 3.7 million signatures in support of Kony's arrest, had mixed results due to the rhetorical strategies used in the film.

The following is Theodore's introductory paragraph and thesis statement. In it, he contextualizes the situation and connects some of the rhetorical strategies in the "Kony 2012" video with its intended audience, purpose, and overall effectiveness:

> See section 13.6 of the *Guide* or section 1 in *Writing Public Lives* for more examples of Rhetorical Analysis essays.

> Even though the video was clearly popular and its message reached many people worldwide, critics have argued that the "Kony 2012" video was inherently flawed and presented a simplistic, stereotyped, and ethnocentric view of the African conflict, instead of encouraging viewers to learn more. Critics have also argued that the film promoted a form of political activism for the truly lazy where viewers were given the naive idea that all they had to do was click on an icon, sign a petition, or post a sign to bring a warlord to justice. However, I argue that the film was a success in raising awareness about an important conflict. The same factors that made the "Kony 2012" video a huge success amongst its target audience of American youth also created the video's failures and controversies. The film's simplistic conclusions and focus on its American narrator allowed the filmmakers to connect with their young American audience. While the film's request that viewers share the video seems like a simple or naive solution for fighting against Joseph Kony's brutality against children, the video did create worldwide awareness of Kony and his brutal army and did build a community of youthful activists who might otherwise be unaware of the conflict.

Following up on student writing:

- Locate the elements of the rhetorical situation that Theodore identifies in his introduction. How does he manage to mention all of this information in just one paragraph?

- Underline Theodore's thesis statement. What information does he include in it?

- What rhetorical strategies do you think he will discuss in this essay?

- Notice how Theodore does not use the terms *ethos*, *logos*, or *pathos*, and instead focuses on the specific strategies used by the producers. Based on this introduction, what do you think is the main rhetorical appeal being used by the producers?

In his body paragraphs, Theodore demonstrates how the simplicity of the film, the use of an American narrator, and the request for viewers to share the video helps the video creators connect with American youth and create a community of young activists. Then, he explains how and why some viewers of the video conclude that it is overly simplistic or naive. Ultimately, he reaches his conclusion—that while the film hasn't yet resulted in the arrest of Kony, it did raise awareness on the part of the American people—through his analysis of the rhetorical strategies the video employed to reach its intended audience.

Drafting

While drafting your rhetorical analysis, you might choose to organize your essay in any number of ways. You may focus on a separate rhetorical strategy in each paragraph, or you might group multiple strategies into a single paragraph based on the similar appeal they are making or their level of effectiveness or ineffectiveness. Regardless of the organizational pattern you choose, keep your thesis statement in mind throughout the entire drafting process, for you may need to add, delete, focus, or rearrange paragraphs to match your thesis. Or, you can take the reverse approach, in which you might need to revise your thesis to support what you are actually arguing.

No matter how you choose to organize your essay, you should always have well-focused paragraphs that use plenty of textual evidence. This evidence might include quotes, paraphrases, contextual information, or even references to outside research. For example, it is not sufficient enough to just point out that the author of a children's book, like Dr. Seuss, uses rhymes and conclude that this rhetorical strategy helps him effectively reach his audience of children. You should include specific examples that show the use of rhyme in the text and then thoroughly explain how and why these particular rhymes connect the author with his young audience. Why rhymes? In what way does he connect with the children? Is he connecting with them like a teacher might connect with students? Like parents connect with their children? Is he connecting with them emotionally? What purpose do the rhymes serve? How does this relate to the overall message or purpose of the whole book?

You might notice that many of these questions start with "how" or "why." Answering these types of questions is what will move your essay from a summary to an analysis.

Take a look at the following body paragraph from Theodore's rhetorical analysis of the "Kony 2012" video.

> Prior media coverage of the conflict between the Lord's Resistance Army and the Ugandan government may have been more complete and realistic in describing the complexities of the war, but this coverage did not impact an audience outside of a small, politically informed group. The "Kony 2012" video presents a simplistic view of the conflict in

Uganda that ignores many of the war's political and diplomatic complexities, and perhaps reinforces stereotypical views of Africa. But a simple message is sometimes more clear and effective than a complex one. The video used one child, Jacob, to represent the story of all the children victimized, or living in fear of the LRA. While Jacob's experience might not be representative of all the LRA's victims, it is easier for us to relate to the story of one individual. Jacob's story appeals to our emotions. When he says he doesn't want to go on living if things don't change, the viewer can clearly see the need for action. Then Russell, the narrator, tells viewers how they can take action. While the actions are simple, they are actions that most people could easily do. The video does focus on an idealistic, but ultimately unsuccessful goal—the arrest of Kony by the end of 2012. Although the goal was unmet, the video is successful in making viewers aware of the LRA problem and prompting many to take some action.

Following up on student writing:

- Underline Theodore's main point. Does it relate to the thesis (see "Invention" section)?

- Highlight the evidence used to support the main point. What makes this evidence convincing? Do you see a need for further evidence?

- How does the author analyze this evidence and connect it back to the main point? Is he answering the "how" and "why" questions? Does it feel like too much summary?

- What questions are you left with as a reader? What could make this paragraph more convincing or clear? (For example, what type of emotional appeals is the author referring to? And why is it "easier for us to relate to the story of one individual"?) What could the author further explain?

- Can you tell where the author is headed from here? Is there a transition present?

Your paragraphs should do more than just point out a rhetorical strategy. To get beyond a summary of the text and move toward analysis, you should explain how and why this strategy serves the author's purpose, makes the text effective for a particular audience in a particular way, and/or is relevant given the context.

Now, let's take a look at Theodore's conclusion. As you read, pay attention to the way he wraps up his argument without merely summarizing or restating his thesis.

Cameron Hudson, former director of African Affairs on the 2005-2009 United States National Security Council, has said that "If their aim is to raise awareness, they have done that in spades" (Rozen). Although "Kony 2012" has become controversial, the film could not have had the success that it did while fulfilling the desires of its critics. The same factors that made the film successful also created the film's failures. Ethnocentric or not, the focus on the film's narrator and his American life allows the film to better connect with its audience, establish credibility, and springboard to emotional appeals. Ignoring the greater political context of the war allowed the filmmakers to paint a simple good versus evil story that would energize the audience and spark them to action. The focus on Kony and his crimes furthermore provided the audience with a simple, easily stated goal to strive for— his arrest. While the actions haven't secured Kony's arrest, they have definitely created awareness of the LRA problem. Ultimately, this is the film's great success. The millions that watched the video became aware of this serious conflict. They took action to make others aware and called on the U.S. government to take action. Additionally, they may have exposed millions who never watched the documentary to its message. Being aware of a problem is the first step in solving it and that is why "Kony 2012" is successful despite its many flaws.

Referring back to the "Tips for Writing Conclusions" Tips & Strategies Box in Chapter 3, think about the following:

- What approach did Theodore use to conclude his essay?

- Why might he have chosen to include evidence in his concluding paragraph?

Tips & Strategies: DRAFTING

Avoiding the *"Ethos, Logos, Pathos"* Five-Paragraph Essay

When writing a Rhetorical Analysis essay that analyzes a text in terms of the three Classical appeals (*ethos*, *logos*, and *pathos*), many students may fall into the trap of writing a five-paragraph essay that looks something like this:

Paragraph 1: Introduction

Paragraph 2: Appeals to Credibility/ Character (*ethos*)

Paragraph 3: Appeals to Logic (*logos*)

Paragraph 4: Appeals to Emotions (*pathos*)

Paragraph 5: Conclusion

The first problem with this approach is that there is often much overlap between and among these three appeals. For instance, if an audience recognizes that a speaker is blatantly and carelessly manipulating their emotions, it would undermine her/his credibility. Similarly, an audience will not look favorably upon a speaker's character if she or he uses deceitful or illogical reasoning (fallacies).

This approach also limits your ability to analyze a text with sophistication; there is so much more to a text than just *ethos*, *logos*, and *pathos*. These three appeals are present in all rhetorical acts and are a good starting point for your analysis, but remember your focus should be on how specific strategies or choices work to serve the author's purpose, not simply to identify particular examples of an appeal in the text. Consider how the different strategies employed operate in relation to other elements of text.

See sections 9.1 and 9.2 in this chapter for different elements or strategies of a text to look for as you write, and see the sample essays in section 13.6 for an example of how to structure and organize your Rhetorical Analysis essay.

- How does he extend the conversation further rather than just restating the fact that the film was both successful and unsuccessful in various ways?

- What advice would you give Theodore if you were conducting a peer review of his essay?

As you write your own conclusion, think about your overall goals for your essay and how you can extend the conversation by leaving your readers with something interesting to think about.

Revision

As you revise the Rhetorical Analysis, keep your instructor's specific assignment guidelines in mind. You might perform peer reviews or attend teacher conferences as well, so listen carefully to any and all feedback that you receive. As mentioned in Chapter 4, you will want to think critically about the comments you receive. In the end, you are the writer who gets to make the final decisions about your work.

> See Chapter 4 for more ideas on re-envisioning your work.

As you revise, use the following checklist to make sure you have included all the elements you need for an effective Rhetorical Analysis:

✔ Do you have an identifiable thesis? Does it point to the specific rhetorical strategies you analyze in your essay, or are you merely using vague terms like *ethos*, *pathos*, and *logos*?

✔ How have you decided to organize your essay? Does each paragraph have a central point that is supported with evidence from the text and in-depth analysis?

✔ Did you identify and analyze the five elements of the rhetorical situation?

✔ Did you explain how and why certain rhetorical strategies were employed? Did you discuss what effects these strategies have on the intended audience and overall effectiveness of the text?

✔ Are you thoughtfully using evidence in each paragraph? Do you mention specific examples from the text and explain why they are relevant?

✔ Do you leave your reader wanting more? Do you answer the "so what" question in your conclusion?

After addressing some of these global concerns, take a look back at Chapter 4 for tips on making local revisions before handing in your final draft.

9.4 Reflection

In this chapter, you have explored how authors/speakers make specific choices to help them achieve desired effects, reach specific audiences, communicate messages, or even prompt audiences to act or think a certain way. Hopefully, you have started thinking about how context and audience affect how you write, speak, and even behave in certain situations.

As you continue analyzing texts in your first-year writing class, in other classes, or your daily life, understanding the rhetorical situation and common rhetorical strategies will help you come to a deeper understanding of why some texts are more effective than others. Consider the following questions:

- How does an understanding of the rhetorical situation influence your communication strategies?

- Which rhetorical appeals are emphasized most often in your UA classes? With your family? At your favorite store or public location?

- How can you use the skills and strategies you learned in this chapter in other writing situations?

Works Cited

"Advertising: Exposure and Industry Statistics." Media Education Foundation, 2005. Web. 11 Nov. 2012.

Eisner, Will. *Graphic Storytelling and Visual Narrative*. New York: W. W. Norton & Company, 2008. Print.

Herrick, James. *The History and Theory of Rhetoric*. 4th ed. Boston: Pearson, 2008. Print.

McCloud, Scott. *Understanding Comics: The Invisible Art*. New York: Harper Perennial, 1993. Print.

Exploring a Controversy

10.1 Controversy Analysis: An Overview

There is **controversy** everywhere in the world. When you hear political pundits arguing over health care reform, historians presenting their perspectives on the events surrounding 9/11, or sports commentators trying to decide who deserves the Most Valuable Player award, you are listening to arguments that make up a controversy. Although controversy can be generally defined as debate, contention, or dispute, you might also think of a controversy as a social issue or **topic** that is being shaped by various perspectives and viewpoints. In a controversial topic, there is something at stake that has an impact on a community or those living within it.

The **Controversy Analysis** assignment requires you to research an existing controversial argument and to employ your analytical and rhetorical skills to demonstrate your understanding of the key arguments surrounding your selected topic. These are necessary steps before making an informed argument of your own in this class, in your chosen field of study, or even in professional or personal situations that involve controversial topics. In this chapter you will be guided through:

- Choosing a topic for analysis

- Developing a research question

- Drafting a research proposal

- Making connections between sources

- Drafting your Controversy Analysis assignment

The Controversy Analysis Assignment in Context

The research you do in this project will inform your third major assignment in the 102/108 course, the Public Argument, in which you will make your own argument about an issue. Keep in mind, though, that while the Controversy Analysis and the Public Argument assignments are linked, they are still separate assignments with different goals. The following images may help you understand the primary difference between the Controversy Analysis and the Public Argument.

The Research Process

You

The figures in the image represent the ongoing conversation of a particular topic. They have already presented or are presenting an argument on that topic, whether through a newspaper editorial, an article in a magazine, a documentary film, or an essay in a **scholarly source** (such as an academic journal within a discipline). Notice that you are simply observing—not participating directly in the conversation. During the research stage, you are responsible for compiling and organizing what has already been argued in regards to your chosen topic. You might think of this stage as the listening stage, in which you are still an indirect observer getting to know the controversy or debate.

The Controversy Analysis

Once you have conducted a considerable amount of research, you will analyze the individual arguments or viewpoints that you have encountered. At this stage, your task is to describe, analyze, and evaluate the multiple perspectives; you are not yet adding your input in the conversation. You might think of this stage as the listening, synthesizing, and evaluating stage. As an observer, you are seeking to more fully understand the major arguments within the debate or controversy to prepare yourself to "enter the conversation." The skills you practiced in the **Rhetorical Analysis** assignment will be useful for analyzing the purpose, audience, context, and strategies of each argument.

The Public Argument

Chapter 11 of this *Guide* and Chapters 11–16 of *Writing Public Lives* offer more comprehensive guidelines on the Public Argument assignment. You might think of the Public Argument as the "participant" stage, as you are now actively contributing to the controversy or debate you have been researching for some time. For now, keep in mind that it is not until the next assignment that you are entering the conversation by presenting your own argument. Before you can do that, you must develop a certain expertise on the topic by conducting research and investigating and analyzing existing arguments.

10.2 Approaching the Controversy Analysis

In order to write a Controversy Analysis, you must first locate a controversy. Although you might start with a broad topic or "hot button" issue, you should strive to find a manageable line of inquiry for your analysis.

See Chapter 6 for advice on finding an interesting research topic.

For example, you might be interested in exploring the issue of childhood obesity, but this topic is too broad for your controversy analysis. Several smaller, more manageable debates emerge under this broad topic. The following lines of inquiry are all related to childhood obesity, and each one could serve as the subject of a controversy analysis:

- Which programs claiming to fight childhood obesity have already been implemented (such as Michelle Obama's *Let's Move*) and how successful have their outcomes been?

- What kinds of changes should be made to school lunch programs (if any) and how much change is needed (offering more options, offering substitute options, banning certain items, etc.)?

- Would healthier school lunch initiatives be cost effective for taxpayers?

- What is the role of fast food companies in rising childhood obesity rates?

- What effect (if any) does economic status, race, or gender have on obesity rates?

See pages 93–94 in *Rules for Writers* for a discussion of counter-argument.

As you can see, there are many lines of inquiry into the larger controversy of childhood obesity, and you could choose any of those to investigate in your Controversy Analysis assignment. The following sections will guide you through the process of finding a topic using childhood obesity as an example and then narrowing this topic down to a line of inquiry. You will then start to consider the various perspectives surrounding your specific issue.

As you develop a line of inquiry in the following section, consider these questions carefully:

- What do you want to find out? What is your purpose for exploring this controversy?

- What is at stake in the issue? Who are some of the stakeholders, key groups, or people who are impacted by the issue?

- What is the larger social significance? Besides the stakeholders, who else might be impacted by various outcomes?

- What else do you know about this issue? What do you need to learn more about in order to understand all the different perspectives?

Choosing a Topic

See Chapter 9 in *Writing Public Lives* for advice on identifying a local issue for research.

Most instructors require students to use the research they gather during this assignment as the basis for the Public Argument. Since you will be spending so much time on the topic you choose, you will want to select something that interests you and is manageable for the assignment. This section will answer some of the questions you may have about choosing a topic and help you choose a topic that will make this assignment a productive experience.

Building a Personal Interest Inventory

This activity, adapted from Bruce Ballenger's *The Curious Researcher*, is called a "personal interest inventory." When you start the research process, it is a good idea to spend a few minutes brainstorming potential ideas by considering your many interests both academically and personally. By taking an inventory of your interests, you might discover a topic that you would not have otherwise considered. This might lead you to a more interesting, engaging analysis. In the following activity, you will brainstorm your interests, refine those interests into potential topics, and consider research questions that might emerge from those topics. Remember that research is an ongoing process of analyzing, focusing, and revising, and you will often find yourself altering your research question as you dig deeper. These alterations are often encouraged and even necessary. For now, begin by working on building a personal interest inventory:

Step One: Brainstorming Subjects. In the columns on the following page, begin by listing anything that comes to mind under each category. You can be as specific as "economic incentives and drawbacks to the Tucson streetcar" or as vague as "online communication." At this point, you are simply brainstorming, so just write down anything that comes to mind. To help get you started, there is an example in italics under each heading.

10.2

People	Places	Trends
Barack Obama	*Tucson streetcar*	*Healthy living*

Hobbies	Technologies	Professions
Hunting	*Specialized medicine*	*Bilingual education*

Step Two: Refining Subjects into Topics. Now that you have thought about some of the broader subjects you might consider researching, the next step is to flesh out those broader subjects into topics. But what is the difference between a subject and a topic? The most important difference is that a subject is not something you can write a research paper about; it is simply too large to cover. Something like "healthy living" is a subject. You need to further narrow your subject into a topic, which is a smaller thread of inquiry within that larger category.

See page 5 in *Rules for Writers* for tips on narrowing a subject.

Here is an example:

SUBJECT: Healthy living

POSSIBLE TOPICS: School lunch programs for children, extreme diets, childhood obesity, improving access to higher-quality, more affordable foods in poorer areas, the use of GMOs in food production, marketing efforts to sell fast food to youth, success/failure of putting nutritional information in menus, cross-cultural examination of nutrition education programs for children

As you can see, there are plenty of topics under the wider umbrella of "healthy living." When narrowing from a subject to a topic, you will want to consider what aspects of the subject interest you the most. To brainstorm topics, choose three of the most interesting subject ideas you wrote down in "Step One" and write them in the top box of each column below. Next, write down what you know about the subject, what questions you have about it, and what you would like to know about it. These ideas can help lead you to discover a topic. Use column one as a model:

Sample Subject: Healthy Living	Potential Subject 1:	Potential Subject 2:	Potential Subject 3:
Potential Topics: – school lunch programs – extreme diets – childhood obesity – improving community-wide access to nutritional food – use of GMOs – fast-food marketing efforts – nutrition information in menus – advertising – cross-cultural food programs in schools	Potential Topics:	Potential Topics:	Potential Topics:

10.2

Step Three: Asking Questions. At this point, you should have at least one or two research topics that interest you. Think carefully about these options and consider what questions you might ask to guide your research. See the "Evaluating Potential Research Questions" Tips & Strategies Box in this section for important tips on creating focused research questions. Since it is sometimes difficult to research a topic without a clear focus, this step can help you come up with a solid research question that will act as a springboard into your investigation.

See section 1b in *Rules for Writers* for more strategies for exploring a topic.

In the box below, try creating a research question or two based on the subjects and topics you wrote down in Step Two:

Sample Subject: Healthy Living	Potential Subject 1:	Potential Subject 2:	Potential Subject 3:
Topic: *childhood obesity*	*Topic:*	*Topic:*	*Topic:*
Related Research Question: *What are the consequences of regulating school lunch programs in an effort to fight childhood obesity?*	*Related Research Question:*	*Related Research Question:*	*Related Research Question:*

Once you have a workable question, moving on to your library and database research will be much easier and more enjoyable.

See pages 202–207 in *Writing Public Lives* for help with generating a question.

Other Approaches

If you are still having trouble generating topic ideas, here are some additional ways you can find a topic of interest. Consider trying a few of these activities:

1. Surf the internet to see what people are discussing in the news.

2. Search the U of A Library's Course Guide: libguides.library.arizona.edu/engl102-108.

3. Browse Wikipedia using the "Random Page" function.

4. Consider essays you have already written: could the topics of any of the essays you have written for other classes be further developed into a researchable topic?

5. Pay attention to what you read, including debates on social media sites. What controversies seem to be happening around you?

6. Ask friends, parents, coworkers, classmates, or other people what news they are interested in right now.

7. Think about issues you have been discussing in other classes.

10.2

8. Look close to home, within Tucson's borders. Is there anything going on here in Tucson or at the U of A that might be interesting?

9. Collaborate with your classmates. Get inspired by what some of them have come up with and consider how you might add to those conversations.

10. Ask yourself: What is something you have always wanted to know more about? What is a question you have always had, and could research answer it?

Identifying Stakeholders

Most controversies are more complex than simple pro/con, for/against, or yes/no arguments. Determining these binary distinctions is a good first step in understanding a controversy, but it rarely provides a full understanding of the issues important to various stakeholders in the controversy. When you explore a controversy, part of your goal is to ascertain the in-between positions that exist within the controversy—the arguments that fall in the gray area and may not be as simple as "for" or "against."

As you narrow your topic and begin to conduct research, your instructor may ask you to identify the various stakeholders, those who are invested in the controversy for some reason. Consider individuals or groups who are affected directly by the controversy as well as those who control some part of it. Think about what interested parties might gain or lose if an action or decision is implemented.

Consider the topic of regulating school lunch programs with the intention to fight childhood obesity. Although it may seem as though there are only two sides to the issue (change school lunch guidelines or keep them the same), there are actually many different groups that have a stake in this controversy, each with distinct motives. Consider the different reasons why parents, school and school district administrators, teachers, cafeteria workers, nutritionists, government officials, food distributors, the agriculture industry, taxpayers, and students might be interested in this issue. How does each stakeholder approach the controversy? What is motivating their particular argument? Some teachers, for example, may have an opinion motivated by their interactions with students after lunch. They may see more healthy lunch options as a way to improve classroom behavior and, as a result, improve learning and test scores. Some government officials may be motivated by political philosophies about the role of government in local issues and may want to encourage parents to take responsibility for the health of their children rather than changing school lunches. Some students might be motivated by their desire for tasty food and dislike the healthier food options or even refuse to eat, leading to wasted lunches. As you locate common lines of argument, it is important to recognize that not everyone in each of these groups shares the same viewpoint. Not all students, for example, would complain about healthier food options. Consider the different perspectives that may even exist within each of the stakeholder groups you identify.

10.2

See Chapter 10 in *Writing Public Lives* for a discussion on identifying ideology and values in arguments.

In the box below, try identifying the stakeholders in your potential research topic. At this point, you are simply identifying who is affected by the issue at hand. You can build and clarify your list of stakeholders as you conduct your research and begin to see why they are motivated to engage with your controversial topic.

Sample Topic: *school lunch regulations* *Stakeholders:* • *Teachers* • *Students* • *Nutritionists* • *School district administrators* • *Agriculture industry* • *Taxpayers* • *Parents* • *Politicians and government officials* • *Cafeteria workers*	*Topic:* *Stakeholders:*	*Topic:* *Stakeholders:*	*Topic:* *Stakeholders:*

Evaluating Potential Research Questions

H ere are some questions you might ask yourself to test potential research questions. Based on your answers to these questions, consider if you want to move forward with the research question you have developed or if you should revise your line of inquiry.

1. What draws me to this particular inquiry? Why am I interested in this?

2. Is this a complex question—a question that does not lead toward a generally accepted "right" answer and cannot be answered with just basic research and statistics?

3. What "work" do I want this question to do? That is, what kind of conversation, meanings, and feelings do I imagine this question will evoke in those who will be reading it?

4. Does the wording of the question imply a certain belief or make a biased assumption?

5. Is this question likely to generate imagination, engagement, creative action, and new possibilities?

6. Does this question leave room for new and different questions to be raised as the initial question is explored?

10.3 Research

Conducting Research

You will want to consult Chapter 6 as you research your controversy. Your research process will likely even begin before you solidify your research question or identify your stakeholders. You may find yourself returning to the research stage repeatedly throughout the writing process as you draft and revise your essay. You may start to identify gaps in the conversation that you need to fill with a new stakeholder or source, or you may feel the need to revise your initial research question altogether. The following are some tips to remember about the research process:

• Keep track of your sources—You might consider keeping a research log or journal to record where you found each source and make notes as you read (see Chapter 6).

• Find a variety of academic and popular sources—See the following Tips & Strategies Box for ideas on how to find sources. Your instructor may have specific expectations for sources, so make sure to follow your assignment guidelines carefully.

• Read abstracts and summaries first—This step might help you avoid reading sources unrelated to your controversy.

• Be patient—Research is often a process of trial and error. Try new key words, modify your research question, look in unexpected places, and pay close attention to titles and abstracts. Librarians, instructors, and your classmates are there to help you through this process.

• Know when to move on—It's easy to get caught in the research process because there is so much information out there. Sometimes doing more research also has the benefit of postponing the difficult act of writing an essay. Keep your deadlines in mind and remember the goals of the assignment.

• Re-evaluate your sources—You will probably have to collect more sources than you will put in your paper. At first glance, a source might seem to be making an argument about your topic but, as you read further, you discover that the author/speaker is not making a claim or that the source is really discussing a different issue. Don't try to make your sources fit your controversy; instead, try finding new sources that actually engage in the debate of your choice.

Drafting a Research Project

Your instructor may prompt you to write a research proposal as part of your Controversy Analysis assignment. Proposals help people in various fields plan complex research and collaborative projects. Scientists write proposals for grant money, instructors propose new courses, students lobby for proposed changes in policy, manufacturers and designers pitch new products in business proposals, and managers offer proposals for reorganization. Proposals are common in many fields and are likely to be a genre you continue to encounter throughout your college career and beyond.

See Chapter 8 in
Writing Public Lives
for different ways
to approach the
Controversy Analysis.

Writing a research proposal for a Controversy Analysis will give you practice in writing a concise projection of your intended work. Your proposal will also help you to think globally about the different voices you wish to represent in your analysis. Additionally, your research proposal will enable you to receive feedback from your instructor early in the process about important components of the project, including the quality of your sources, the feasibility of your topic, and the overall coherence of what you plan to investigate.

10.3

Tips & Strategies: **RESEARCH**

Finding Sources

When first researching a topic of interest, you may consult Wikipedia or conduct a broad Google search and explore the first few websites that come up. Provided below are some additional resources you might consider using when conducting research for the Controversy Analysis:

- *Library databases*: These contain collections of academic journals and popular sources such as newspapers made available to you online. Some popular databases include *Academic Search Complete* and *JSTOR*. Some databases contain only journals specific to a particular subject area. Explore the various databases on the University of Arizona Library webpage, especially when trying to locate academic sources.

- *Online magazines or newspapers*: Many print publications also have an online format. Look at the online *New York Times* or *Arizona*

Daily Star, for example. Online magazines like *Slate* or *Inside Higher Ed* are updated frequently and maintain similar journalistic standards as print publications.

- *News broadcasts*: Investigate local and international news sources such as CNN, MSNBC, NPR, or Arizona's Channel 12 News. Consider live broadcasts from the radio or television as well as their websites.

- *Podcasts*: Search the iTunes store or Google for podcasts related to your topic or the news. Podcasts are web episodes consisting of audio and sometimes video covering a variety of topics.

- *Google News*: Use Google News to find popular news stories or news related to your specific topic.

- *Documentaries*: Explore an online movie provider, your local video store, or YouTube for documentary films related to your topic.

Your Controversy Analysis research proposal will likely include the following components:

- A brief description of the controversy you plan to investigate.

- A demonstrated awareness of the range of stakeholders and their positions.

- A discussion of which arguments you will analyze and why as well as how you intend to perform the analysis.

- An annotated bibliography or other account of the research that you have already completed.

- Questions for your instructor and/or peers about your project.

Even after you write your research proposal, you may find that your understanding of the controversy changes as you learn more about it. While your instructor likely understands and even expects your ideas to evolve throughout the project, you might want to check in with her or him if your research begins to veer too far from your proposal. Once your proposal has been approved, you can start organizing your research and closely analyzing your sources.

> See Chapter 7 in *Rules for Writers* for advice about evaluating arguments.

10.4 Thinking through the Process

Invention

Before and even during the drafting process of your Controversy Analysis, it is important to carefully conduct research and read, analyze, and organize your sources.

Analyzing Sources: Writing a Rhetorical Précis

Some of your instructors may assign a Rhetorical Précis or an Annotated Bibliography as part of this assignment. (See section 6.6 for more on the Annotated Bibliography.) In French, the word "précis" (pronounced "pray-see") means "**summary**." The purpose of the rhetorical précis is to offer a short account of an article that does more than summarize the content. The rhetorical précis, which is generally four sentences long, accounts for the author's main assertion as well as an explanation of how the author develops or supports the **thesis**. The précis also includes the author's purpose for writing, a description of the intended audience, and the relationship the author establishes with that audience (Woodworth 156–64). Examining issues of audience and purpose are essential to writing descriptions that analyze rather than summarize the content of a source.

Sentences of the Précis:

1. **Name of author, [optional: a phrase describing author], genre and title of work, date in parentheses; a rhetorically accurate verb (such as "assert," "argue," "suggest," "imply," "claim," etc.); and a "that" clause containing a major assertion (thesis statement) of the work.**

2. An explanation of how the author develops and/or supports the thesis, usually in chronological order.

3. A statement of the author's apparent purpose, followed by an "in order" phrase indicating the change the author wants to effect in the audience.

4. A description of the intended audience and the relationship the author established with the audience.

For the Controversy Analysis assignment, you will be asked to provide an overview of several arguments that comprise a larger controversy, which requires you to fully understand individual arguments. The Rhetorical Précis can be helpful because it requires you to think about what an individual author is arguing and how that author develops his or her central claim(s).

Sample:

In a *New York Times* opinion article entitled "Finally, Good News About School Lunches" (2011), food writer Mark Bittman argues that while the new federal guidelines for school lunches are not perfect, they are

10.4

Craft Box: ANALYSIS

Reading for Controversy

One of the most important aspects of writing a Controversy Analysis is understanding how to read critically for controversial issues in sources you encounter in your research. Utilize the skills you practiced in the Rhetorical Analysis assignment to identify the rhetorical situation, appeals, and strategies your sources and stakeholders are relying upon in their arguments. As you compile and sift through your sources, you should consider the following questions:

- What is the medium? A newspaper article? Website? Scholarly article? How does this medium impact how the audience is receiving the message?

- Who is the author? How does the author speak to her or his particular audience? Does she or he represent a larger organization or group of people in this piece?

- What is the main argument?

- What persuasive appeals and strategies are used to enhance the argument and appeal to the audience? See Chapter 9 for more information about identifying appeals and strategies.

- What are the strengths and weaknesses of the argument?

In this activity, you will practice your critical reading skills by examining *The Daily Wildcat* for current controversies in the news and determining how those controversies are presented to readers. Alternatively, you can work with your instructor to choose a different source.

Reading your sources in this way will help you to identify how and why the stakeholders in your chosen controversy are constructing their arguments. You will want to analyze each argument/source/stakeholder individually (like you practiced in this Craft Box) before you begin to synthesize the various perspectives.

Use an issue of *The Daily Wildcat* (or another source of your choosing) to fill in the following boxes:

effective and are a positive step forward. Bittman supports his thesis by outlining the pros and cons of the new bill, comparing the new guidelines to previous ones, and placing the new guidelines in the context of a larger cultural and political conversation about health and the food industry. **His purpose is to persuade potential supporters who may be disappointed by compromise that the new bill is indeed a victory. Bittman establishes an informal tone ("let's remember") and places his argument in political terms in order to connect with similarly-minded readers.**

See section 1b in *Rules for Writers* for more strategies for exploring a topic.

Synthesizing Sources

As you locate and analyze individual sources, you can start to put your sources in conversation with each other. Consider the following questions to help you synthesize the many perspectives of your chosen controversy:

- What stakeholder does each source represent?

- Which writers are making similar arguments? How are their arguments similar?

- Which writers are positioned against each other? In what ways do their arguments differ, and why?

Title	Medium	Rhetorical Situation (Author, Audience, Context, Purpose)	Main Argument

Persuasive Appeals and Evidence	Strengths and Weaknesses

213

- Are any writers using similar rhetorical strategies in making their arguments?

- Are there informational or conceptual gaps in one source that are being covered in another source?

At this point, it might help you to visualize the "conversation" that is taking place around your chosen research question. Consider making a drawing like the one below to help you organize your sources and map out the connections between/among your sources. Consider points/rhetorical strategies of similarity and difference.

See pages 13–17 in *Rules for Writers* for more ideas for invention.

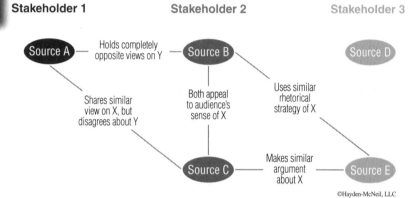

©Hayden-McNeil, LLC

Drafting

As you read in section 10.1, a Controversy Analysis incorporates research on the key arguments made by people who have a stake in an issue. More than just outlining these arguments, however, a Controversy Analysis should also do the following:

- Evaluate the validity of specific claims.

- Examine the persuasive strategies employed by key stakeholders using your rhetorical analysis skills.

- Explore the similarities and distinctions between diverse viewpoints.

Remember, the purpose of a Controversy Analysis is not to assert a position on the issue, but rather to demonstrate a thorough consideration of a variety of viewpoints on a topic and to rhetorically analyze the arguments made by others.

See Chapter 10 in *Writing Public Lives* for further discussion about thesis statements for this assignment.

A major goal for your analysis is to demonstrate how the various texts you cite are in conversation with each other. By showing how different writers develop their lines of argument, comparing the lines of argument, and evaluating the effectiveness of their persuasive strategies, you are essentially developing a rhetorical analysis of the range of opinions that figure in a controversy. The difficult part of framing this conversation, however, will be maintaining control of your analysis. Because you will be relying heavily on research, it can be tempting to let the "voices of authority" dominate your essay, or to merely write a summary of their ideas and opinions. A well-written Controversy Analysis should forefront your analysis, synthesis, and evaluation of the sources.

As you begin to draft your essay, think about how you can forefront your analysis by demonstrating your understanding of the relationships between arguments. Rather than simply reporting your research ("Writer X says this, Writer Y says that"), you may consider organizing your essay based on the kinds of arguments being made and the rhetorical strategies used by different stakeholders. Take a look at the beginning of this paragraph from UA student Melissa Quiceno. Here she distinguishes between two different kinds of arguments being made in the reproductive rights controversy.

> While tax money is considered a primary concern of the birth control debate, there are those who take a moral stance against women being able to access contraception. It is thought that providing more women with affordable family planning resource would just encourage promiscuity, something still heavily frowned upon in religious communities. In his passionately anti-contraceptive book *Aborting Planned Parenthood*, author Robert Ruff advocates moving away from birth control distribution, and moving towards what he sees as the solution for the lack of morality in our modern culture, "The birth control approach is a failed attempt to mitigate the fallout from sexual sin by technical or medical means" (Ruff 163). Ruff maintains that advocating sexual abstinence before marriage is the only solution to the high number of women facing unwanted pregnancies.

Thesis Statement for the Controversy Analysis

Typically, a thesis statement functions to 1) introduce your argument to your audience and 2) provide a "blueprint" of how the essay will proceed. Depending upon your assignment, you may be asked to write a Controversy Analysis without making any argument yourself regarding the controversy or the effectiveness of the arguments. In this case, should you include a thesis statement? The answer to this might depend upon your teacher's expectations. You should also consider the following:

- Does my introductory paragraph offer an overview of the controversy and the main issues under consideration?

- Have I explained the controversy in precise and succinct language?

- Have I demonstrated, through my organization of the introductory paragraph, how the essay will be organized?

- Does the transition between introductory paragraph and body paragraph feel natural?

If the answer to any of these questions is no, consider crafting a thesis statement at the end of your introduction. Your thesis statement might include a concise description of the controversy, a brief reference to the different sides of the issue, a mention of common rhetorical strategies you will be addressing, or other ways that you have organized your analysis.

Following up on student writing:

- How does Melissa demonstrate the complexity (i.e., not a simple pro/con) of Ruff's argument?

- How does Melissa use transition words to show connections between viewpoints?

Questions to consider as you draft:

- Can you group your sources together by position on the issue, the kind of argument used, or common rhetorical strategies?

- Can you make any connections between the role of the stakeholders (concerned parent, politician, citizen activist) and the kinds of arguments being used?

Guidelines for Recognizing Bias in Your Writing

While there is nothing wrong with disagreeing with a particular author, you should always try your best to maintain objectivity as you compose your Controversy Analysis, even if that seems difficult. Remember, you will have the opportunity to present your own argument in the next major assignment. One purpose of the Controversy Analysis assignment is to demonstrate your ability to step back from an issue and maintain a critical distance as you analyze it.

The following chart provides examples of phrases that make an argument that subtly reveals a writer's bias, along with examples that help to maintain a more critical distance.

Phrases That Reveal Bias	Phrases That Demonstrate Objectivity
Author X does not seem to realize that…	Author X's argument might have been strengthened had he or she addressed…
Author X loses his credibility when…	Author X may seem less credible to some readers when she or he says…
Author X mistakenly believes that…	Author X argues that…
Author X fails to mention that…	Readers might find Author X's argument more persuasive if it included…
Author X's argument is not convincing because…	Some readers may find Author X's argument unconvincing because…
There is an obvious logical fallacy in Author X's argument.	An analysis of Author X's argument reveals a logical fallacy.

- Is there a narrative trend (historical, cultural, political) or central event to consider as a framework for your analysis?

Avoiding Common Pitfalls of the Controversy Analysis

1. **Don't Argue (Yet).** The point of the Controversy Analysis is to analyze an existing controversy. However, a common mistake some students make is to present an argumentative essay. Remember, you will have an opportunity to craft your own argument in the next major assignment, the Public Argument. See section 10.1 in this chapter for an explanation about the difference between the Public Argument and the Controversy Analysis.

2. **Don't Polarize the Issue.** Another common mistake is to present issues as "black and white," or as having only two perspectives that are polar opposites. Just because there are extreme perspectives on an issue does not mean that there are only two possible positions. Some stakeholders may have similar opinions on the issue, but they probably present these opinions in nuanced ways.

3. **Don't Avoid Academic Research.** A common mistake students make is going to Google, typing in some key words on their topic, and clicking on only the first five search results. If you do this, you will likely end up with a Wikipedia page, an About.com overview, and a few random blog pages. Almost anyone can do that kind of internet research, and almost no one will be able to effectively summarize or analyze a controversy from such a cursory examination of viewpoints. A key element of this assignment is to learn the basics of conducting academic research. Academic research is not easy to do, and it might even be a bit intimidating, but learning how to conduct academic research is a central goal (and an essential component) of your first-year writing course. And try not to worry—your instructor and the librarians are more than willing to help you with research.

> See Chapter 7 in *Rules for Writers* for advice about evaluating arguments.

> See Chapter 6 for more on conducting research.

10.4

Revision

As you revise your Controversy Analysis, make sure to keep your specific purpose in mind. The following questions for global revision from section 4.2 are especially applicable to this assignment. Try answering these questions by yourself or with a peer:

- What do I hope to achieve with this writing? (Have I demonstrated complexity in my analysis of the controversy?)

- What are the requirements of the assignment? (Have I met them?)

- Does my essay have a thesis? How does my thesis relate to my purpose? (Have I provided enough synthesis and analysis?)

- In what ways does my essay achieve my purpose? In what ways does it fail to achieve my purpose? (Is my essay an analysis or a summary? How am I representing the "conversation" among sources?)

> See Chapter 11 in *Writing Public Lives* or Chapter 13 in this book for more samples of student writing.

10.5 Reflection

In this chapter you generated a line of inquiry, narrowed your idea from a subject to a topic, identified multiple stakeholders invested in an issue, conducted research on these perspectives, analyzed your research, and composed your Controversy Analysis. Before you move on to making your own argument in the Public Argument assignment, consider the following questions as reflective practice:

•   What challenges did you face during the research process?

•   What kinds of arguments or rhetorical strategies did you find most effective? Why?

•   Which perspective(s) would you like to explore further?

•   What did you learn about your own research and writing process?

•   How can you use the skills and strategies you learned in this chapter in other writing situations?

Works Cited

Ballenger, Bruce. *The Curious Researcher: A Guide to Writing Research Papers*. New York: Pearson/Longman, 2004. Print.

Bittman, Mark. "Finally, Good News About School Lunches." *Opinionator: Exclusive Online Commentary From The Times*. The New York Times, 31 Jan. 2012. Web. 22 Sep. 2013.

Woodworth, Margaret K. "The Rhetorical Précis." *Rhetoric Review* 7.1 (1998): 156–64. Print.

Public Argument

- **11.1** Public Argument: An Overview
- **11.2** Approaches to the Public Argument
- **11.3** Thinking through the Process
- **11.4** Reflection

11.1 Public Argument: An Overview

What does it mean to create a public argument? Consider this: The word "public" derives from the Latin term *publicus*, or "belonging to the people." "Argument," on the other hand, comes from the Latin *argumentum*, or "evidence, ground, support, proof" ("Public"). Though these terms might have meant something very different from how we conceive of them today, the notion of crafting an argument for a particular audience or "public" using compelling evidence remains as important today as it did in ancient Rome. While the development of digital technologies has radically changed our understanding of where, how, and when arguments can take place, it is important to remember that all public arguments intend to present a particular message to a particular audience in a particular way.

An argument's success depends on many factors, such as how well the writer has analyzed the **rhetorical situation**. Understanding how and why arguments work (and why they may not) is critical to your success both in the academy and outside the classroom walls. Whether in the form of a website, a video, an academic essay, a photograph, a multimedia presentation, or even a poster, public arguments are everywhere—and they influence everything we do.

See section 3 of *Writing Public Lives* for a detailed description of how "publics" are defined.

CHAPTER 11

For your Public Argument assignment, you will design your own public argument by learning to:

- Choose a position to argue.

- Analyze the rhetorical situation of your public argument.

- Select and analyze a **genre** and/or medium that will be most persuasive to your audience and most fitting for your argument.

- Create and present your argument to your intended audience.

See Chapter 12 in *Writing Public Lives* for more on public argument strategies.

11.2 Approaches to the Public Argument

In the **Controversy Analysis** you learned how to locate and analyze the arguments that other people have made about a controversial issue. For the Public Argument assignment, you will now "enter" the debates and craft your own argument, likely in response to those discoveries you made in the last unit (see the images in section 10.1 for a visual reminder of this sequence).

See Chapter 6 in *Rules for Writers* for advice on constructing arguments.

Depending on your instructor's particular assignment requirements, you might be asked to construct a public letter, speech, or essay. Other instructors might ask you to create a digital argument, drawing on your skills of rhetorical analysis and knowledge of multimedia arguments. Whichever assignment you are asked to complete, your primary job will be essentially the same: to take what you learned from your Controversy Analysis and create an argument that targets a real, tangible audience for a specific purpose.

In this section you will find three ways English 102/108 students and others have sought to align their argument with a rhetorical situation. As you review these examples and others your instructor may provide, consider the different ways students have used their research, their understanding of audience, and different rhetorical strategies to convey a purpose.

Letter Argument: "Letter to the Honorable Janice K. Brewer"

For an example of how letters to public officials can function as public arguments, take a look at the following letter written by UA student Kassandra Esmeralda Díaz. During her research on Arizona's 2011 budget cuts for Medicaid, Kassandra explored other possible solutions to help balance the state budget that would not impact Medicaid recipients as severely. In her Controversy Analysis, entitled "Is Medicaid a True Safety Net?", she came to the conclusion that the Arizona legislature should not cut spending on Medicaid from its budget. She determined there were viable alternatives to the budget cuts other than those to Medicaid, so she decided to write former Arizona Governor Jan Brewer a personal letter to present her research and offer an alternative solution.

Dear Governor Brewer,

I am a freshman attending the University of Arizona writing to you in the hopes of discussing Arizona's recent budget cuts on Medicaid. In this letter I will offer solutions to prevent these cuts while still balancing the state budget. As you know, the idea of implementing these cuts has caused controversy for many Arizonans. A primary topic for discussion has been the negative consequences resulting from the proposed cut of $1 billion.

Cuts to the state budget will cause an average of 250,000 people to lose coverage from the Arizona Health Care Cost Containment System (AHCCCS), the state-funded Medicaid program. In addition, the cuts will freeze Medicaid enrollment for potentially tens of thousands of Arizonans, forcing Arizona patients who rely on healthcare coverage into serious debt, and, in some cases, poverty. Patients will fall into debt when they are suddenly cut from Medicaid and are later expected to pay the healthcare expenses that Medicaid had previously covered for them. These cuts target the most vulnerable population: the disabled, the elderly, and the needy. Another area of concern is the effect of the budget cuts on Medicaid hospitals.

As you have rightly pointed out in your 2011 state budget proposal, continuing with the process will save the state approximately $542 million, which can be used to finance larger scale public projects requiring additional funding. Choosing to cut the state budget is a very tough decision. I understand your commitment to save the state money while ensuring access to healthcare for the people of Arizona; however, I believe that there are other approaches that reach this goal without cutting back on the state budget. When considering enactment of the cuts, the short-term savings that can be achieved do not seem to be the primary area of consideration. Instead, Arizona should steer its attention toward setting a spending limit to prevent having to make cuts to healthcare in the future. Setting a spending limit will help limit the size of the cuts and prevent further damage to the system.

A second approach to consider is increasing oversight on high medical costs. The cost of Medicaid could be less if research went into tracking unnecessary fees such as those administered by specialty doctors to Medicaid-insured patients who require care beyond basic diagnostic testing and treatment. Arizona can reapply the money saved from ridding itself of unnecessary fees and use the money to ensure healthcare accessibility without offsetting Arizona's current financial crisis.

A third initiative is to set up a healthcare tax that will increase federal payments and relieve Arizona of some of the debt it currently incurs. In the future, this tax will provide the state with more money and reduce state costs, as you have endorsed before. Lastly, Arizona can set up an affordable safety-net program that improves the way healthcare is delivered and financed. This program will function as a safety net that provides for people who face immediate harm from complete or partial loss of coverage.

I urge you to reconsider cuts to the Medicaid budget and consider the above alternatives.

Thank you for your time and consideration. I am available and eager to help and have provided a contact email address if necessary. I look forward to further discussion on the issue.

Sincerely,

Kassandra Díaz, College of Science, Biology Department

Following up on student writing:

- What is the tone of this letter? Why and how did Kassandra convey this tone?

- What are some conventions of this genre (a formal letter) that you see Kassandra using? Is this an appropriate genre for Kassandra's argument?

- How does Kassandra establish her ethos? Is it effective? Why/why not?

- What is her overall claim? How does she support it? What evidence does she use?

- What is her call-to-action? Is it clear what she wants from this letter?

- What suggestions would you have made to Kassandra if you were reviewing her work?

See the Tips & Strategies Box on page 224 for tips on composing a video.

11.2

Video Argument: "Suffering in the Desert"

Now let's look at an example of an English 102/108 student's video public argument. After researching whether or not it is appropriate to assist undocumented immigrants crossing the U.S./Mexico border, this English 102/108 student created the video "Suffering in the Desert" to advocate her position. This viewpoint was the result of extensive interviews with people involved in the controversy, including members of No More Deaths (No Más Muertes), who work to provide humanitarian aid to undocumented immigrants crossing the border through the Southern Arizona desert, and the Minutemen, a vigilante group that patrols the border in efforts to stop undocumented immigration. After the student created her video, she decided to make it public by placing it on YouTube. In the following days, several area non-profit organizations, including No More Deaths, provided links to the URL, earning the video praise and recognition.

Suffering in the Desert

Image courtesy of Suffering in the Desert, *No More Deaths*

Now view the video at http://www.youtube.com/watch?v=-dVuTiOK2Vg and respond to the following questions. You can also visit www.youtube.com and search for "Suffering in the Desert."

• What is the overall tone of the argument? How do the text, visuals, and audio contribute in creating this tone? How would this tone change if any of the elements were different?

• Does the video rely more heavily on one type of appeal? Why do you think this is?

• How does the producer establish credibility?

• How is the argument structured? How is this similar to or different from the structure of written arguments?

• Think about the arrangement as logos. Can you see a storyline in the order in which the images are presented? What does this story say? How might changing the order of images alter the effects of the argument?

• Is there a call to action? How is it presented? How do the images add to the sense of urgency?

• How would you present this argument in your own video? In other words, what would you do differently?

Website Argument: The University of Arizona

Take a minute to think about your favorite website: Why do you go there? What do you like about it? What choices did the web designer make that keep you coming back? When you think about it this way, all websites are public arguments. Whether or not they are trying to convince you of a political opinion or to buy a product, websites are always trying to persuade you to come back and spend time on their site.

Creating Your Own Video Public Argument

Video can provide an effective means of communication with your audience when developing your Public Argument. Like websites, video can incorporate text, audio, and visual elements, all working together to create a more persuasive piece. Pay attention to the things that draw you in when you watch videos shared by others on sites like YouTube. When you watch videos, consider what causes you to keep watching them and also take note of what makes you lose interest and move on to another video or something else entirely. All of this is integral to understanding video as a genre, because in order to convey a persuasive message, you must gain and keep your audience's interest.

Creating a video means thinking not only about what images portray your meaning, but also what music or sounds convey that message. With video, you strive to engage as many of the viewer's senses as possible. Commercials are great at this strategy, and restaurant commercials are particularly good at engaging the senses. Restaurant commercials will often depict the food close up, similar to how it would appear if you were eating it, but they also include sounds we associate with that food in the audio: the sizzling of steak, the crunch of lettuce, or the fizz of opening a soda.

Think about commercials when you are creating your own video—you want to use every aspect of this medium to draw in your audience. You want the images to be meaningful to the viewer, so think about how the viewer might see the situation in real life. The images can come from a variety of sources: filmed interviews or scenarios, clips of stock footage, or even a slide show of still photography. Similarly, your audio might include elements such as music, dialogue, or environmental sounds that contribute to the meaning in some way.

Before you begin creating your own video, you will want to think carefully about your topic and the best way to frame it. Ask yourself these questions:

1. Who is the specific audience you are trying to target? As the earlier sections of this chapter suggest, the general public is not a sufficient target audience. Analyze your audience carefully using the strategies in section 11.3.

2. What kind of emotions do you want your video to raise in your audience? Sadness? Joy? Anger? How can you connect these emotions to your audience members' lives? How can you use the visual medium to evoke these emotions in a way that is both responsible and clear?

3. What text is needed in the video, and how should it be incorporated? How can text add to the meaning being conveyed by the images and audio?

Now Break It All Down

1. What different visual elements are required to create your argument? Video? Interviews? A series of photos?

2. What auditory (sound) elements do you need? Music? Taped conversation or environmental sounds?

3. Whom do you need to consult to make this happen? Make a list of everyone you would like to appear in or be involved with the creation of your video.

4. Where do you need to go to get the resources (video, photos, or sounds) you want? What do you need to do in advance to prepare?

5. What software and hardware do you need to gather the pieces you need? Cameras? Tripods? Tape recorders? Video editing software? Where can you access this?

For an example of how text, images, and sound can work together to convey an argument, let's consider The University of Arizona's website. The UA depends on a highly successful webpage in order to attract potential students, offer a positive glimpse into life in Tucson, and convince parents and guardians that they should encourage their children to apply. Type in the URL (www.arizona.edu) and think about the following questions:

- What is the first thing you see when you load the page? The university logo? The tabs at the top? The numbers at the bottom? The colors? Or something else?

- Where do you feel your eyes drawn to next? Why do you think this is?

- What is the overall "feel" of the page? Professional? Fun? Stuffy? Clean? Try to determine what makes you feel this way. Compare this to other school or university websites you have seen.

- How would you describe this site's ethos? How does it try to establish a relationship with the audience? Pay close attention to the use of color, graphics, and text used on the front page.

- What is the largest element on the page? An image? A word or name? What is the smallest? Why do you think this might be?

- Click on some of the most prominent links. Where do they lead you? Why do you think those links were placed on the front page of the website?

> See Chapter 9 for more information on rhetorically persuasive evidence.

To this point we've only looked at the visual design of a homepage. If you plan to design your own website, however, you'll also want to think about the content on each page or tab within the website. Click on the "About the University" link on the UA homepage and consider these rhetorical choices:

- What is the purpose of this page? How do you know?

- What might the audience expect to find on this page? How does the webpage meet or challenge these expectations?

- What words, terms, or phrases are repeated? Why do you think this might be?

- Describe the visual appeal of this page. Consider the arrangement of text and visuals. How does the appearance of the page impact the audience and/or argument?

- What strategies does the writer use to persuade the audience?

- What is the relationship between this page and the homepage? Do you notice any changes in visual style or language choices?

Now go to a website that you visit frequently, perhaps a blog or a vlog. How are the answers to the questions above similar? How do they differ? How do the differences between the sites reveal the **rhetorical** purposes of each? When you design your own website, you'll want to carefully consider your audience before you start making choices in regards to content and form.

See section 6e in *Rules for Writers* for a discussion of supporting claims with specific evidence.

11.3 Thinking through the Process

Invention

After you have determined the position you would like to take in your argument, there are several rhetorical factors you should consider as you develop your Public Argument. Here are a series of steps you should take to make your argument persuasive to your chosen public audience.

Step One: Identify Your Audience. Before you can make any choices about how to construct your argument, it is essential to decide to whom your argument will be directed. Keep in mind that you may not always know or control the members of your specific audience—that is precisely what makes it public. What you can do is appeal to most of your readers or listeners based on what you know about your target audience. It may benefit you to review your Controversy Analysis as you consider your audience. Do you want to direct your argument to any of the stakeholder groups you have already identified?

Keep the following tips in mind as you identify an appropriate audience and devise appropriate rhetorical strategies.

- **You already analyze audiences on a daily basis.**

  Think of how, in ordinary conversations, you often express the same opinion differently when talking with a friend as opposed to talking to your professor or your parents. You should bring this same rhetorical awareness to this assignment, as choosing a specific audience makes your task much more manageable and also enables you to reach those readers or viewers best suited to your purposes for writing. From the beginning, your target audience helps shape your argument's goals and intentions, your choice of medium, the tone you adopt, the persuasive strategies you choose, and the level of sophistication you bring to the conversation.

See Chapter 11 in *Writing Public Lives* to read more about choosing a specific audience within the "general public."

- **There is no "general public."**

  In order to simplify the process of selecting and analyzing an audience, it might be tempting to write for the "general public," but does this group really exist? Think again about the example above: if your friends and your professor are part of the same "general public," why do you express your opinion differently to them? The same principle can be applied to this assignment. While you might initially think that the articles you have come across in your research are directed to a general audience, the fact is that most journals, newspapers, magazines, and even websites cater to specific populations. The targeted audience for *Time* is different from that of *Rolling Stone*. While, on the surface, the writing may appear to reach the same general magazine-reading audience, the authors have made choices about the types of topics they will explore, the visuals they will include, the relative depth of their analyses, the examples that will be most appropriate, and so on.

- **Not all audience members who belong to a similar group share the same beliefs.**

  The U.S. is made up of many diverse groups. Individuals come from different racial, ethnic, religious, and socioeconomic backgrounds, have different sexual orientations, and speak different languages. Even as you begin to narrow your audience—like "parents of high school students," for example—you will still want to explore the differences that may exist within this group. Do parents of private school students share the same beliefs as those who send their students to public schools? Do parents in Tucson have the same concerns as those in Yuma, in Nogales, or in Berkeley, California? Additionally, when you create an argument for a particular audience, do not assume that they will have the same views as you. Stretch yourself to think about views that are drastically different from your own. Keep in mind that you can address your Public Argument assignment to different publics—you just have to spend time reflecting and discovering where and, more importantly, why your views on a particular issue might diverge from theirs.

See Chapters 11 and 12 in *Writing Public Lives* to read more about stakeholder relationships.

Step Two: Determine Your Purpose. The purpose of an argument is usually to move an audience in some way, potentially inspiring them to act or think about your topic differently. For example, if you are making an argument about a proposed water conservation law to a group of Tucson voters, your purpose might be to persuade your audience to vote a certain way. Other public arguments might have less clear-cut purposes. Take the time to answer these crucial questions about the reason you are making your argument. Ask yourself:

See pages 3, 6, and 7 in *Rules for Writers* or section 9.1 in this book for advice about determining purpose.

- Am I moving my audience to *act*, to *react*, to *know*, or to *feel*, or all of the above?

- What do I want my audience to *do* in response to my position?

- Am I making it clear *how* my listeners or readers can take the action I want them to take?

Step Three: Select a Medium. There are many modes of argument that might appeal to your audience, such as a speech or performance, a compilation of images accompanied by text, or a digital argument that engages the users of a specific website. While academic audiences and some other public audiences might expect to read a twenty-page research paper, many audiences are more likely to pay attention to other types of communication. For example, an audience of college students rushing to class would be unlikely to listen to a ten-minute speech about animal rights, but they might glance at an installation of large photographs with shorter snippets of written text. The medium you choose should complement your purpose and be appropriate for your audience. If you hope to evoke your audience's sympathy about animal rights, for example, photographs might be helpful to gain an emotional response. By considering the rhetorical situation of your argument, you should be well prepared to decide the best medium for your claims. As you consider your medium, ask yourself:

11.3

- How much time will my audience have to interact with my argument?

- What format is most likely to serve the purpose of my argument?

- What media are most familiar to my audience members? Will they know how to interact with my chosen medium, or will I have to teach them?

Ultimately, the choice of medium is also a choice of genre. A genre is a category or group of texts that share similar characteristics and perform similar functions. For instance, an obituary is a genre used to announce someone's death. Most obituaries include important information about a person's life and inform readers about the funeral services. Obituaries share patterns of language, such as "the deceased is survived by" followed by a list of family members' names. Readers of obituaries would probably expect to find these conventions. Different genres of writing conform to different conventions in terms of style, format, tone, structure, purpose, and use. As you prepare to form your argument(s), you may find it helpful to think about the form or genre that would be most fitting and persuasive for the purpose of your message and the audience you would like to reach.

For instance, if you were making an argument opposing tuition increases, you could choose to write a letter to the editor of the *Arizona Daily Wildcat* or a business letter to the President of the University of Arizona. Each of these choices would serve a different purpose, reach a different audience, and require different choices in everything from tone to type of evidence used.

> See the sample approaches in section 11.2 of this chapter to review the kinds of questions you'll want to ask yourself as you examine your chosen genre.

Once you have identified a genre appropriate for your rhetorical situation, you should spend time researching that genre. Try collecting samples of the genre and looking for common features. You may think you know what a brochure looks like, for example, but have you ever taken the time to examine its unique features—the characteristics that distinguish it from a flyer or an advertisement? There are certain conventions that you should consider when writing a brochure, such as choosing a tri-fold design, writing in bulleted points instead of large paragraphs of dense text, and using pictures to help convey your claims. Analyzing a genre by breaking it down to see how the parts work will help you to compose that genre effectively using appropriate rhetorical strategies.

Step Four: Consider Your Character and Credibility. For the Rhetorical Analysis assignment in Chapter 9, you analyzed the ways in which an author establishes character and credibility to reach a desired audience and achieve a purpose. Now you must consider how to build a relationship with your audience. Think carefully about the tone you wish to take toward your subject and your audience, about the type of voice you wish to develop to characterize yourself, and about how to present yourself as a credible researcher, authority figure, or participant in the conversation surrounding your subject matter. Following are some questions to help you develop your ethos:

- What is my relationship to the issue? Do I have experience that makes me an authority on the subject, or am I relying mostly on outside research? How will this affect my audience's engagement with my argument?

- Will I be making the argument in person? If so, how should I dress and present myself? How will I carry my voice, utilize props or visuals, or gesture with my hands?

- What is my relationship to the audience? Do they already know who I am? What level of formality should I use?

- How will I explain my stake in the issue?

- How do I want my audience to see me? As a friend? A colleague? A teacher? An official? What rhetorical strategies will help me achieve this goal and meet the conventions of my chosen genre?

Step Five: Think about Your Rhetorical Strategies. The level of knowledge and expertise of the public you are targeting will ultimately determine the kinds of rhetorical strategies you use. For example, if you are seeking to convince your local hospital to buy an MRI machine, you would likely use technical language about the medical benefits of magnetic resonance imaging to a group of doctors and nurses, but that same language might frustrate a less scientifically minded and more financially motivated administrator. Always consider your audience's needs and use your rhetorical strategies accordingly.

- What kind of language will my audience be most comfortable with? Specialized terms/jargon that allow for more precision? Generalized language that is more understandable but less exact?

- How will my choices reflect my ethos?

- How will my medium affect my rhetorical choices?

As you can see, writing for a public audience builds on the skills you have been developing in your first-year writing courses. You will want to draw on what you know about rhetorical analysis in order to be as persuasive as possible to your chosen audience and within the genre and medium you have selected.

Drafting

The Logic of Arguments

Now that you have thought through your audience, your medium, and your purpose, let's think about how you can create a strong argument based on thoughtful research and compelling evidence. To do this, here is a sample process of how you might take the research from your Controversy Analysis and turn it into a Public Argument.

See pages 202–207 in *Writing Public Lives* for more on formulating research questions.

11.3

Analyzing Your Audience

As you begin planning your Public Argument, consider the following questions to help you analyze your audience:

1. Who might be interested in or impacted by this issue? Review your sources and the stakeholders from your Controversy Analysis to remind yourself who is affected by your topic.

2. What ages, locations, educational levels, races, genders, and/or political tendencies might be likely of people involved with or interested in this issue? What specific values or beliefs might members of the audience for this argument hold?

3. How do you plan to make your argument "public" and who would have access to or be likely to engage with that medium? How familiar will your audience be with your topic?

4. Aside from your ideal audience, who else might encounter this argument? How would someone who disagrees with the perspective you offer be likely to respond? What would someone who has little or no experience with this issue need to know to understand your argument?

Keep in mind that establishing, analyzing, and responding to your audience is one of the most crucial components to generating an effective Public Argument. Pay attention to arguments you might notice in your own life or in current events. Notice how authors and speakers react to different types of audiences.

In the Controversy Analysis, you identified an issue or point of concern (such as childhood obesity) and then formulated a research question that narrowed this issue into a more manageable and focused line of inquiry. As you formulate your stance in the Public Argument, it often helps to revisit your question as you frame the perspective you wish to support.

Consider the following example:

NATIVE AMERICAN MASCOTS

Topic
Native American mascots for sports teams (such as the Cleveland Indians, Washington Redskins, Florida State Seminoles)

Controversy Analysis Research Question
Should the governing bodies of sports organizations (Major League Baseball, the National Football League, the National Collegiate Athletic Association, etc.) ban the use of "Indian" mascots?

Argument For
Yes, professional and collegiate sports organizations should ban the use of "Indian" mascots.

Argument Against
No, these institutions should not ban the use of Indian mascots.

As you discovered in your Controversy Analysis, an issue might have more than just two sides. Perhaps there are several solutions to a problem or sources agree on an action but for completely different reasons. A strong Public Argument should consider the benefits and disadvantages of the action or idea proposed, and reflect on the various needs of different stakeholders. It is possible that your Public Argument will combine elements from differing stakeholders to produce a new and original solution to your issue like the one below.

New Argument
The governing institutions of sports teams should establish strict ethical guidelines for mascots (not quite a ban, but could be used to initiate dialogue about the effects of this social practice).

What's the thesis?

In the Public Argument, your thesis should contain your primary claim(s). It should not merely present a well-known fact, but it should be arguable, meaning that it is open to debate. In the following sample thesis, the primary claims are marked in blue.

11.3

See *Rules for Writers* sections 6b and 6c for advice on stating a position in an argument. See also the sample argument essay in section 6h.

Using "Indian" mascots demonstrates that contemporary U.S. society has an inadequate understanding of both the history of Native Americans and their continued presence as active members in local and national communities; therefore, these "mascots" should be challenged, and people living outside of these communities should work to increase their understanding of Native American history and contemporary life.

This example shows that the thesis of the paper can include a series of claims that must be further developed. This particular thesis sets up a problem that exists and then proposes a specific solution. In a public argument, your thesis might not be stated in the same way it is in an academic essay. You should still ensure, however, that your audience clearly understands your thesis and primary claims.

Developing Supporting Claims

To develop an argument, you will need supporting claims with sufficient evidence that help prove your central argument. Closely examine your thesis and consider what information your audience will need to understand your perspective. It is often useful to re-read your thesis with these questions in mind: "How so?" or "In what way?"

Consider the example of the mascot controversy. The author suggests that U.S. society has an "inadequate understanding" of Native American life. The development of supporting claims can help to prove this point. In this example, one might ask: How do "Indian" mascots demonstrate a lack of understanding? The answer to this question becomes a supporting claim.

Supporting Claim 1
Using names such as "Indians," "Savages," or "Seminoles" as mascots demonstrates an ignorance of the historical realities experienced by indigenous peoples of North America.

Supporting Claim 2
"Indian" mascots freeze representations of Native Americans in time; they are always "braves," "savages," and "warriors," rather than real people experiencing everyday life.

The sample thesis also suggests that these mascots should be challenged. To develop a supporting claim in response to this primary claim, one might ask, "In what way?" or "Why?" Answers to these questions become supporting claims.

Supporting Claim 3
State legislators have a responsibility to protect the cultures of Native American citizens.

When making a claim, it is also important to consider the **counterclaims** that could be raised by either the primary, secondary, or even tertiary audience. If you are further developing the work you did for your Controversy Analysis, it could be useful to return to the various stakeholders you identified and consider who might disagree with all or some of your argument and why. Identifying and responding to potential counterarguments can help you build your ethos as a well-informed participant in the debate. Acknowledging that not everyone will agree with you also shows that you understand the complexity of the issue and that you have listened to other perspectives.

In the mascot example, some members of your audience might point out potentially high costs (financial and in public opinion) of changing the mascots. If this student argues that Native American mascots demonstrate an ignorance of historical realities and damage the perception of a culture and its people, for instance, she might want to address how the potential costs of changing mascots would be worthwhile.

Incorporating Evidence

A balanced argument features strong claims supported by compelling evidence. You should always keep the audience in mind when considering the kinds of evidence to use. For example, does your audience expect compelling anecdotes? Or do they prefer strong statistical evidence?

> See Chapter 9 for more information on rhetorically persuasive evidence.

As you go through this list, mark the items that might make good evidence for your own public argument. You might also refer to the rhetorical strategies listed in Chapter 9 for more ideas. Don't forget to keep in mind the types of evidence commonly used in your chosen genre.

- ❐ **Bulleted lists of information:** Bulleted lists provide quickly accessible facts, statistics, and examples to bolster a claim.

- ❐ **Facts or statistics presented in charts, graphs, and tables:** Like bulleted lists, graphical representations of information allow audiences to take in a great deal of information quickly and efficiently. Graphs and charts can also show relationships between different types of information.

> See section 6e in *Rules for Writers* for a discussion of supporting claims with specific evidence.

- ❐ **A public opinion poll or survey:** You can find reliable public opinion polls in your research, or you can conduct your own. Polls and surveys can offer a grassroots perspective for your argument, but they often work best when paired with other types of evidence. When offering findings from a poll or survey, be sure to acknowledge the limitations of your findings. Interviewing 100 UA students may seem sufficient, but not when you consider that this campus has almost 40,000 students with a large variety of backgrounds and experiences. In addition to making sure the sample size is adequate, it is also important to ensure that the population you are sampling is appropriate to the claim you are making. For example, if you are conducting a poll on the reasons why retention rates at UA are lower for out-of-state students than for students from within the state of Arizona, you would want to make sure that the students you interview represent those populations proportionately.

11.3

Craft Box: INVENTION

Investigating Public Genres

By Ashley Holmes

Choose one of the genres from the box on the next page. Then, find three realistic examples of that genre. For instance, walk through the student union and collect three brochures, stop by a telephone pole and collect three flyers, go online and find three websites, or grab a newspaper and find three obituaries. Examine your examples and use them to help you answer the following questions:

1. What purpose(s) does this genre usually serve?

2. Where, how, or in what context do readers usually find this genre?

3. Who is the typical audience for this genre?

4. What are some of the key features or characteristics that are unique to this genre, distinguishing it from other texts?

5. Based on your answers to the questions above, come up with a definition in your own words for this genre.

6. How can the genre you have selected fulfill your argument's purpose and your target audience's needs and expectations? Write a plan (1–2 sentences) on how to construct your argument using this genre.

11.3

Below is a chart of various kinds of genres. Consult this chart as you consider the genre you would like to use for your public argument.

Public Genre Types			
Professional or Business	*Publications (Newspaper or Magazine)*	*Technology*	*Spoken*
• business card	• editorial	• e-mail	• eulogy
• business letter	• article	• text message	• speech
• application	• letter to the editor	• phone conversation	• dialogue
• memo	• obituary	• blog	*Lists*
• brochure	• advice column	• Facebook page	• pro/con list
• résumé	• tabloid article	• wiki	• top ten list
• flyer	• advertisement	• website	• to do list
• proposal	• book or movie review	• podcast	• directions
	• interview (Q & A)		
	• biographical profile		

Academic Genre Types		Personal Genre Types	
• report		• personal letter	
• abstract		• personal narrative	
• essay		• scrapbook page	
• syllabus		• diary/journal entry	
• tutorial		• memoir	
• diagram		• blogs or vlogs	
• summary			
• call for proposals			
• outline			

Visual/Design Genre		Miscellaneous Genres	
• cartoon	• graph	• petition	
• photograph	• certificate	• poem	
• travel poster	• poster	• recipe	
• award certificate	• concept map or web	• song	
• comic strip	• calendar	• bumper sticker	
• collage	• greeting card	• restaurant menu	
• illustration	• invitation		
• movie	• postcard		
• map	• infographic		
• timeline			

11.3

Software, Programs, and Apps for Your Public Argument

Text-based arguments—such as speeches, letters, essays, and articles—are excellent choices for public arguments. However, you might decide that creating a digital argument best suits your message and audience. If you would like to try creating a digital argument but are not familiar with the many technologies available, it can be difficult to know where to start. To help you find the right technology to use, here is a list of programs, software, and apps that are easy to learn and intuitive to use. All of the programs listed here are completely free, have free options, or have free trial periods, so make sure to double-check before you purchase anything!

Presentations & Brochures	**PowerPoint:** This software is part of the Microsoft Office Suite. **Prezi.com:** Prezi is similar to PowerPoint, but it has a different spatial orientation. **SlideRocket.com:** This program is similar to PowerPoint, but it has a fun and different option if you want to try a cloud-based program. **Microsoft Word Templates:** Once in Word, click on "File" and then "Project Gallery." You can alter all templates.
Web-Based Texts	**Storyjumper.com:** Create online books that users can flip through. This is a great program for creating interactive children's books. **Glogster.com:** "Glogs" are interactive posters loaded with text, graphics, music, video, and other elements. **Meograph.com:** A site that allows you to create "four-dimensional stories" using different media.
Websites/Blogs	**Weebly.com:** This is a very easy and intuitive drag-and-drop website creator. **Wix.com:** Drag-and-drop website creator that also allows for Flash animation. **Blogger.com:** This is a very easy-to-use blog creator, and you can use your UA Net ID to create one. **Wordpress.com:** Many professional blogs use Wordpress to host their sites, and it is easy to see why: it is intuitive and has more design options. **Yola.com:** Another drag-and-drop website creator that is used by many small businesses.

Slideshows/Movies	**Slide.com:** A cloud-based program that allows you to upload photos, add text, and create graphics in a presentation format.
	Smilebox.com: Another cloud-based program that allows you to create visually stunning slideshows.
	iMovie or Windows Movie Maker: Great choices for creating and editing video on a Mac or PC.
	Masher.com: This cloud-based program allows you to create a video by mixing together video clips, music, and photos.
	Animoto.com: This cloud-based program is similar to Masher but gives additional options.
Graphics/Cartoons	**Powtoon.com:** A DIY animated presentation tool that is really user-friendly and intuitive. You can sign up for a 14-day VIP free trial and then cancel after that if you wish.
	XtraNormal.com: Another choice for making storyboards and cartoons. Make sure to avoid the options with money signs ($) next to them, as only some characters and locations are free.
	ToonDoo.com: Choose ToonDoo (the free option), NOT ToonDoo Spaces. Click on Toons and then "create toons."
	Easelly: You can create charts, graphs, and infographics with this beta site. (http://www.easel.ly/)
	Wordle.com: You can use this to create word clouds with key words and phrases. See the example in *Writing Public Lives*, pages 238–239.

11.3

University of Arizona Resources:

Computer Labs: Type the following link into your web browser to view the UA's computer labs and hours: http://uits.arizona.edu/locations

Gear-to-Go: For school projects, you can check out digital cameras, digital video cameras, lighting kits, tripods, microphones, audio gear, and more through Gear-to-Go. Just type this link into your web browser for more information: http://www.uits.arizona.edu/departments/oscr/locations/gtg/

See section 58a in *Rules for Writers* for detailed information on integrating quotations.

□ **Quotations:** You can use quotations to demonstrate the breadth of your research and establish your credibility, to add to the emotional appeal of your argument by evoking a particularly charged bit of language from another writer, or to draw on an authority in the matter at hand. The best time to use a quotation is when the source says something uniquely and/or more precisely than you could say in your own words. Quotes should usually be contextualized by your own writing, but in visual arguments (like an infographic) it can be effective to list a quote by itself. As always, think rhetorically about your choices.

□ **Stories or anecdotes from individuals affected by the issue at hand:** Stories and anecdotes can add a personal quality to arguments that are otherwise steeped in facts and statistics. It is especially helpful to include stories from individuals who have been directly impacted by the controversy you are discussing. Think of how often politicians will bring in an "average Joe" to show how a specific policy might influence people's lives.

□ **References to commonly known cultural sources:** Referencing a popular or familiar cultural source, such as a film or television show that your audience is likely to be familiar with, can help you establish rapport with your readers or viewers. Think of this like sharing an inside joke, but be careful; like inside jokes, cultural references risk excluding people who might not be familiar with the **text** you are referencing. Other examples of cultural sources include poetry, song lyrics, and idioms.

See page 90 in *Rules for Writers* for a section on using visual evidence.

□ **Images:** Images can elicit a quick emotional response in audience members, and they can help to illustrate points that have also been made textually or verbally. In multimedia presentations, images can be paired with most of the other types of evidence on this list.

□ **Color, font typeface, style, and size:** Each of these choices can help make a document more visually appealing, but they can also invoke emotional responses from audiences. For example, consider what you might think if you saw the word **Earth** written in large green letters versus what you might think if you saw **Earth** in large red letters. In addition, you can use font typeface choices to help establish your relationship with the audience. Think of the different feelings evoked by **Comic Sans,** which is playful and found frequently in comic strips, and by **Century**, which is formal and found most often in newspapers.

□ **Sounds and music:** Sounds can draw an audience into a presentation by evoking a particular mood. Audio stimulation can be soothing, exciting, or impart a sense of danger or fear. To get an idea of how important sound can be in audience response, try watching a scene from your favorite scary movie with the sound turned off. Is it as suspenseful without the music helping to generate tension?

11.3

Developing Thesis Statements for Public Arguments

By Kenneth Walker

As you produce your Public Argument, remember that there are already a significant number of existing arguments with which you will be engaging. You might even say that you are entering an ongoing conversation on the topic. Listed below are three models that may help you articulate a position within this ongoing conversation for an audience with multiple perspectives. Try to enter your claims into the models to see which works best for your particular Public Argument. A sample thesis follows each model.

1. **A thesis can *correct false impressions*.**

   If you believe the topic you are arguing on has somehow been misrepresented or misconstrued, the following types of thesis statements can be useful.

   Model: Although many believe X, a careful examination suggests Q and Z.

   Sample: Although credit card companies appear to offer special services to college students, evidence suggests that these companies aim to exploit students' inexperience with buying on credit and often charge students comparatively high interest rates while offering limited benefits.

2. **A thesis can *fill the gap*.**

   If you believe that certain information or perspectives have been neglected from the topic you are arguing on, these thesis statements are particularly effective.

   Model: Although many people talk about X, many people miss the importance of Q and Z.

   Sample: Although many people talk about financially inexperienced students being exploited by credit card companies, people neglect the fact that these students are legal adults and, therefore, should be capable of making their own decisions and dealing with the consequences.

3. **A thesis can *argue through extension*.**

   This thesis often takes a qualified position toward the conversation by invoking the arguments of others while demonstrating the writer has something new or important to say that will bring the conversation to a different level.

   Model: I agree with people who argue X, but it is also important to extend/refine/limit their ideas with Q and Z.[1]

   Sample: Although I agree that all adults, including college students, should be held accountable for their financial decisions, it is also important to consider that many college students are just learning about financial responsibility, and credit card companies should be required to educate inexperienced customers on how credit and credit cards work.

Once you've found a model you think will work for your purpose and the multiple perspectives of your audience, edit your thesis for clarity and style.

[1]Adapted from Stuart Greene and April Lidinsky's "Developing a Working Thesis: Three Models" in *From Inquiry to Academic Writing: A Practical Guide.*

11.3

❑ **Spaces and places:** Where you choose to make your argument is just as important as how you convey it. The kind of space you choose for your argument will determine the range of your audience and, often, how your argument will be contextualized.

Revision

Let's return to our earlier example of the Native American mascots. Again, this is the thesis we are working with:

> Using "Indian" mascots demonstrates that contemporary U.S. society has an inadequate understanding of both the history of Native Americans and their continued presence as active members in local and national communities; therefore, these "mascots" should be challenged, and people living outside of these communities should work to increase their understanding of Native American history and contemporary life.

After considering her issue, thesis, claims, and evidence, imagine that this student decided to create a website rallying for public support to include a unit on Native American history and contemporary life in K–12 curriculum. Perhaps

Tips for Giving Oral Presentations

By Rachael Wendler

At the end of the Public Argument unit, many instructors will assign an oral presentation in which you must present your argument to your classmates. Because some communication is nonverbal, how you present your ideas matters almost as much as what you say. In fact, the ancient teachers of rhetoric considered delivery one of the five key points of effective communication, so these tips will help you deliver your presentation with confidence.

Three-Point Eye Contact

Eye contact builds a connection with your audience. For the majority of the audience to feel as though they've made personal eye contact with you, look at three points in the room: front left, back center, and front right (see diagram by Semay Johnston). Pick a person in each place, and alternate looking at each one during your talk. Practicing your talk can help you focus on your audience rather than your notes or slides.

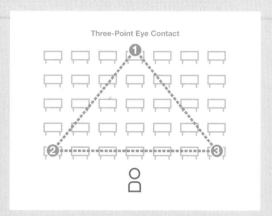

Image courtesy of Semay Johnston.

Open Posture

Your body posture can either communicate openness with your audience, or it can place obstructions between you—or your voice—and your

she decided to create a fictional nonprofit organization, Overcoming Prejudice, and then used her understanding of ethos to develop the site around the major goals of the nonprofit, which is to teach all U.S. citizens (especially children) about Native American life. As an example, here is a screenshot of the homepage she might have created:

listeners. For example, you place a barrier between you and your listeners when you cross your arms or hide behind the teacher's station, and your voice cannot carry as well if you are speaking down into your notes. You can increase connection by using your hands to emphasize points and speaking directly to the audience with your face forward.

Acing the Q&A

Responding to audience questions in the moment is an art, especially when you receive challenging questions or criticism. Remember to always thank people for their questions, and watch your tone carefully (avoid sounding defensive). If you don't know the answer, it's okay to say, "That's a great question! I'll have to look into this idea some more to find out." Also, practice thinking of questions or counterarguments and how you would address them before you present, so you will be prepared to answer most of the questions.

Film Yourself

The best way to improve your delivery is to video record yourself giving your presentation and watch the video. You can reserve a room through the library: A120 in the Main Library and 214 in the Science and Engineering Library have equipment for you to both present and record, and many rooms in both libraries will allow you to practice and have a friend record you on a personal device. Reserve at http://www.library.arizona.edu/services/study-spaces. As you watch your video, pay special attention to:

- Distracting movements such as twirling your jewelry or playing with coins in your pocket

- Shifting your weight rapidly

- Talking too fast

- Fidgeting unnecessarily

You might find it helpful to remove some of these temptations by taking off jewelry, wearing your hair back, or removing coins from your pocket before your presentation.

11.3

Tips & Strategies: PRESENTATION

See Chapter 13 in *Writing Public Lives* for more on writing visual arguments.

Try evaluating the Overcoming Prejudice webpage using the following questions and then include a short rationale for why you evaluated it the way you did. These criteria are taken from Sonya C. Borton and Brian Huot's chapter "Responding and Assessing" in *Multimodal Composition: Resources for Teachers*. Marking 1 means the draft did not meet the criteria; marking 5 means the draft met the criteria exceptionally well.

1. The text conveys a specific purpose.

    1   2   3   4   5

2. The text identifies a specific audience—either explicitly or implicitly.

    1   2   3   4   5

3. The text employs a tone consistent with the designated purpose and audience.

    1   2   3   4   5

4. The text is organized around an appropriate controlling idea. This idea is clear to readers/viewers/listeners.

    1   2   3   4   5

5. The text uses transitions to guide the audience effectively from one set of ideas to another.

    1   2   3   4   5

6. The text synthesizes relevant information from research efforts with composer's own ideas and arguments—in a way that increases the rhetorical effectiveness of the whole.

    1   2   3   4   5

When you are working on revising your own public argument, you might want to use these same criteria to guide your own revision. You can also return to the questions in section 4.3, "Tips for Successful Workshopping," to help guide your peer review and revision process. Depending on the kind of public argument you have created, revision can be tricky, so make sure to leave time to edit and revise after you receive your peer and instructor feedback. Draw your comic in pencil, for instance, or make sure you choose an easily editable website template.

See the Revision section in Chapter 8 for more on anticipating reader/viewer responses.

After you receive peer and instructor feedback on your public argument, go back to section 4.4, "Receiving and Making Sense of Comments," and think about the major patterns, questions, and comments that your peers noticed.

Then, start putting together your revision plan. What will you specifically work on to improve your draft?

11.3

Personal Public Argument Checklist

As you revise your Public Argument, it may be helpful to ask yourself pointed questions to ensure your project is effective and meets the criteria for the assignment. Try answering the following questions to help you get started with your revision.

- What is the purpose of this text? What do I want it to accomplish? What difference do I hope it will make?

- Who is my primary audience? Secondary audience? Tertiary audience? What can I predict about how these different groups will respond to my argument?

- Have I selected an appropriate medium for my argument? Why is this medium the best medium for my message?

- Is my argument coming through clearly and effectively?

- Did I follow effective design principles? Did I follow conventions of grammar, organization, arrangement, and design for my genre?

- Which areas still need improvement? How can I improve them?

- What kind of relationship am I trying to build with my audience? How am I doing this?

- What are my primary rhetorical strategies?

- Is my arrangement effective? How might my argument be different if I reorganized or tried something different?

- Are the messages being conveyed by my print-based and/or visual choices consistent with one another?

11.4 Reflection

The Public Argument assignment required you to craft your own argument concerning a controversy. Instead of merely reporting about the controversy, you entered the conversation and aligned yourself with a specific position. You applied your understanding of rhetorical analysis to your own writing in order to have an effect on others. As you wrap up your work for this assignment, think about how you would respond to the following questions:

- How does an understanding of genre affect my choices as a writer?

- How did my public argument "enter" an existing conversation and add a new perspective?

- How did what I learned in this chapter help me become more critical of the arguments I hear/see/create?

- How will I continue to interact with public arguments in the future?

Works Cited

Barton, Sonya C., and Brian Huot. "Responding and Assessing." *Multimodal Composition: Resources for Teachers*. Ed. Cynthia L. Selfe. Cresskill: Hampton Press, 2007. 99–111. Print.

Greene, Stuart, and April Lidinsky. "Developing a Working Thesis: Three Models." *From Inquiry to Academic Writing: A Practical Guide*. Boston: Bedford/St. Martin's, 2008. 85–87. Print.

"People, *n.*" *Oxford English Dictionary Online*. Oxford UP, 2011. Web. 11 Mar. 2011.

"Public, *adj.* and *n.*" *Oxford English Dictionary Online*. Oxford UP, 2011. Web. 11 Mar. 2011.

11.4

Reflective Writing

12.1 Reflective Writing: An Overview

"Reflective writing helps you to grow as a writer and a thinker. Intellectually, you push your ideas further and your work develops."

—Amanda Fahey, UA Student

Whether writing a reflective end-of-semester essay, **freewriting** to help you brainstorm for a particular assignment, or composing a discussion post, blog, or journal entry, you will produce some form of reflective writing in your first-year composition courses.

Your instructor may ask you to reflect on something you have read, an activity you have completed, or your semester experiences in the course. Alternatively, you may be asked to write an essay in which you use your own life as a context for a larger discussion about a text you have read and discussed. The questions at the end of each of the assignment chapters in this book have asked you to reflect on your writing process, your approach to specific assignments, and the ways you see your writing skills used in other situations. These are all examples of prompts that lead to reflective writing.

12.2 Approaches to the End-of-Semester Reflective Essay

At the end of the semester, your instructor may ask you to write a reflective essay on how your understanding of reading and writing has developed throughout the semester (or year). While the assignment parameters will vary, it is important to remember that the analysis you write should focus on process—the writing process, the process of becoming a writer, the peer-review process, the revision process, and the editing process. While **textual analysis** focuses on a text, reflective analysis focuses on your experiences producing texts, a topic on which only you can provide your unique insights.

Discussing your own writing can be difficult, of course, because many of the strategies that you used during the semester might have been compulsory (your

Discovering Your Writing Process (Revisited)

Chapter 3 introduced four different types of writers, including Heavy Planners, Heavy Revisers, Sequential Composers, and Procrastinators. Return to these descriptions and consider your writing identity now that you have taken one or more semesters of first-year writing. Do you consider yourself to be one of these types of writers? In what ways has your identity as a writer shifted throughout the semester?

The following questions are similar to those asked in Chapter 3. As a reflective exercise, consider your answers in comparison with how you may have answered them at the beginning of the semester.

- What type(s) of writer do you consider yourself to be?

- Have you changed your process to incorporate approaches from different writer identities?

- In what ways has your approach to writing changed because of a particular assignment, activity, or concept you have learned?

- What does your writing process look like? Has it shifted throughout the course of the semester? Does it change for different writing situations?

- Did you try any new or different approaches to writing this semester? What worked? What didn't work? What might you try in future writing situations?

instructor required you to do something) or unconscious (you just did some-thing because you always have). However, the reflective process asks you to think critically about what you did and why you did it. Why do you think your instructor asked you to do something in the writing process, and was it useful? Why or why not? Why did you choose to revise your second paper differently than your first paper? What worked and what did not work?

As you brainstorm topics, you might find it useful to revisit the "Reflection" sections at the end of the assignment chapters presented earlier in this book. Consider investigating the following topics to start generating ideas for your reflective essay:

> Return to Chapters 3 and 4 in this book for a reminder of some of the strategies you have learned for draft-ing and revising your work.

- Your assumptions and ideas about writing before taking your first-year writing courses and how these assumptions were reinforced or challenged

- The most important lessons you have learned as both a reader and a writer as a result of taking your first-year writing courses

- The ways you generated ideas, narrowed down topics, and worked on thesis statements

- The peer review process, including feedback you offered and feedback you received

- Individual or group conferences with your instructor

- The discussions you had about your paper with people who were not in your class

- How you approached the revision process for each essay

- Your understanding of reading and writing in different genres

- What you would do differently if you were to take your first-year writing courses again

- How college writing fits into your life now and how it will fit into your major and future career

Once you have generated some topic ideas, you will want to find a common thread between your reflections so that you can write a cohesive and focused essay. You have had many writing experiences during the course of the semester, but in your essay you may choose to just focus on one experience, or one con-cept or strategy that you practiced. Remember to always read your instructor's assignment sheet carefully so that you can adequately meet the expectations for the assignment. The following topics and questions might help you focus your reflections and develop a **thesis** statement for your reflective essay:

> See section 1b in *Rules for Writers* for more on generating ideas for writing.

- **Focus on an assignment, experience, or concept:** What did you learn (from a specific writing assignment, from a specific experience, or about a particular writing strategy or concept)?

- **Compare to past writing experiences:** Did the choices you made, or writing experiences you had, reinforce or challenge something you thought you knew about writing?

- **Reflect on strengths and weaknesses:** If you did not gain as much from a particular project as you had hoped, what are the possible reasons for that and what might you do differently the next time? What are some of your strengths as a writer? How did you practice or improve on your abilities throughout the semester?

- **Focus on course objectives:** Think about the course objectives listed on your syllabus as you consider your success in the class. What course objectives did you meet? What objectives are you still working on?

- Return to the "Discovering Your Writing Process" Craft Box in Chapter 3. Has your perception of yourself as a writer changed throughout the course of the semester?

Reflective writing provides you with an excellent opportunity to analyze yourself as a writer, noting your own strengths within the larger scope of the writing project, the course, or your ongoing development as a writer. Keep in mind that addressing disappointments or even failures can also help you gauge what you have learned and how you can continue to develop your writing abilities.

12.3 Thinking through the Process

Invention

The previous section introduces many questions and ideas to help you begin the process of reflection for your final reflective essay. As you begin to narrow your ideas and prepare to write your essay, you'll also want to consider the rhetorical situation for this assignment.

Audience and Purpose for Reflective Writing

Like all writing, starting a reflective writing project involves establishing an awareness of your audience and purpose. In other words, the reflective writing process is intricately linked to the rhetorical situation as discussed in Chapters 3 and 9, and the **rhetorical analysis** skills discussed in Chapter 9.

The left column in the following table shows how one UA student, Christopher Tursi, might have identified the **rhetorical situation** for his reflective essay. Use the right side to generate ideas about the rhetorical situation of your upcoming assignment.

Sample Student Answers	Your Essay
What topic do I want to discuss with my readers? What do I want them to understand about the topic? I want to explain the ways I have grown as a writer over the course of my first semester. Looking back I realize that my first essay was mostly summary not analysis, and I want to show my reader that I understand what would make it better.	**What topic do I want to discuss with my readers? What do I want them to understand about the topic?**
Who is my primary audience? Who is my secondary audience? My primary audience is my instructor. He read the first essay and will be reading and grading this one. My secondary audience is my classmates because I'll be discussing this with them.	**Who is my primary audience? Who is my secondary audience?**
What do my audiences already know or believe about the topic? Well, they already know me and my writing, and they have already seen my first essay. My instructor and my classmates also know the strategies that we have focused on this semester, so I should really highlight those.	**What do my audiences already know or believe about the topic?**
How will I organize and develop my ideas to make them convincing to these readers? Because my main audience is my instructor, I'll want to show specific aspects of the original and explain exactly how I would change it. Since we have talked so much about analysis and using evidence in class, I'll make sure to take specific examples from my essay and explain clearly how I would improve them.	**How will I organize and develop my ideas to make them convincing to these readers?**

Once you have a central purpose and primary audience in mind, you can shape the content and the overall presentation of your writing accordingly. For example, as a writer you get to shape the voice or voices that emerge in your writing. Having a voice in writing does not mean that you strive to transfer your speaking voice onto the page. Instead, your goal is to construct voice(s) in your writing to create an **ethos**, a sense of character or credibility, that suits your purpose. Just as credible sources are important in a research essay, the voice and ethos that you create are fundamental to the success of your reflective essay. The relationship you build with your audience and their perception of you will depend on your rhetorical choices.

> Your instructor may or may not use the term *ethos*, but you will be asked to think about the ways writers establish a relationship with their audiences. See Chapter 9 for more information on *ethos* and rhetorical strategies.

Let's look at an example of how Christopher builds a relationship with his audience within the first few sentences of his essay. His ethos plays an important role in making an **argument** about an assignment he disliked writing because he could easily come across as unmotivated, bitter, or even whiny, especially to his teacher. As you read Christopher's opening few sentences, note the specific details, **tone** of voice, and sentence construction that he uses to create his ethos:

> It is impossible to enjoy every essay that you are assigned in school. There will always be at least one that you hate writing and the resulting essay will reflect that. A reader can feel your disdain for the paper. That was the problem I had with essay two.

Following up on student writing:

- What kind of relationship is Christopher trying to create with his audience?

- In what ways do his choices reflect an understanding of his rhetorical situation?

- Can you think of ways this opening could be improved?

Thinking about the ethos you want to create in your writing can help shape your choices as you begin drafting. Here are some questions to consider as you plan your writing:

- What kind of relationship do you want to create with your audience(s)?

- What choices can you make in your writing to earn your audience's trust or encourage them to view you in a certain way? Consider content, structure, and style.

> You can read more about using emotional appeals in your writing in Chapter 9.

Drafting

Though there are many ways to approach this assignment, your reflective essay should do the following:

- Analyze your writing process in terms of the experiences, writing assignments, or the concepts you have learned. You are not merely offering a report on the class. You are demonstrating how your writing or your view of writing has been affected by what you have learned or experienced through your composition class.

- Provide concrete examples from your own writing (either quotes from your writing or rich descriptions of your writing process) as evidence. For help with integrating quotes, see Chapter 5.

- Explain why you made certain choices (not just "it was on the assignment sheet"), and evaluate whether those choices were effective.

- Use the language of writing. For example, if you explain that you revised something, name what sort of revision it was (local, global, stylistic, and so on). Use *Rules for Writers* and the glossary terms from this book to help you discuss writing concepts more precisely.

Drafting the Thesis Statement

Your thesis for this assignment should focus your reflection on a particular assignment, experience, or concept of writing and help you to organize your thoughts. In the following sample, Christopher decides to focus his reflection essay on one particular assignment that he struggled to compose and knew he needed to revise in specific ways. The following excerpt is from the introduction to his end-of-semester reflection:

> While I was writing the assigned paper, I knew it was bad. I wrote sentences poorer than I thought possible for me, but I had to push out ideas I didn't fully believe in anyways in order to try and receive credit for this monster I was creating. I couldn't even make the designated amount of words; I was so unmotivated. Moreover, I was coming off a fantastic essay-one that I backed with my entire heart. I hated myself more and more with every word and every sentence I put into this essay-two. That is how I knew this was the one I needed to revise. My essay-two needed to be revamped from beginning to end by rewriting the introduction, including more complete ideas in my body paragraphs, and to fill my conclusion with the requirements needed like a summary of the main argument and an answer to the reader's "So what?" question.

Following up on student writing:

- What is Christopher's thesis? If you were in a peer review with Christopher, how might you suggest he revise his thesis?

- Why do you think Christopher uses the personal pronoun "I" in this introduction? Is it an effective strategy? Why or why not?

- Where do you expect Christopher's essay to go from here?

Drafting PIE Paragraphs in a Reflective Essay

Since your end-of-semester reflection is an analysis of your writing and writing experiences, you can continue to use the **PIE** paragraph structure you have practiced in your other analytical writing. After all, while you are not necessarily analyzing an outside text, you are analyzing your own writing and experiences, which can be considered evidence for your claims. When writing your end-of-semester reflective essay in PIE structure, you might want to take the following approach:

<table>
<tr><td>

See the "Model Papers" area of the *Rules for Writers* website: <www.hackerhandbooks.com/rules> or the sample essays in section 13.9 for models of reflective writing.

</td></tr>
</table>

- Open your paragraph with a topic sentence (**Point**) that states a specific area or feature of your writing you wish to address that relates to the overall thesis of your essay.

- Present examples (**Illustration**) of this feature of your writing as evidence, either using quotes or specific moments that illuminate an idea. You might also include evidence from *Rules for Writers* or this book to help you explain certain writing concepts.

- Clearly connect each example to the overall point of your paragraph (**Explanation**). In other words, show how your illustration proves the claim you are making in the paragraph.

The following paragraph from Christopher's reflective essay includes his reflection on challenges he faced during first-year writing using PIE format.

See section 4a in *Rules for Writers* for advice about and examples of topic sentences.

> The biggest problem with my body paragraphs was that I didn't complete the PIE (Point Illustration Explanation) idea. I barely explained anything—leaving out any detail or depth—and most of the explanation I offered was inaccurate or unimportant and unrelated to the neighboring reasoning. I needed to introduce further explanation and tie it together with shared ideas of both the stories. For example, when writing about the use of repetition in Moody's story my analysis read, "This shows the different benchmarks the boys hit while growing up." With virtually no detail the reader is confused on how this shows anything, not even having a chance to worry about its relation to my main claim and the rest of the support. After revision it read, "This phrase is placed before and after the main idea of almost every sentence. Each sentence explains one more event or occasion the twins encounter. They act as benchmarks in a way. Every time they enter the house, they arrive at or have just competed another happening in their life. They enter the house from the point they are brought home as babies, being carried on their parents shoulders, until their father dies tragically and they leave the home permanently." This can be considered a different paragraph instead of a revision, because it is so changed. The entire feeling of my analysis is transformed with the added corrections and ideas and it is now much more effective at explaining what I am trying to say.

In this paragraph, Christopher first identifies an area of his writing that he wanted to analyze: paragraph development. Then, he moves into a brief discussion of his general tendencies, noting that he needed further explanation to tie together his evidence and claims. He offers a concrete example of one of the weaker explanations, explains why he wanted to revise it, and includes the revised sentences. This strategy gives his readers a detailed sense of his process and how he improved in this particular area. To end the paragraph, he offers an explanation for why he changed the paragraph the way he did and what he learned from doing so. Doing this kind of analytical work and crafting well-developed and organized paragraphs will help ensure a successful reflective essay.

Following up on student writing:

- What kind of evidence is Christopher using? How well suited is his evidence to his point?

- What suggestions would you give Christopher if you were peer-reviewing his paper?

Revision

As you revise your essay, keep in mind the goals of this assignment:

- Did you demonstrate an ability to think about your writing and yourself as a writer?

- Did you provide analysis of your experiences, writing assignments, or concepts you have learned?

- Did you provide concrete examples from your own writing (either quotes from your writing or rich descriptions of your writing process)?

- Did you explain why you made certain choices and whether those choices were effective?

Evidence in Reflective Writing

To effectively analyze a particular experience, or your growth as a writer over the course of the semester, it is important to include proper evidence to support your claims. The following list—while certainly not exclusive—represents some of the ways you can include evidence in personal or reflective writing:

- Anecdotes or stories

- Quotes or paraphrases from texts or sources such as this book, *Rules for Writers*, a class handout, or PowerPoint

- Dialogue (perhaps part of a conversation you had with your instructor or peers during office hours, peer review, or class discussion)

- Photos, charts, or illustrations (if appropriate)

As in other writing assignments, make sure to properly introduce your evidence with a signal phrase or other cue for your reader. If appropriate, also explain how your evidence connects to the claims(s) you are making. Chapter 5 contains tips on integrating quotes and evidence.

Tips & Strategies: DRAFTING

Writing Vivid Description

In *On Writing*, Stephen King describes writing as a form of telepathy, a "meeting of the minds" in which an image is transmitted from one person to another. After providing an elaborate description of a strangely painted rabbit in a cage, King writes, "[W]e all see it. I didn't tell you. You didn't ask me. I never opened my mouth and you never opened yours. We're not even in the same year together, let alone the same room… except we are together. We're close" (106). Vivid description and concrete details can bring people closer, creating a moment of telepathy in which an image or a moment travels from one mind to another. Or, as is the case in Dave Eggers' writing, description can carry personality, fostering a connection between author and audience. For example, when looking at San Francisco through Dave Eggers' eyes, the traffic over the Bay Bridge becomes "a string of Christmas lights being pulled slowly, steadily" and foggy mornings in Berkeley are "filmstrip white" (51). His unique descriptions allow readers to experience the city in a new way.

Description becomes especially vivid when an author uses sensory detail to breathe life into places and personalities. For example, in her essay "Words of My Grandmother," UA student Rachel Park doesn't just tell the reader that she felt stuck inside as an eight-year old. Instead, she compares herself to a butterfly in a collector's frame, "stuck, helpless, trapped, and only there because someone wanted me to be there…to gratify its owner with its beauty, and nothing more." Through the use of this metaphor, Rachel creates an emotional connection with her reader. Concrete and sensory details create living moments on the page, moving a reader to see, feel, or experience something differently.

Of course, it is important to keep in mind that there is a fine line between effective detail and description abuse. Unless the description is strategic and purposeful, it can easily clutter your writing. Figurative language (e.g., metaphors and similes) can enliven writing; however, if overdone, the details become roadblocks that interrupt the flow of the writing. Here are some revision tips to help bring your reader closer with vivid description.

1. **Include vivid sensory details:** "his hands were like sandpaper" is more interesting and entertaining than "his hands were dry." Always strive to make interesting connections when you use figurative language.

2. **Use discerning details.** Make sure your descriptive writing differentiates in a way that is informative. If you write, "the automobile has four tires, a steering wheel, and two bumpers," that does not help distinguish the car from any other your reader is likely to encounter. If, however, you describe a sedan with rusted paint, a broken back window, and stained upholstery, it creates a much more vivid picture.

3. **Avoid vague adjectives** such as "interesting," "beautiful," "nice," "good," "bad," or "weird." These words can mean very different things to different people. Your definition of beauty might differ drastically, for instance, from someone else's definition of beauty, so it is best to stay away from these overused words. Instead, aim for more precise adjectives such as "adventurous," "brash," "curious," "unfortunate," or "eccentric."

4. **Keep organized.** One of the biggest mistakes first-year students make in their descriptive writing is being less structured, believing that reflective writing does not have a clear structure. In fact, descriptive writing needs to be extremely organized. For example, the

order in which you offer details impacts how successful your descriptions will be: "The delicate, silver, etched with flowers from you mother's garden antique spoon was so beautiful" is confusing, whereas, "The delicate silver spoon, etched with spring garden flowers, was a stunning antique" includes much of the same detail in a more reader-friendly way.

5. **Keep your purpose in mind.** Remember that you are translating an experience onto the page and not giving a news report. Instead of trying to give your readers a sequential rendering

of events, spend time thinking about which aspects of your story need more description. Should you spend more time describing what it was like to have your mom read to you in bed as a child? Should you pare down on that one scene from your ninth-grade literature classroom and instead summarize it in a sentence? Keep in mind that your readers will assume that highly descriptive language is emphasizing an important moment in the story, so it should be used strategically and mindfully.

Now try your hand at writing vivid description. First, find one sentence from a draft of your personal or reflective essay draft that you would like to revise. Write it here:

Next, eliminate any weak or vague words, decide if anything sounds redundant or unnecessary, and remove any problematical language from the sentence. Rewrite the sentence here:

Now that your sentence is grammatically streamlined, go back through and insert strong, descriptive adjectives and clear, appropriate verbs. Rewrite the sentence one final time:

Lastly, describe the major revisions you did to this sentence that you could do to other sentences in your draft:

- Did you use specific terms and concepts related to writing and the writing process?

Because this is likely the last assignment you will submit in this course, consider this an opportunity to show all that you have learned about the revision process. It may be wise to revisit the revision sections of the previous assignment chapters, Chapter 5, and any other revision activities or peer reviews you did in class and attempt to apply what you learned from those experiences to this writing assignment. Consider working on your draft with a classmate, a friend, or a tutor at the Think Tank.

12.4 Reflection

Reflective writing, like the **academic writing** you composed in this course, is a process—one that calls on your skills in rhetoric and research and requires an openness to the sometimes "messy" process of getting from an idea to a final product. In this chapter, you identified a purpose and audience for your writing, considered your ethos as a writer, and saw that the concepts of analysis can be applied to reflective writing. Before you move on to your next assignment or course, consider the following advice from Dr. Anne-Marie Hall, former director of the UA Writing Program, about the "habits of mind" necessary for writing success in all situations:

> Be curious—desire to know more about your world.
>
> Be open—there are lots of diverse people and ideas and ways of thinking in the world.
>
> Be engaged—find a way to get invested and involved in your own learning.
>
> Be creative—think outside the box—are there new ways you can generate and investigate ideas?
>
> Be persistent—you need to sustain interest in short- and long-term projects.
>
> Be responsible—if you said it or did it, you own it. Think of the consequences of what you do.
>
> Be flexible—college requires you to adapt to new situations and demands.
>
> Think about your own thinking, understand your decisions, and reflect on your work.

- In what ways did your personal or reflective writing engage these habits of mind?

- What challenges did you face in your personal or reflective writing assignment?

- What did you learn about yourself in this assignment? What did you learn about your writing process?

- How can you use the skills and strategies you learned in this chapter in other writing situations?

Works Cited

Eggers, Dave. *A Heartbreaking Work of Staggering Genius*. New York: Vintage, 2001. Print.

King, Stephen. *On Writing: A Memoir of the Craft*. New York: Scribner, 2000. Print.

PART IV

STUDENT WRITING AND AWARDS

Sample Essays

13.1 Essay Contest Information

For over 30 years, the Writing Program has held an essay contest for students enrolled in first-year writing courses. Not only does the contest give instructors the chance to read the year's best essays and students the chance to share their best work, but prize-winning essays often become samples for future students as well. Even if your essay doesn't win a prize, the editors might ask your permission to print it in the next edition of the *Guide* or on the online Teacher's Guide to the *Guide*.

Entering the contest is easy. Go to the Essay Contest Instructions online in the Writing Program section of the English Department website: http://english. arizona.edu/writing-program/student-essay-contest.

The Writing Program accepts essays year-round and judging happens around the middle of each spring semester.

The Hayden-McNeil Difference and Inequality Student Essay Award

The Hayden-McNeil Difference and Inequality Award was established by the University of Arizona Writing Program's Difference and Inequality Committee in 2008. This award recognizes student writing that either explicitly or implicitly brings readers' attention to issues of difference and inequality in the classroom, the individual's experience, the campus, or the world at large. A candidate's essay should demonstrate an awareness of the D&I Committee's main objectives, even though the essay may not have been written with those objectives specifically in mind. **This year's winner is Joshua Ambre for his essay "Wordplay Before Foreplay: Rhetoric's Role in Sex Ed Curricula."**

Winners of the Annual First-Year Writing Essay Contest

13.3 Textual Analysis

First Prize: **Alec Coles**, "Dreaming of the Demon: A Visual Analysis of *The Nightmare.*" *Instructor Elizabeth Labiner* (page 265)

13.4 Literacy Narrative

First Prize: **Katherine Scarafiotti,** "Finding a Voice Through Tragedy." *Instructor Sarah Wilhoit* (page 268)

13.5 Text-in-Context

First Prize: **Trudy Eaton,** "The Revolution and Evolution of Love." *Instructor Christine Wald-Hopkins* (page 271)

First Prize (Honors): **Jennifer LaMoureaux,** "The Power of Myth and Naming in Defining Communal Identity." *Instructor Emily Lyons* (page 274)

13.6 Rhetorical Analysis

First Prize: **Mikayla Gerdes-Morgan,** "Wanted: Emotional Response for the End of Sex-Trafficking." *Instructor Maria Conti* (page 277)

First Prize (Difference and Inequality): **Joshua Ambre,** "Wordplay Before Foreplay: Rhetoric's Role in Sex Ed Curricula." *Instructor Casely Coan* (page 280)

13.7 Controversy Analysis

First Prize: **Andrea Fulgham,** "The Great Corn (Syrup) Debate." *Instructor Nicholas Greer* (page 284)

13.8 Public Argument

First Prize: **Steven Chin,** "Along the Border of Free Speech." *Instructor Katherine Standefer* (page 290)

13.9 Reflective

First Prize: **Joshua Rubin Abrams,** "The Art of Being." *Instructor Matthew Kundert* (page 294)

We want to thank the talented judges who helped with this year's contest:

Daniel Bernal	Maureen McHugh
Rachel Buck	Ted McLoof
Sylvia Chan	Miguel Angel Ramirez
Casely Coan	Joanna Sanchez-Avila
Krista Ferguson	Jenny Slinkard
Jenna Altherr Flores	Clare Sudak
Sarah Fredericks	Jessamyn Swan
Rafael Gonzalez	Sarah Wilhoit
Al Harahap	Kimberly Wine
Elizabeth Labiner	

13.2 Sample Essays: An Overview

This chapter includes essays created by first-year writing students at the University of Arizona. You can approach the student work included in this chapter in a number of different ways. Like most writing, the samples found here contain features to emulate and learn from, as well as areas that could be improved with further revision. Consider them samples rather than models; if a "model" can be seen as providing a formula to follow (write exactly like this and you'll get an "A"), "samples" encourage you to identify the different choices made by different writers so that you can examine what works well and what could work better. To this end, we have not corrected any spelling, grammar, or Works Cited errors in the student essays, nor made changes to larger global concerns. This choice was deliberate; we believe that these samples provide a great opportunity to look at what worked, what mechanical errors were made, and what can be revised. Because they accurately reflect student writing as submitted to instructors, you can critically engage with the essays to help you think through writing choices, revision strategies, and different genres.

Since students from first-year writing classes at the University of Arizona provided these samples, the essays featured in this chapter reflect the shared assumptions and course guidelines adhered to by the UA Writing Program. However, the writing represents the fact that individual instructors tailor each essay assignment to fulfill slightly different visions of the course or to meet criteria representing different emphases. For example, some instructors may ask students to work with films and focus on visual analysis, while others focus on analysis of written texts, and still others might ask for autobiographical writing as a way to analyze identity or culture. Given this set of considerations, students will have individualized responses to a particular assignment. Like these writers, you will need to be aware of your own particular situation as you set out to produce writing appropriate for your class.

As you read the sample essays, examine the choices each author has made and consider what you might do differently or what you might try to emulate in your own writing.

Here is a list of questions to ask yourself as you examine each of the sample student essays:

- How does the author introduce the topic of the essay or project? Is it broad or specific? How does that lead into the thesis/point?

- Is the thesis explicitly stated ("This paper argues…") or implied (the claim of the paper becomes clear but is not directly spelled out at the beginning)? Where is the main idea presented and how is it communicated to the reader?

- How do language and style work in the essay? Are sentence lengths and word choices effective? Are there any places where language and style break down or distract from the essay's purpose/meaning? How would you revise those sections?

- As you are reading, do you notice how the author transitions between paragraphs/sentences? How does the author link ideas? Are there any places that the transition is abrupt or does not exist? How might you revise the paper so that the connections between ideas are clearer?

- How does the author use evidence? How are quotations or paraphrases introduced and integrated into the paper? Do you find the evidence useful in supporting the main idea of the essay?

- Does the conclusion of the essay simply restate the introduction or does it suggest any larger implications that open up as a result of the research/writing? How would you revise the conclusion?

In addition to these questions, your instructor may want you to look at how an essay fits (or does not fit) a particular assignment. You may also notice strengths or weaknesses in a paper that we do not prompt you to notice. When you notice something interesting, bring it up in classroom conversations; show your peers and instructors what you noticed so that you can start to think through how you can respond to these observations in your own writing choices. This is what the student essays are about: helping you to become a stronger writer by learning from what others have done and adapting these lessons to suit your own writing purposes.

13.3 Textual Analysis

Dreaming of the Demon: A Visual Analysis of *The Nightmare*

By Alec Coles

Henry Fuseli, was notorious for his vulgar and unusually terrifying paintings. Heavily contrasting with the early romanticism of landscapes and portraits other artists created during his time, Fuseli, 1741–1825, focused his career on the world of the supernatural and freakish. One of the most well known of these paintings is *The Nightmare*; the painting portrays a dark chamber, in which a ghoulish creature is sitting atop the body of a seemingly lifeless woman, with his companion, an eyeless horse, standing behind them. In *The Nightmare*, Henry Fuseli utilizes dark images, striking colors and juxtaposition of character to depict the nightmare of the loss of innocence.

The first image of horror is found in the creature on top of the woman. Through the use of an almost identical creature in Fuseli's other works, such as *Incubus Leaving Two Sleeping Women*, it can be inferred by the audience that the creature in *The Nightmare* is, in fact, an incubus. The incubus, or imp, is a devilish creature in medieval folklore that preys upon sleeping women, and robs them of their virginity while in their slumber. Derived from the Latin terms "incubo" and "incubare," the word can be ultimately broken down to be defined as a "nightmare" that "lies upon the sleeper" (Online Etymology Dictionary). Described to "impede respiration and all voluntary motion," the incubus instilled terror in the masses with its threat of sexual violence and "untimely suffocation" during one's sleep (Waller 10). The incubus demon became a symbol of fear, causing the "approach of night a cause of terror" and making "life itself miserable" for its potential victims (Waller 9). The image of the incubus is strategically used by Fuseli to set the grim, threatening tone of the painting. In addition, Fuseli creates an emphasis on the imp by placing him as the most centric image in the painting. By positioning the sexual predator above the sleeping woman, Fuseli suggests the power of the imp over the woman in the current scene, further implementing the subconscious notion of an attacker. The use of an animalistic and threatening creature suggests the immediate presence of evil in the woman's chamber. This strong sense of danger contributes to the nightmare of the loss of innocence that Fuseli is depicting.

The demonic incubus is further supported by the black horse, which is another dark image used by Fuseli to portray the horror in his painting. The horse's coat is a jet black. As a color, black is symbolic of the dark, simultaneously representing sinful and malevolent behaviors or circumstances. In conjunction with the horse's coat, Fuseli gives the horse opaque eyes that seem lifeless. The eerie image of the eyes, and the black coloring, suggest that the horse in the painting has a negative connotation. In folklore, the black horse is a known companion of the incubus. Through this knowledge, as well as their dark coloring and crude characteristics, it can be inferred that the incubus and his steed are sinister in nature. Fuseli utilizes the demonic duo's presence in the depicted scene to portray a mood of terror and evil. The evil pairing, and their appearance in the bedroom, suggests their motivation to steal the innocence of the woman.

Fuseli develops the mood further with the colors he utilizes in depicting the sleeping woman. The woman in the painting is clad in a white night gown. White is a color that is used to symbolize purity and innocence, as well as suggesting at virginity. White is also symbolic of the light, or the good, that can be discovered within the world, especially within religious affiliations. By showing the woman clad in a gown of white, Fuseli indicates that the woman in his painting is therefore good in nature, and is symbolic of an angelic presence. Through this, Fuseli portrays her as the protagonist counterpart of the incubus. The pairing of the innocent woman in white and the contrasting darker images such as the imp and the horse further envelops the sense of peril in the scene; the evil characters in the painting are creeping up to the woman in white, implying the takeover of the goodness within the woman.

Color is further used to suggest a dangerous mood through the red blanket. Located on the bed in which the woman in laying, the painting depicts a red blanket that has been draped over the woman's midriff, and sweeps over the side of the bed to the floor. The red is a striking contrast to the monochromatic background setting surrounding it, drawing further focus to the blanket and the woman beneath it. However, the positioning of the blanket begins beneath the woman's bosom and cascades to the floor. The pairing of the movement-like qualities and the crimson coloring of the cloth makes the blanket suggestive of blood. The presence of blood symbolism in the painting further indicates the horror of the painting. Through blood surrounding the lifeless woman, an inference of death and murder can be derived. The end of the woman's life in the painting essentially recreates the termination of the goodness within the scene, further developing Fuseli's nightmare.

Fuseli displays juxtaposition of character through his use of lines in his painting. When illustrating the sleeping woman, Fuseli uses stark, hard lines to create a definitive shape. This representation of the woman presents an image of the female anatomy that viewers can easily identify and recognize. This is contrasted with the lines used to exemplify the incubus. Fuseli leaves half of the incubus shrouded in shadows, while allowing the rest of the incubus to be drawn with softer, indistinct lines. The imprecision of the incubus's form creates an aura of mystery and allusion for the creature. This effect creates an unnerving mood for the piece. While the viewer is familiar with the image of the woman, the strange visage of the incubus is psychologically uncomforting. By implementing a creature of unknown origin, and further veiling its appearance to the viewer, Fuseli's monster creates an innate feeling of fear. This visceral reaction augments the impression of sexual violence that is presented by the incubus's presence.

Fuseli's combination of color and character creates further juxtaposition that expresses a darker theme of the work. The contrast between the colors used in the characters, as well as the opposition of the symbolism suggested by their images, shows a struggle between two ideologies. Showcasing the sleeping woman in white as the protagonist, and the black incubus as the antagonist, both the literal and figurative light and dark of the characters is used to draw parallels between the battle between good and evil. The demonic nature of the incubus and the purity of the woman can produce inherent reactions from viewers who hold religious affiliations, especially that of the Christian belief. Reputable in medieval folklore for being "sent by the Devil," the incubus is used as a satanic tool to "frighten, tempt, and contaminate the righteous" (Edwards & McClenon 8). The painting suggests the overcoming of sin above righteousness, manifested in the power the imp holds over the woman. The amorous horror in the scene and the themes presented in the painting strike viewers as terrifying or unsettling. The mood is further developed by the thematic elements suggested by the colors and images in the painting.

In Henry Fuseli's *The Nightmare*, Fuseli uses images, lines and color to portray a mood of horror in the painting, perpetuating the nightmare of the loss of innocence within oneself. The use of color and images dictates the scene, and give indications of characters, their motivations, as well as larger themes of the piece as a whole. The notions of good versus evil, sin versus virtue, and the domination of hell over humans lend themselves to much darker messages than the typical painting in Fuseli's era. As an artist, Fuseli was reputable for these paintings that held complex themes. Because of this, it can be inferred that Fuseli used his art as way to challenge the societal norms of artistic creation.

Works Cited

Fuseli, Henry. *The Nightmare*. 1781. Switzerland. Detroit Institute of the Arts.

Fuseli, Henry. *Incubus Leaving Two Sleeping Women*. 1810. Zurich. Web.

"Incubus." Online Etymology Dictionary. Douglas Harper, Historian. 07 Dec. 2014.

McClenon, James, and Emily D. Edwards. "The Incubus in Film, Experience, and Folklore." Southern Folklore 52.1 (1996): 3-18.

Waller, John Augustine. *A Treatise on the Incubus, Or, Nightmare, Disturbed Sleep, Terrific Dreams, and Nocturnal Visions; with the Means of Removing These Distressing Complaints*. London: Cox, 1816. Print.

13.4 Literacy Narrative

Finding a Voice Through Tragedy

By Katherine Scarafiotti

I always took for granted the fact that I could communicate with the world around me. It wasn't until I was faced with the choice to speak that I understood how important communication with one another is. For months I remained silent and void of the world around me. My only sense of language happened to be writings in a small leather journal embossed with a tree on the cover. In time my words that once only belonged on a journal page wanted to belong in the world. The words within my soul begged and pleaded to escape. It was through learning to heal in the form of writing, which helped me to speak again.

"I love you and always will, but I'm not ready for this, you'll end up being a great mother". Those were the last words I heard before I felt my body jolt forward, watched the phone fly out of my hands, and felt my head slam into the steering wheel. Time froze and darkness consumed my vision. I'm unaware exactly how long life was a big black abyss for me. All I know is the next sign of life I remember was the sound of panicked voices and sirens in the distance. I felt a warm sticky wet substance drip down my forehead and the taste of iron stained my bottom lip. A tingling sensation swept across my body and a sharp pain, unlike anything I had experienced in my life, stabbed my stomach. "Can you hear me?" questioned a man in what looked to be a white buttoned up shirt. Well I thought I could hear him, though I wasn't quite sure what was going on. I drifted in and out of consciousness. I heard a mix of words that I didn't understand, and I saw flashes of people I didn't recognize. I finally woke up to the steady beeping of machines, the feeling of cords coming out of every inch of my body, and white walls surrounding me. I didn't need the doctors to explain the pain I was feeling. I knew in my heart that a piece of me was gone, the piece that made me whole. In that moment I lost my voice along with my little girl.

When someone would come in to communicate with me, to see if I had made any progress, I would simply shut his or her voice out. When I wouldn't answer, he or she would simply leave me alone. I spent a week in the hospital completely withdrawn to all that happened around me. No words dared to escape my mouth. Family and friends would visit me on a daily basis claiming all the memories of that dreadful night would slowly fade away and in time I would become healthy again. I tuned everything they were saying out. However, things didn't improve once I was discharged even though I knew the people around me wanted it to so desperately. A month passed by and the most I had accomplished was lying in bed and taking a shower. Every day was the same. I would sleep till three in the afternoon, eat lunch, or at least attempt to, and then resume sleeping. After the month passed and nothing changed, my parents thought going back to school was the best option for me. Going to school would get me out of the house and hopefully my friends would break the barrier that engulfed me. However, every morning when they would wake me I would remain in bed. This went on for another month. I spent a total of two months away from school, and it wasn't looking like passing junior year was going to happen. The time came when my parents could no longer bear to see me withering away. So, with lots of hesitation from me, I was sent to a therapist.

I sat there staring at the perfect room in front of me where not a single item was out of place. I, however, was nowhere near being as put together as the room I was sitting in. It took all my parents had to get me out of bed. So, it was no surprise that my hair was sticking out in every direction and my clothes were mismatched. I felt like a huge contradiction being in this beautiful room when I was exactly the opposite of that. The woman who emerged into the room seemed nothing less than perfect. The suit she wore appeared tailored to fit her slim body, her hair was neatly pinned back in a bun, and her makeup was applied flawlessly. No wonder this woman helped others with their problems for a living since, on the outside, it looked like she had none. She sat poised in the black leather chair across from me. She didn't ask for me to talk because she knew I didn't want to. She instead handed me a small book with blank white pages and proceeded to explain to me what it was intended for. After the accident I refused to talk and that set me back on my healing process. This new book, with a beautifully engraved tree on the cover, would contain every hurtful memory that I wasn't able to verbalize. She explained that if I never let go of the hurt I'd never be able to move on to the future. After my session I left with the book, which burned a hole through my hand. The need to write was strong. So, each new day I would make sure to write a new page.

Surprisingly the more I wrote the better I felt about what happened that night. Even if on some days it seemed hard to formulate my thoughts into words. The once blank pages were now filled with black ink. Had someone decided to read the writings, within the binding, they would know everything about me. My faults, my depressing thoughts, my weaknesses, my joys, my loves, and everything else I felt on a daily basis. They'd have a play-by-play on who I am, which at times was scary to think about. Writing was my escape until one day when I came to a realization. This was ultimately the realization that brought me back to the real world.

I had finally realized just how much my silence was hurting my parents, my friends, and myself. It was stopping me from growing. In that moment I knew I had to find my parents and explain this new revelation. When I saw their faces looking so down and defeated I knew that the simplest of words would make them happy. "I'm sorry" was all I could bring myself to say, but it was those simple words that changed everything. The light in my parent's eyes had retuned. In that moment of silence all of us had come to the conclusion that things were going to get better and this was the start. As days passed the more my vocabulary expanded. It went from simple phrases like " thank you" to carrying out conversations. Before I knew it I was back in school making the grades I needed to pass my junior year. By the time summer came I had made up all my missing work and things at home were going smoothly. Life seemed livable and I was on the path to becoming healthy.

The people around me saw the change, along with the growth, I was making. Even if on some days it seemed hard to notice this change within myself. Though I couldn't see the change, the administration at my school did. They believed that since I was able to overcome the challenge it would be inspiring for the rest of the student body. The dean of students thought the best way to inspire people was with a talk, and so he proposed a speech. Of course I had a different outlook on the situation, and wasn't quite sure if a speech in front of 300 students was plausible for me. I mean here I was just learning how to talk to my family and close friends. How did they expect me to talk to 300 strangers about a tragedy that tore me up on the inside every time I thought about it? The answer to me was simple, no.

With lots of persuading, and I mean lots, my school finally got me to accept giving the speech. It wasn't completely my choice to go through with it; my therapist thought it would be beneficial for my future development. So, I began to write. Speech after speech I would write and each new one seemed worse than the last. I was at a standstill and had no idea how to write on, or about, a touchy subject as the one in front of me. The more I thought it through the more I realized the problem wasn't necessarily the subject, but in fact the person writing on the subject. I had not fully come to terms with my accident and loss. That is why the speech was so hard to formulate. My challenge had not yet been conquered—I was still fighting it. That is what, in the end, helped me to write the speech. It wasn't the speech everyone thought it would be, but it was the truth.

I cannot just simply forget the night that changed me to the person I am presently. I remember the gruesome details of that night like it happened recently and in reality not two years ago. The scars that tagged my body, like an unwanted tattoo, may have slowly healed in time, but the scar on my heart still leaves an imprint that will remain there forever. I wish I could say it's easy healing, like all the others told me it was, but that would be a lie. Healing is the most challenging aspect of life because it means forgiving the mistakes made and learning to live with them. I never expected to watch my life fall apart right in front of my eyes but it only took milliseconds. My focus was momentarily impaired and I lost the most precious gift of all. I didn't just lose one person that night, I also lost myself. However, with every word I wrote on paper my heart slowly began to heal and my voice found its way out. There was no more hiding and feeling sorry for myself. I realized that being able to speak is a gift that some people never get to experience and no one should take it for granted. I am a woman with a newfound voice after a year of living in silence and depression. I have a voice and I use it because my little girl never got the chance to use hers.

13.5 Text-in-Context

The Revolution and Evolution of Love

By Trudy Eaton

Spearheaded by the Supreme Court decisions in the lawsuits *Lawrence and Garner v. Texas* and *Goodridge v. Department of Public Health*, the Lesbian Gay Bisexual and Transgender (LGBT) community made great strides towards marriage equality in the early 2000's. In the *Lawrence* (2003) decision, the Supreme Court struck down a Texas sodomy law therefore legalizing homosexual activity in the U.S. and its territories. Five months later, the Supreme Court decided in *Goodridge v. Department of Public Health* that state law did not have the power to deny same-sex marriages—this decision marked the first Supreme Court ruling on behalf of same-sex couples' right to marriage. However, with a majority in Congress and the power of the presidency (Congress Profiles), Republicans were able to block the progressive actions of the courts until the Supreme Court directly confronted the issue of same-sex rights a decade later.

Elliot Ruchowitz-Roberts' poem "Revolution," written in celebration of a friend's same-sex marriage in February of 2004, sheds light on the issue of same-sex equality. The early 2000's were a time characterized by a growing liberal society, exemplified by the increase of literature on the topic, controlled by a conservative government that desperately clung to ideologies of the past. Though stifled by congressional actions, progress towards equality was made through the previously mentioned Supreme Court decisions and expanding readiness of liberal groups to find solutions to the discrimination against homosexuals. These actions opened the discussion of same-sex rights and began the decade long drive for equality. With hope and courage, Ruchowitz-Roberts seized the opportunity to chime in and reveal his support for same-sex equality in his poem "Revolution." The poet develops his purpose through an extended metaphor stemming from his idea of "love as revolution's heart" (line 5); utilizing a double meaning of the term "revolution" regarding the emotional effects of love, and an ultimately optimistic tone to convey to the reader the scale of impact they possess and to encourage them to employ their power to enact change.

The extended metaphor that comes to fruition in the second stanza with the line: "love as revolution's heart," allows the poet to make claims about human dependency on love (line 5). Inspired by the concept of gravity and its effect on Earth's rotation, Ruchowitz-Roberts makes the connection between the revolving world and how love can keep humans "revolving" (line 7). Love, the author writes, is the greatest freedom humans can experience if they "open themselves" to it, yet the gay community, who want to experience love, are not allowed to express and share their love freely due to social constraints (line 22). Embedded within the piece are the similarities between love and the effects of gravity; the pull to be near to loved ones as the Sun exerts control on the Earth to stay in orbit, the head-spinning emotions that can mimic the weightlessness of zero gravity, and the motivation for humans to continue the same cycles as the Sun rises in the east every morning. Ruchowitz-Roberts presents the argument that love is why humans wake up each day—an idea that without love humans would die in bitter darkness cradling "rage and hatred," (line 1) never able to experience being "bathed in light" or the warmth of love (line 14). It is this, a miserable, terrifying thought of loneliness that the author utilizes to inspire his audience to allow themselves to fall into the unparalleled effects of love and to fight for equality for every person to share this experience. The poet believes that his readers will better understand why the LGBT community has fought relentlessly for the past decade for the right to marriage and the right to express their love by experiencing love personally. In this understanding of the love and the power each person obtains in deciding to support or oppose the equality of love, the poet hopes that his audience will respect and aid in the continued protest for same-sex rights.

Revolution is key to the author's argument concerning love and same-sex marriage. Through multiple contextualizations of the word "revolution" the author is able to examine lighter and heavier emotional levels in the fight for equality. The first contextualization, the idea of an orbital revolution, was explored in the previous paragraph in relation to gravity. However, the second contextualization, revolution as a forcible overthrow of government, carries a much heavier emotional burden, evoking mental images of the blood and passion thick enough to spark wars. While the rotational definition of "revolution" explained briefly the feelings of being in love, the extreme passion of forcible revolution is applicable to the struggles same-sex couples have encountered in the attempt to gain equal marital rights. For decades, homosexuals have experienced the extremes of social ostracism and intense physical and verbal abuse; forced to fight everyday to be tolerated in an unaccepting society that fears and shames anything dissimilar. Ruchowitz-Roberts argues that the LGBT community cannot combat the intolerance aimed at them with violence but instead should exemplify the acceptance and love they wish to receive. He writes, "yours is not a revolt but a revolving," explaining his idea that the affection that buds from the LTGB community will breed further acceptance in society until there is no distinction between heterosexual and homosexual love (line 6). Revolution, in its second meaning, requires passion and willingness to sacrifice old beliefs for new ones. The poet is not suggesting physical violence, but he is pushing his audience to fight against social norms that lack validity and accept others because he believes "all people who open themselves to love" deserve to be proud and joyous about their love (line 22). While "revolution" evokes greatly different emotions depending on the word's connotation, both responses of "spinning" and "whirling" associated with rotation and the rushing passion that brings about change are central to the human experience of love (lines 26, 27).

In 2004, Ruchowitz-Roberts identified a change in the culture around him; society was willing to discuss the issue of same sex equality, a significant contrast from previous eras—and with the Supreme Court's support, the author believed real social change towards equality could be possible, the poet clearly joined his friends in the fight for a legal and social acceptance of their love when he stated, "your love turns our world on its axis" (line 13); a bold statement that same-sex love is not abnormal and its power can drive the world round as naturally as gravity can. Similarly, in the third stanza the poet celebrates the two women and the gay and lesbian communities for their bravery to stand against cultural norms saying, "here's to love that makes history" (lines 15, 16). This statement stands as an encouragement to his audience to stand alongside these men and women to bring about change. Love broadens a person's perspective of the world; it can overthrow previous ideas, changing the outlook people carry through their life. The poet believes the power of love is strong enough to change protesters' opinions and bring about social change; that is why he challenges his audience to seek love personally. He is optimistic that if his readers feel love's effects, they will understand the LGBT community's motivation in the continued fight for acceptance and aid the community's call for a universal respect of all forms of love.

Ruchowitz-Roberts ends the poem with a hopeful vision for the "revolution of love" established through the revelations he makes regarding the "tangible freedom of spirit…dictatorship of the heart…and power to all people who open themselves to love" (lines 21, 22). The previous quote mimics the third line of his poem in which Ruchowitz-Roberts labels the ideals of freedom, dictatorship, and power as "pristine and unattainable" (line 2). However, the abstract ideals become "tangible" in the last lines, signaling the change Ruchowitz-Roberts has identified previously as the gay community moves closer to equality. The poet also described the acceptance of same-sex marriage and love as "bring[ing] such joy to our hearts" (line 17); a joy of seeing two hearts promise everything to each other for forever. Ruchowitz-Roberts argues against the conservative view that gay people should be excluded from creating that happiness. But now, power lies in "all people who open themselves to love" and those who lead with hatred will be overthrown and forgotten (line 22).

Through various literary tools the author is able to convey huge ideas about abstracts such as love and equality in such a short text. The extended metaphor praises same-sex couples and their drive to receive equal rights as the double meaning within the poem reveals the various aspects of love. Ten years after Ruchowitz-Roberts penned "Revolution," same-sex marriage is still not recognized nationally in the United States. But the same passion and love that began the revolution in 2004, burned fervently in 2014. The poet encourages the same-sex community and its allies to continue fighting to be the "love [at] revolution's heart" (line 5).

Works Cited

"Congress Profiles | US House of Representatives: History, Art & Archives." *Congressional Profiles*. History, Art, & Archives, n.d. Web. 27 Oct. 2014. <http://history.house.gov/Congressional-Overview/Profiles/108th/>.

"Goodridge v. Department of Public Health." *Wikipedia*. Wikimedia Foundation, Web. 20 Oct. 2014. <http://en.wikipedia.org/wiki/Goodridge_v._Department_of_Public_Health>.

"LAWRENCE AND GARNER v. TEXAS." *Lawrence and Garner v. Texas*. N.p., n.d. Web. 26 Oct. 2014. <http://www.oyez.org/cases/2000-2009/2002/2002_02_102>.

Ruchowitz-Roberts, Elliot. "Revolution" *Fire and Ink: An Anthology of Social Action Writing*. By Frances Payne Adler, Debra Busman, and Diana García. Tucson: U of Arizona, 2009. 346. Print.

The Power of Myth and Naming in Defining Communal Identity

By Jennifer LaMoureaux

In his essay, "Aztlan: A Homeland Without Boundaries," Rudolfo A. Anaya details the value of ceremonial naming for defining and unifying a nation. While Anaya's essay specifically addresses the ceremony of naming that took place in the southwestern United States in the late 1960s when the Chicano community named Aztlan as its homeland, Anaya more generally defines a naming ceremony as the expression of any self-defined group's history, identity and purpose. Says Anaya, "The politicians of the group may describe political relationships and symbols, but it is the artist who gives deeper and long-lasting expression to a people's sense of nation and destiny" (230). In applying this viewpoint to Ansel Adams' photograph, "Grand Canyon National Park" (1941), a deeper understanding of the image's power over, and value for, the collective American psyche emerges. Contracted by the Department of the Interior just prior to America's official involvement in World War II to photograph America's National Parks, Adams managed to capture, or, more precisely, create an iconic vision of America as both wild and honorable at a time when, following the Depression and heading toward war, the country was in need of redefinition. In doing so, he re-imagined (renamed) his country as surely as the Indohispanic community named Aztlan. A closer look at the works of Anaya and Adams will show that, despite their differences in backgrounds and methodologies, both Adams and the Aztlan Movement embraced the power of myth and legend to infuse their compatriots with renewed pride and sense of purpose.

"Various circumstances create the need for national or tribal definition and unity," writes Anaya. "The group may acquire cohesion and a feeling of nationhood in times of threat..." (230). In this statement, Anaya explains the necessity of a renaming. For the Indohispanic community of the late 1960s, the threat was not physical *per se*. Rather it was the fear of extinction through assimilation. Without a conscious effort to preserve their nation, the Indohispanos were doomed to exist as a tourist commodity, "…admired for its quaint folkways but not taken seriously by the world of nations" (233). For Adams, in 1941, the threat was, indeed, physical. America was on the brink of war; the world was full of uncertainty. In the eternal and majestic landscape that is Adams' Grand Canyon, however, one senses a moral universe, rugged, uncompromising, and incorruptible. Though there are gradations of gray, the predominant *feel* is of a black and white universe, a metaphorical representation of right and wrong. The balance is perfect, like the scales of justice. One can almost hear that most American of phrases, "In God We Trust." America, as represented by this balanced but boundless image, is the answer to the time's uncertainty: America, like her landscape, is timeless. She will prevail against peril. Thus, it can be seen that it was this *national peril* for both the Indohispano community of the 1960s and post-Depression/pre-war America, which gave rise to the need for redefinition for each.

"The naming ceremony creates a real sense of nation, for it fuses the spiritual and political aspirations of a group and provides a vision of the group's role in history" (230). Here, Anaya explains the purpose of a naming. For the Mexican-American community of the 1960s, the naming ceremony helped to bond the group at a time when its new awareness of self demanded a need for self-definition. By naming the group, it became a single entity that could use its formerly diffuse energy in a concerted direction. In looking at Adams' Grand Canyon, one initially finds a carved landscape. Like the Mexican-American community pre-Chicano, post-Depression/pre-war America was psychically scattered. A unification in both cases was required. Necessarily, though Adams' canyon winds, he chooses a perspective that allows the viewer to follow its course. A clearly defined path emerges despite the dangerous terrain. (With war approaching, America was also carving her niche in the world.) The canyon's steep walls drop into bottomless crevasses; one false step would mean disaster. The white quartz caps of the mountains, however, appear as cairns marking the trail. The journey is immense. The viewer cannot see the end of the canyon in any direction of the photograph. Emotionally, however, there is no question as to what direction to follow; the viewer's eye cannot help but follow the winding course marked by the canyon walls. There is unity in this singular path whether or not one can see the end of it. It is this unification of spirit that allows the individual to approach the daunting task ahead, to tread through this dangerous landscape. Anaya echoes this sentiment of the individual being empowered by the unity of the group when he writes, "…the naming ceremony was reenacted wherever Chicanos met to discuss their common destiny" (231). Thus, the purpose of the naming: an agreement to proceed as one nation with a common destiny.

Finding the commonality, choosing the name or icon, is critical to the success of the unification. Writes Anaya, "For too long the Indohispano community had projected only its Spanish history and heritage… It was in Mesoamerica that we rediscovered the legend of Aztlan, a story of mythic proportions, rooted as it was in the tribal memory of the Aztecs" (234). Of note is that the Grand Canyon winds through the same southwestern region of the United States as the mythical Aztlan, and looking at the sheer scale of landscape as depicted by Adams, the viewer cannot help but be awed. Of equal note is the fact that Adams' depiction is as much a creation as any mythological tale. Seemingly naturalistic at first sight, Adams' landscape is artificially created with filters and processing manipulations to produce heightened contrasts, darker shadows, brighter whites, which is to say, a scene which does not actually appear in nature, but, rather in the heart and mind of its creator. It speaks to Adams' skill that, for many Americans, this mythical creation has become fact, the iconic image brought to mind whenever the name "Grand Canyon" is spoken. In parallel fashion, Anaya writes, "Yes, there was a real Aztlan, but there was also the spiritual Aztlan, the place of the covenant with the gods, the psychological center of our Indian history" (236). "Those of us who saw the potential of myth as truth, or myth as self-knowledge, argued that it was indigenous America that held the tap root of our history; its mythology was the mirror by which to know ourselves" (238). Adams' portrayal of the Grand Canyon similarly reflects America's vision of her best self: beautiful, but rugged; tough, but fair; free, but disciplined. The stern but generous hand of a sublime force, a force that resides in *our homeland*, is clearly apparent in the ever-receding, never-ending vistas, and immeasurable depths within the canyon walls. Adams' Grand Canyon, like Aztlan, exists in mythical time as well as historical time, the former of which, as Anaya points out, is continuous. Despite differences in race, culture and eras, these two intentionally manufactured ideas represent and address "...the need for homeland inherent in the collective memory of any group" (239). The *intentionality* of these ideas further reflects Anaya's belief that during certain stages of communal awareness, a group may create the context of its destiny in time. Quoting Miguel Leon-Portilla, the renowned Mexican philosopher, Anaya asserts that the group becomes, "'senores [masters] of their own time'" (233).

"Myth," explains Anaya, "is our umbilical connection to the past, to the shared collective memory" (236). Through myth, a nation may access the noblest aspects of its character thereby releasing, "...a chain reaction of new energy, initiative and originality" (240). He goes on to say, "The spiritual yearning for homeland is encompassing, but because the geography of the earth is limited, homelands rub against each other and create friction. We have not yet moved to a new consciousness where the Earth truly becomes the homeland of everyone" (239). This move to an inclusive homeland, however, is Anaya's true vision. "This is a most difficult proposal," writes Anaya, "the idea that we can move beyond our ethnocentric boundaries, that we can envision the limitation of ethnicity even as we extol our self pride" (241). In Aztlan, the legend goes, the seven tribes emerged from the seven caves of a mountain. This introductory line of the fable could be substituted into one of a thousand similar tales embedded in all cultures and times. That is the nature of myth, its universality. Adams, as apparent in "Grand Canyon National Park" believed in capturing the mythical, eternal quality of nature: adjectives for the work include darkest, brightest, boundless, bottomless, edgeless, limitless—all superlatives which matches Anaya's description of Aztlan in its, "mythic proportions." Though Adams created this iconic image of the Grand Canyon for the United States government at a time when the country needed unification to face a common enemy, his understanding of the power of myth allowed the image to transcend its original purpose. Any human being on the planet could look at this Grand landscape and say, "Look at the majesty of Earth, my home." It is that very conception which is Anaya's Aztlan.

Works Cited

Adams, Ansel. *Grand Canyon National Park*. 1941. National Archives, Washington D.C. Archives.gov. Web. 20 October 2014

Anaya, Rudolfo A. "Aztlan: A Homeland Without Boundaries." Anaya, Rudolfo A., and Francisco Lomeli. *Aztlan: Essays on the Chicano Homeland*. 1991. New Mexico: El Norte Publications/Academia UNM Press edition, 1998. 230-41. Print.

13.6 Rhetorical Analysis

Wanted: Emotional Response for the End of Sex-Trafficking

By Mikayla Gerdes-Morgan

Human sex-trafficking, referred to as modern day's slave trade, has become a multi-billion dollar industry (Nolot). It thrives on the exploitation of individuals, especially women, and traffickers use these individuals as commodity in their trade of "business." *Nefarious: Merchant of Souls* (2011), a documentary produced and written by Benjamin Nolot, brings insight to what human sex-trafficking is, as well as how sex-trafficking affects the individuals directly within the system. Through the use of reenactments and cinematography, Nolot effectively illustrates the dire need for the cessation of human sex-trafficking and appeals to his viewers' emotions.

When describing the lives of victims to human sex-trafficking, Nolot dramatically appeals to his viewers' emotions, for he displays images of these victims being used and labeled as material or capital objects. For example, Nolot successfully uses dramatized reenactments to portray how traffickers dehumanize their victims when they purchase them from the black market. In this scenario, girls are shown walking down a "runway" as owners of trafficking companies observe these girls from seats nearby. This take on runway paints a façade over the entire scene, for a fashion show is typically used as a means for selling clothing; however, in the sex-trafficking industry fashion shows consist of the selling of one's body. Thus, this reenactment shocks viewers because fashion shows are no longer representations of an accepted common practice, but instead a means of dominant control and a way to exploit someone's body in a negative manner. Nolot furthers this emotional appeal by simultaneously incorporating a metaphorical comparison to evoke the dehumanization of sex-trafficking victims. He states that sex-trafficking victims are treated worse than dogs, for the dogs are taken out three times a day; whereas, the victims are forced to remain in their room like caged animals (Nolot). By using a metaphorical comparison to compare human sex-trafficking victims to dogs, victims are belittled because they are not acknowledged as being equivalent to the majority of the human beings. As a result, the victims' are explicitly displayed as a lesser entity than the trafficker's dogs, emphasizing the ideology that these victims are merely a commodity within the system. By referring to sex-trafficking victims as lesser beings than animals, Nolot is able to appeal to his viewers' emotions because he is able to explicitly depict the hypocrisy of the sex-trafficking industry. Because of this, Nolot is able to bring awareness to this skew in perspective and advocate for the necessity in ending sex-trafficking.

Nolot also appeals to his viewers' emotions in another scenario by including commentary from clinical psychologist and Executive Director for Prostitution Research and Education, Melissa Farley. In doing so, he gives viewers insight on the desperate nature of these victims. She describes that victims will lie down on the ground upon command of their trafficker—similar to a dog. This description becomes the epitome of a power complex, for the victim is willing to follow her trafficker's demands, and as a result, the trafficker is able to extend his absolute control over her (Nolot). Farley's commentary also appeals to the viewer's emotions because the victims are being treated and portrayed as lesser beings when described to behave in a manner similar to a dog. Through the use of explicit dialogue and reenactments to pictorialize the metaphorical comparisons of victims to animals, Nolot effectively brings focus to the violating factors within the industry in an unnerving manner, and resultantly forces his viewer's to strive to make a difference.

Unlike a typical written text, Nolot's video text is also able to incorporate cinematography effects to appeal to the readers' emotion in furthering the conceptual idea of the power complex. For instance, Nolot incorporates a discussion with psychologist and anti-trafficking advocate, Dan Allender, who described the idea that having power over an individual causes that individual to feel as if their only hope for survival is to disconnect from their "engagement with the surrounding world" and experience a "dissociation from reality" (Nolot). In order for a victim to escape the trauma that they have experienced in the surrounding world, they resort more and more into their interior self and leave the exterior world as a means for other people to control. As a result, Nolot portrays the images of a man beating a woman in a narrowing rectangular viewing frame. The camera angle of the scenario pictured in the rectangular frame is from a woman's perspective as she is being beaten, and as Allender describes the concept of "a soul dwindling to invisibility," the rectangular viewing window slowly decreases in size (Nolot). Eventually, this rectangular viewing field fades to blackness, signifying a visual representation of the soul actually dwindling to invisibility because the woman's perspective is no longer visually apparent. Through the incorporation of a diminishing visual field, Nolot is able to appeal to his viewers on an emotional level because the visual field creates the illusion that the viewers' own visual perspective is fading to a sense of invisibility. This allows the viewer to subconsciously connect with the victim being described on a more personal level because they are essentially experiencing a similar haze in dissociation from reality. Consequently, Nolot successfully uses visual appeals as a means of emotional appeal because the images force the viewer to place themselves in the victim's situation, and therefore; see where they are coming from.

In addition to the narrowing rectangular image, Nolot also incorporates the image of a narrowing circle to act as a visual metaphor for a tunnel. In this scene, a previous sex-trafficking victim provides an account on the broken emotional outlook victims experience during their prostitution careers. In doing so, she compares this mindset to being within a tunnel lacking vision—a dead end (Nolot). While the previous sex-trafficking victim elaborates on this last stage of prostitution, accompanied by feelings of absolute despair and depravity, a girl is seen from above sitting on a bedroom floor, leaning against her bed, crying. Simultaneously, the screen's visual field narrows into a circular shape, framed by a black background, as it hones in on the girl and her room. As the scene proceeds, the image of the girl becomes more distant, as if the circular viewing field is travelling further away from the scene. This perspective tool in imaging functions as a visual representation to show that hope in finding a way out of the business—a light out of the tunnel—is diminishing. The diminishing circular lens further supports the previous sex-trafficking victim's commentary as she explains that everything one thought that they could make from prostitution was just a mirage (Nolot). With this commentary, the circle border fades to blackness, a visual representation expressing the blackening of the light at the end of the tunnel. This visual comparison, representing the loss of light (or hope), successfully stands as an emotional appeal towards viewers because it places the viewer in the victim's situation. By having the camera angle looking from above, the viewer is able to look upon the victim from a heightened perspective. Thus the victim is again placed at a lower standing, which appeals to the viewer's empathetic emotions. This drives the viewer to want to help the victim, pull her out of the darkening tunnel, and bring her back into the "light."

Brazenness is the driving force for the documentary because it allows Nolot to create an empathetic emotional response within his viewers. Through his exposure of the maltreatment and emotional despair within sex-trafficking victims, Nolot provokes a desire within his viewers to assist sex-trafficking victims because they are essentially unable to help themselves. By exposing the emotions and situations these sex-trafficking victims experience, Nolot provides reasoning for the need of action and the importance of helping these victims. Additionally,

Nolot proves that sex-trafficking victims deserve a chance at a renewed future by advocating that they are humans too. In doing so, Nolot rehumanizes these victims, proving their equivalence to other human beings around the world. He also provides his viewers justification for having the desire and wish to change the sex-trafficking industry, as well as, a newly developed emotional outlook focused on why change is so imperative. Ending sex-trafficking is by no means an easy task; however, in order to initiate a change, society must take action. Thus, Nolot infuses his documentary with visual appeals to influence his viewers to join together in allegiance and fight for the termination of human sex-trafficking across the globe, as well as, the emancipation of its victims.

Works Cited

Nolot, Benjamin. Nefarious: Merchant of Souls. Exodus Cry, 2011. DVD.

Wordplay Before Foreplay: Rhetoric's Role in Sex Ed Curricula

By Joshua Ambre

Of all the games, sports, and competitive activities that have risen to the height of popularity in today's world, there is one that goes consistently unnoticed: the game of language, otherwise known as rhetoric. Unlike most sports, rhetoric boasts few spectators and many participants, most of whom are completely unaware that they are playing a game at all. However, for those who do count themselves as active participants—politicians, salespeople, lawyers, and countless others—language becomes a tool not only for expressing their own thoughts, but for manipulating the thoughts and actions of others through persuasive techniques and linguistic sleight of hand. Nowhere are the effects of such techniques more apparent than in sex ed curricula, whose sensitive subject matter and immature, adolescent audience render them all the more vulnerable to the already potent influence of rhetoric. Thus, when reading allegedly informative texts like "I Got Game," a sex ed curriculum that attempts to marry sexual abstinence with professional success, it is almost impossible to turn a blind eye to the artifices it employs to achieve its purpose.

In the case of this text, it is perfectly feasible to "judge a book by its cover," so to speak, and still walk away with a comprehensive understanding of its contents. The action shot of the two basketball players vying for control over the ball, coupled with the familiar sex ed jargon that urges the reader to think about "what choices and decisions" they will need to make in order to achieve their goals, is more than enough to drive the author's message home: the message that, in order to attain success, it is necessary to exercise tremendous self-control. Excellent motor control is a necessary attribute of any successful athlete, and by emphasizing the basketball players' *physical* self-control on the court, the text is able to seamlessly transition into why it is equally important for everyone, not just athletes, to exhibit the same degree of *emotional* self-control off the court. The author takes an overt approach to this task by displaying the testimony of NBA superstar A.C. Green in a sprawling script at the bottom of the next page. "I made a decision… I resolved not to be with a woman until I married" (2). Clearly, the author of the text is using Green's reputation to add weight to their argument that abstinence is the only way to exercise self-control. This shameless celebrity endorsement of A.C. Green calls to mind similar endorsements of Olympic athletes on cereal boxes, the only difference being the author's purpose. In the case of the cereal boxes, the goal is to establish a link between the physical fitness of the athlete and the product on which the endorsement appears. In the case of "I Got Game," the goal is to establish a link between A.C. Green's professional success and his practice of sexual abstinence. Given the fact that this particular text was written in 2001, when basketball icons like A.C. Green and Magic Johnson were continuing to grow in popularity, this claim is especially effective. The teenage boys reading the text, many of whom probably idolize athletes like A.C. Green, would be hard-pressed to disregard his advice to save sex until marriage. After all, if abstinence worked for A.C. Green, then by the false causality this text so heavily relies on, how could it not work for them, too?

Directly following the segment on A.C. Green is a story about Tom, a paraplegic who became paralyzed in a car accident after agreeing to ride in the car with a drunk driver. At first glance, this anecdote seems almost comically out of place, but closer inspection reveals that the story was strategically placed in order to highlight the tragic contrast between Tom and A.C. Green. The story about A.C. Green is one of self-driven athleticism, while the story about Tom is one of peer-pressured paralysis. By placing them one after the other, the author insinuates that a person who succumbs to peer pressure will inevitably become like Tom—a person robbed of their mobility in life, completely at the mercy of their body's shortcomings. According to the text, Tom "often thinks about how different his life would be if he had resisted his friends and chosen not to ride in the car that day," (4). Though the author never explicitly states how sex and abstinence fit into the story, the use of the word "resisted" carries various sexual undertones that, combined with the curriculum's overarching theme of abstinence, make the story's underlying message quite clear: failing to remain abstinent will send a person's life spiraling out of control, make them a slave to their libido, and ultimately eliminate every possibility for them to achieve their goals. By the author's skewed logic, a person who has pre-marital sex might as well be paralyzed because, either way, they will have virtually no control over their body and its desires. On the other hand, a person who remains in control over their body through abstinence will become like A.C. Green: a successful, popular, and incredibly talented individual. Of course, the author fails to account for the fact that the rest of the Lakers, many of whom are just as successful as Green, were able to achieve their goals without abstaining from sex. Evidently, the author assumes that the implications of this logical fallacy will be lost on the text's audience, which they assume to be a bunch of star-struck adolescents too caught up in A.C. Green's fame to notice the flaws in this ethical appeal.

With this connection between self-control and success firmly yet implicitly made, the text clumsily transitions back into its original theme of abstinence with an image of A.C. Green kneeling beside a basketball, surrounded by a quote of dubious origin. "Young people are told when they're old enough to smoke, drink, drive, vote, go to school and fight in the military. Why don't we at least tell them how much better off they'll be, physically, emotionally, mentally and socially if they wait until marriage for sex?" (5). In other words, no matter what the law may have to say on the matter, adolescents are incapable of making informed, beneficial decisions regarding their bodies. Once again, the audience is urged to value A.C. Green's celebrity endorsement more highly than their own common sense. This time, however, the author takes that tactic one step further by urging the audience to disinherit their constitutional right to govern the use of their bodies. While it may be inadvisable to start smoking, drinking, and having sex at such a young age, the author's attempt to strip adolescents of their legal rights lays bare their true purpose: to enshrine abstinence as law, and pre-marital sex as a crime against one's future and the future of society as a whole. In an attempt to give their argument a more factual foundation, the author defines abstinence as it might appear in the dictionary, minus all the subjective commentary at the end of the word's definition. "Abstinence is the only 100% effective protection from the possible physical, emotional, mental and social consequences of sex before marriage. Abstinence is the safest and healthiest lifestyle," (6). Surely it is no coincidence that the author fails to mention the fact that anyone, abstinent or not, can still be a victim of rape—an experience that comes with its fair share of physical, emotional, mental, and social trauma. The author even goes so far as to include a statistic, 100 percent, in an attempt to clothe an otherwise defenseless argument in a suit of iron-clad logic. Above all, the author's authoritative tone in defining abstinence belittles the audience's sense of ownership over their own bodies, while exalting abstinence as the only answer to the most pressing question facing adolescents: how are they going to achieve their goals?

In an effort to create a human interest in the practice of abstinence, the author moves on to a story about a young couple, Steve and Tina. After having dwelled for so long on celebrities like A.C. Green and extreme cases like Tom, it appears that the author is finally going to provide an everyday example of how abstinence plays out in the real world. At least, this is what the author appears to be doing, until they proceed to characterize Tina as a malevolent temptress whose sole goal in life is to tempt Steve into having sex with her, presumably so that he will have no choice but to father the child she conceived with another man. The picture of the couple alone is enough to convince the reader that Tina is some sort of demonic presence bent on ruining Steve's life: leaning over his shoulder with a smoky look in her eyes, Tina becomes the proverbial femme fatale, Eve reincarnate. What's more, the questions that follow the story blatantly lead the reader to the conclusion that Tina, and the sexual promiscuity she represents, is the essence of evil. The first question reads, "why do you think Tina was trying to get Steve to have sex with her? What was her real concern?" (7). The emphasis lies on Tina's motive rather than on her unfortunate circumstances, and it is clear that the author, in stripping Tina of any and all human qualities, is trying to muster sympathy for the chaste and honorable Steve. The next question, which asks the reader how having sex with Tina might have affected Steve's future (7), places additional emphasis on abstinence and its role in helping adolescents achieve their goals. Naturally, the author fails to question how any of these events may have affected Tina and her life goals. Instead, the author consigns Tina to the scrap heap of shame and poverty in saying that she "became a single mother at age 18," (7) and nothing else.

As in the case of Tom and A.C. Green, the author seeks to create a contrast with the story of Steve and Tina through the story of Steve and Karen. Karen, Steve's future wife and the mother of their four children, shared Steve's desire to remain abstinent until marriage and, consequently, the two of them now live a perfect life in which they "never worry about sexually transmitted diseases, or unwanted pregnancy, or emotional issues" (8). Not only is this artless appeal to the popular conception of an ideal marriage unrealistic, but it is also unrelated to abstinence. There is no reason that Steve and Karen could not have ended up with the marriage they have now through the use of protected sex. Rather than expose the reality of the situation, the author opts to oversimplify matters instead, hoping to manipulate the optimistic expectations of their adolescent audience to achieve their own ends. Because most adolescents have had little to no relationship experience—certainly not enough to even begin to prepare them for marriage—their expectations of an ideal marriage are bound to be fantastic and whimsical. It is highly probable that many of the adolescents reading the text imagine marriage exactly as the author makes it out to be, and are therefore more likely to believe that such a perfect union can only be achieved through abstinence. In this way, the author emerges as a credible source by virtue of the ignorance of their audience, leaving them no choice but to blindly trust the claims being made in the text. Still, as if this ploy left any room for doubt, the author follows up the story with two more questions, each asking the reader to consider how abstinence allowed Steve and Karen to reach the state of unspoiled, monogamous bliss they now enjoy—a state of bliss that the author assumes everyone aspires to reach, one that anyone would be willing to sacrifice their sexual freedom to achieve.

As it happens, assumptions such as these constitute the bulk of the sex ed curriculum "I Got Game," and serve as the primary link between abstinence and future success throughout the text. Were it not for these assumptions about how people define success and what their "game plan" may entail, the author would never have been able to establish a causal link between abstinence and the fulfillment of a person's goals. In reality, just as basketball is not everyone's career path of choice, neither is abstinence everyone's chosen method to achieve their goals, whatever they may be. In the end, the only claim that the text "I Got Game" successfully supports is the claim that wordplay always comes before foreplay, and that rhetoric always has the first say in the decision-making process, especially where sex ed is concerned.

13.7 Controversy Analysis

The Great Corn (Syrup) Debate

By Andrea Fulgham

It's not easy to imagine that the Chips Ahoy cookies, the A&W root beer, or the Vick's cold medicine in your pantry are actually the subject of a nationwide controversy (after all, who could have anything against something as innocuous Kellogg's Corn Flakes?), but these items are a small part of a much larger whole that has come under fire regarding one of their main shared ingredients, High Fructose Corn Syrup (HFCS). The accusations of critics range from HFCS being the culprit responsible for America's obesity epidemic to the question of whether the human body is able to even digest this substance, which is made from corn and found in a long list of popular foods and beverages. The opposing viewpoint says that HFCS is a product that is made from corn, which is an all-American food that has been ingested by humans for centuries, in many different ways, with no ill-effects that have been definitively scientifically documented. But there are some surprising facts that seem to have missed the invitation to take part in this controversy. It seems that each side of this debate has its own stakes in the outcome, and there is now a question from where, exactly, the information that has maligned HFCS has sprung, as well as whether or not the corn industry is harboring dark secrets regarding the production of their most prolific cash-cow and its by-products. Even now you may be innocently toasting a HFCS-laden Pop-Tart, blissfully unaware of this controversy, and yet it rages…and has raged for much longer than anyone might suspect.

There are many experts on both sides of this debate that have provided a lot of information both pro- and con-High Fructose Corn Syrup over nearly a century, and even longer than that, beginning with the first stages of scientists learning how to transmute corn starch into a sweetener, as "… in the case of the corn industry, wet-millers knew as early as the 1800s the process of converting D-glucose (an aldose) to D-fructose (a ketose)", but "in the process of conversion, excessive by-products were produced, which tended to cause dark colours and to develop off-flavours" (Thomas 29). Since the technology had not yet been developed to deal with these by-products (today known as ethanol, corn oil, and corn feed for livestock), the first spark of controversy was ignited. After all, something that was so unattractive in taste and flavor couldn't possibly be good for you, a philosophy with which the sugar industry whole-heartedly agreed, but they weren't the only ones. Harvey W. Wiley, chief of the USDA's chemistry bureau was embroiled in a controversy in the early 20th century to denounce the use of "processed foods", and began the "issuance of reports condemning the adulterants that were being used to alter practically every food Americans ate" (Levenstein 71), and in 1911 he targeted corn syrup specifically, and "embarked on a campaign to prevent politically powerful corn processors from calling their sweetener corn syrup. (He wanted them to label it glucose)"

(Levenstein 72). This label would indicate to the general public that the very idea of chemical processing was frightening, alien rather than an organic and familiar term regarding food. It seems that Mr. Wiley didn't do much to explain to the public how, exactly, HFCS was "processed": a simple bacterium (Aeromonas hydrophila) produces an enzyme that reconfigures the components of corn glucose into fructose (Beil 22). Perhaps not as frightening a process as the early critics thought it was. After a few decades passed, perhaps due to the lack of scientific evidence that HFCS caused injury to the human condition, the fear of HFCS dimmed to the point of becoming a non-issue, and the corn industry grew larger than ever. Eventually, though, it became an issue again, and now the debate is as hot as ever.

Surprisingly, the most vociferous adversary of HFCS, the sugar industry, had an unwitting hand in the sudden avalanche of mass-development and mass–production of HFCS. Indeed, in the 1970s, "a world-wide spike in sugar prices sent manufacturers scrambling" (Beil 23) for an alternative and affordable sweetener, and "…by the end of the 1980s, high fructose corn syrup had replaced cane sugar in soft drinks, and it soon became popular among makers of baked goods, dairy products, sauces and other foods" (Beil 23). At this point, it seemed that almost every consumer of HFCS believed that tossing back a 60 oz vat of soda in one sitting fine…until approximately 2004, when the blogosphere became popular (Beil 24) and people began to communicate information quickly, if not always (in)accurately, and HFCS was one issue that certainly didn't escape Internet Scrutiny.

In fact, partially thanks to an unknown researcher and nutrition scientist at the University of North Carolina, Chapel Hill named Barry Popkin, and a researcher from the Pennington Biomedical Research Center named George Bray (Beil 24), that scrutiny became an epic battle of the sweetener industries, but may have begun on a false assumption made by some in the general public; in 2004 Popkin and Bray "published a commentary in the American Journal of Clinical Nutrition pointing out that the country's obesity crisis appeared to rise in tandem with the embrace of HFCS by food manufacturers" (Beil 24). What seemed to escape the notice of possibly everyone was the fact that the commentary was "far from an indictment of HFCS" (Beil 25), and that Popkin himself said that the "original article actually was a scientific speculation saying we needed research" (Beil 25). In other words, the researchers had little to no evidence that obesity was directly linked to the consumption of HFCS, but it was too late… Popkin's clarifying statement would never receive the same attention as his commentary, and word of mouth spread like wildfire: HFCS was harmful to human health and welfare, and should be avoided. Using every rhetorical situation known to man, the general public took up their torches and pitchforks and began the march on the evil alchemists who were turning corn into liquid gold. One might think that in such an advanced age as 2004, the early 21st century, internet bloggers and researchers would fully investigate a subject such as whether

HFCS was actually dangerous for human consumption, but apparently the mere suggestion of danger was enough to validate what some already believed, and what others wanted to believe. To add fuel to the fire, it also so happens that the public discovery of the Popkin/Bray hypothesis coincided with another popular diet notion that has slowly grown immensely in popularity.

One of the most vociferous opponents to the consumption of HFCS is the current group of practitioners of the Paleo Diet, which involves eating only clean, organic foods consisting mostly of meats, vegetables, nuts and berries (according to the diet of our Paleolithic ancestors), and avoiding all processed and refined foods, especially grains. One self-proclaimed farmer's daughter and food writer (Planck 1), and fierce clean-eating advocate, Nina Planck, states, "Americans do eat too many grains and refined grains. The main villain is corn, in three forms: corn-fed beef, corn oil, and corn syrup" (Planck 224). There is no citation in this passage, so one might assume that this statement is her own generalization. Miss Planck also goes on to state:

> Corn also becomes high fructose corn syrup, the main caloric sweetener in junk food. Intake of high fructose corn syrup grew by more than 1000 percent between 1970 and 1990, far exceeding changes in consumption of any other food. The rise of corn syrup mirrors the increase in obesity (Planck 224).

Her lone citation is, believe it or not, "Commentary, 'Consumption of High Fructose Corn Syrup in Beverages May Play a Role in the Epidemic of Obesity', *American Journal of Clinical Nutrition* 79, no. 4 (2004): 537-43." That's right, the very commentary that was written and consequently clarified by Barry Popkin, our dietary scientist friend from UNC-CH. The author, Ms. Planck, then makes some other medical claims (sans citation) about the negative health effects of HFCS on insulin, blood pressure and triglycerides (Planck 224), but what she lacks in reliable and definitive sources, she makes up for with a sincerity of tone indicating a desire to help her fellow man eat more healthily, beginning with her audience of like-minded Paleo dieters and people researching the diet to see if it's health benefits outweigh the current trend of packaged and processed foods. Of course, sincerity of tone and good intentions aren't limited to the farmer's daughter; these things can also come straight from the farmer himself.

As someone who hails from the "Tall Corn State", Iowa, it might stand to reason that I know plenty of farmers, and I do. Lance Feuss and his family, friends and most of his community are heavily invested in the growth and sale of field corn on their farm in small-town Baldwin, Iowa; that growth and sale is what sustains their livelihood and pays their bills. I recently interviewed him and his wife, Krisy, about their own thoughts regarding HFCS, and first asked him if he was affiliated with the local Archer Daniels Midland (ADM), a branch of the largest corn processing plant in the world, which is located in Clinton, IA. Lance hooted and asked me if I had turned into a "damn hippy" and replied that of course he was affiliated with them—that I knew that's where they took their corn for "sale". (This would be the first of several times that I had to remind the interviewee that he was helping me with an academic paper, and also the first of several times that he would call me a "damn hippy"—farmer humor.) I then asked him what kinds of corn he grew and he said, "All kinds". This is farmer-speak for field corn and a much smaller amount of sweet corn. When I got to the subject of HFCS and asked him if he thought that it was bad for human consumption. He said, "We've been eating corn for centuries!" and I asked about it being blamed for obesity. He said, "Look, people are going to get fat if they eat too much ANYTHING, butter, sugar, pie, noodles, whatever crap candy and junk food they eat. If they don't want to get off their fat asses and work to stay healthy, that's not corn's fault!" Finally, I asked him why he thought that there was a campaign against HFCS and he said, "Simple…other companies don't want the corn association to succeed." Like who? "Like the sugar people, of course." To Lance, the answer is simple, it's ridiculous to think that corn can be bad for human digestion, and the sugar people want all of the sweetener contracts, edging corn syrup out of the picture. To anyone who heard his answers, it might seem like they were too simple, too heavily laden with pathos, but he may be right about a few things.

Regarding his answer about obesity, as stated in an article from a report from the Center of Food and Nutrition Policy: "…an increasingly popular approach is to blame a specific food or food ingredient for the rise in overweight/obesity in the US population. However, this clearly is an oversimplification because there are many variables that that contribute to obesity" (Hein et al 253). The article goes on to state that, "At this time, there is no scientific evidence to suggest that humans utilize (HFCS) any differently than sucrose, invert sugar, or honey. All disaccharides are completely hydrolyzed in the gastrointestinal tract into their simple sugar (monosaccharide) components prior to absorption" (Hein et al 254). While I looked high and low for any type of scientific evidence that humans are unable to metabolize HFCS, the most that I could find were unrelated claims, mainly about cattle being unable to digest feed corn: "they interview a veterinary scientist, who shows in a particularly graphic segment what eating corn does to a cow's ruminant stomach" (Powell 79), that didn't address human consumption except to make a weak comparison. What Hein et al have is a scientific background to provide ethos and logos to their factually stated article, while the most that could be found to refute it were some comparisons to cow digestion. In other cases, the corn industry is blamed for many ecological problems in the US, especially in the Gulf of Mexico, "that ecologists call the 'Dead Zone'" (Manning 15) an area that is provably problematic as nitrogen pesticides are flowing down the Mississippi river and killing habitat and marine life there (Manning 15), but is not related to human consumption except for a brief statement that says HFCS also "exports obesity to Mexico", with no source citations or other information to make the audience think that humans are in danger of HFCS, besides the author's opinion.

Lance may also have been correct about the "sugar people", and many others have been stating the same opinion for years, but the truth may be that neither industry is pure as the driven snow in this matter. In a recent New York Times article, published in February of 2014, some rather enlightening information has been uncovered. "The corn refinery and sugar industries, bitter rivals in the manufacture of billions of dollars' worth of sweeteners for sodas and other high-calorie food, covertly funded dueling nonprofit groups in Washington in a multiyear effort to grab market share, while also stoking fears among consumers about possible health risks, court records made public in a federal lawsuit between the two parties show" (Lipton 1). The journalist goes on to state that this lawsuit has provided hundreds of pages of "secret corporate emails and strategy documents" that show how these rival industries use corporate lobbying campaigns to damage their competitors or defend their own reputations (Lipton 1). The question now becomes, which industry is doing what to whom? Does it really even matter, in the grand scheme of human health? After all, this lawsuit is really about the loss of profit, and everyone knows that money will propel corporations into a frenzy. Therefore, the accusations are being launched like Tomahawk missiles: the sugar companies "charged that the corn refining companies, in a bid to halt a decline in HFCS sales, had conducted a 'false and misleading' publicity campaign portraying HFCS as a natural product that was nutritionally the same as sugar—including changing the name to 'corn sugar'" (McCarthy 1), and the corn companies returned fire by rebutting that the suit is "an attack on free speech" and that the sugar industry could not prove a loss in profits from the name "corn sugar" being used (McCarthy 1). Both sides have been accused of paying for scientific research to further their own cause, which is a common practice among many different industries (McCarthy 1), and with the corn industry saying that it "had no choice but to defend its product" (Lipton 2) against the allegedly false information put forth by the sugar industry. Perhaps inadvertently, the sugar association used the fear tactic once employed by the very first critic of HFCS, Harvey W. Wiley from the early 20th century USDA… "Back in 2003 (the sugar industry) formally began a secret effort it called 'food and beverage industry replacement of H.F.C.S. with sucrose', meaning replacing corn-based sweeteners with sugar, the court documents show, reproducing a Sugar Association memo" (Lipton 2), and in 2004 a memo stated celebration for having "fed the media with the science to help fuel the public concern and debate on H.F.C.S." (Lipton 2). However, notice that the memo does not state that it was "false science", and perhaps that's the biggest question of this debate. Maybe there is no definite science showing that HFCS is bad for people, but maybe Lance has the right idea when he charges that eating too much of anything that contains a lot of calories will increase your weight gain. Both Lipton and McCarthy use logos to simply state the facts of the lawsuit, leaving the reader to wonder what other "secret documents" might surface in this particular controversy, and to also wonder whether those documents might provide an answer as to whether HFCS is any worse for people than any other sweetener, but the odds don't look good for that kind of closure on the subject.

Basically, it seems that the controversy surrounding high fructose corn syrup is one that was started with sincere intentions regarding human health and digestion, which then evolved – almost a century later -- into a public debate regarding the responsibility that HFCS held in the growing obesity epidemic, and eventually became twisted into a high-profile lawsuit between two competing sweetener industries whose concern extends only to their own monetary gain. Somewhere in the middle is the American farmer and the American consumer. The farmer is doing what he knows, or loves, or what his family has done for generations by growing and selling crops for profit, believing that his efforts are not at all harmful to the people who consume the products made with the corn he grows. The American consumer is someone who trusts that the Special K, or Yoplait yogurt or Wheat Thins that they are eating is carefully regulated, and not made with a substance that might be harmful to them or their loved ones. On the other hand, there are those who are suspicious of any type of "chemical" processing, the Paleolithic eaters and people who are looking for organic and home-made food alternatives to the packaged products on grocery shelves, both perhaps believing that the best thing for their health and the health of their loved ones is down to the types of food that they eat. These two groups of people are engaged in as honest of a debate as they can have, considering the scope of the unknown: Is HFCS scientifically proven to be harmful or not? The biggest problem, it seems, is that these two groups of people are overshadowed by the slavering, monolithic sweetener industry, whose sole focus is to take down their competitor and win the profit war. Embedded somewhere in the epic battle between refined sugar and processed corn syrup is one undeniable truth: maybe HFCS is fine for human consumption, and maybe it's not, but in the end, neither sweetener is beneficial for anyone but the sweetener industry when eaten in large amounts.

Bibliography

Beil, Laura. "Sweet Confusion: Does High Fructose Corn Syrup Deserve Such a Bad Rap?" *Science News* 183.11 (2013): 22-25. *Academic Search Complete*. Web. 2 Mar. 2014.

Feuss, Lance. Personal interview. March 27, 2014.

Hein, Gayle L., et al. "Highs and Lows of High Fructose Corn Syrup: A Report from the Center for Food and Nutrition Policy and Is Ceres® Workshop." *Nutrition Today* 40.6 (2005): 253-256. *Academic Search Complete*. Web. 2 Mar. 2014.

Levenstein, Harvey A. *Fear of Food: A History of Why We Worry about What We Eat*. Chicago: University of Chicago, 2012. Print.

Lipton, Eric. "Sweet-Talking the Public." *New York Times* 12 Feb. 2014: B1+. *Academic Search Complete*. Web. 2 Mar. 2014.

13.8

Manning, Richard. "Against the Grain: A Portrait of Industrial Agriculture as a Malign Force." *The American Scholar* 73.1 (2004): 13-35. *JSTOR*. Web. 31 Mar. 2014.

McCarthy, Michael. "US Food Industry Wages Bitter Fight Over Sugars And Corn Syrup." *BMJ: British Medical Journal* 348.7947 (2014): 5. *Academic Search Complete*. Web. 24 Mar. 2014.

Planck, Nina. *Real Food: What to Eat and Why*. New York: Bloomsbury Pub., 2006. Print.

Powell, Bonnie Azab. "Good Cob, Bad Cob." *Gastronomica: The Journal of Food and Culture* 8.2 (2008): 77-79. *JSTOR*. Web. 31 Mar. 2014.

Thomas, Clive Yolande. *Sugar, Threat or Challenge: An Assessment of the Impact of Technological Developments in the High-fructose Corn Syrup and Sucrochemicals Industries*. Ottawa, Canada: International Development Research Centre, 1985. Print.

13.8 Public Argument

Along the Border of Free Speech

By Steven Chin

Dean Saxton, also known as Brother Dean at the University of Arizona, has brought about a large amount of controversy regarding gender roles, religious beliefs, and rape culture. Brother Dean claims to be a campus preacher, spreading the word of the Gospel in the effort to convert people into Christianity. However, Brother Dean has become a name synonymous with extremist beliefs regarding how women deserve to be raped and how homosexuals, Muslims, and atheists deserve to burn in hell. Through Brother Dean's multiple campaigns with "slut-shaming" messages, and anti-homosexual messages, it is clear why many modern-day students find this offensive and not appropriate for campus grounds. However, as much as the students on campus wish to prevent him from delivering his messages, and as much as the students retaliate through arguments and violence, the fact of the matter is that students should not resort to illegal methods in trying to silence Brother Dean and need to accept the fact that he can freely express his beliefs, as his actions are both protected by law and are fundamental human rights.

Most of the outrage regarding Brother Dean stems not only from how he expresses his beliefs, but that the University of Arizona will not take any action to prevent them in the first place. An article written by Tyler Kingkade for the Huffington Post describes how Brother Dean has been shown through multiple sources yelling statements such as, "You deserve to be raped" and, "All Muslims are pedophiles" (Kingkade). Brother Dean has also been shown in different videos holding signs with messages reading, "Rapists Deserve the

Death Penalty", "Frat Boys are the Rapists," and, "Sorority Girls are Whores" (Kingkade). Kingkade describes how several people lost their tempers and attempted to knock the sign out of Saxton's hands, spat at him, threw food at him, and threatened to physically assault him. While many people may find these reactions normal and justified, physically assaulting an individual due to vulgar and upsetting messages directly violates the freedoms of speech and assembly that the Bill of Rights protects.

The First Amendment prohibits "Congress to make laws respecting an establishment of religion, or prohibiting the free exercise thereof; or abridging the freedom of speech, or of the press; or the right of the people peaceably to assemble" (Archives). The Bill of Rights serves as the foundation for all of the controversy regarding Brother Dean's speeches and actions. Several students feel that Brother Dean's messages extend beyond free speech, and are instead based upon hate speech. These students have argued that by protecting Brother Dean's rights to preach on campus, others' rights are violated. They argue that protecting community interests is more important than safeguarding the rights of the individual. However, the First Amendment does not make exceptions to the rights to free speech, whether or not it is regarded as an offensive message. As much as the students do not agree with Brother Dean's messages, individuals are allowed the right to speech whether or not the listener agrees and whether or not their messages are offensive and hateful.

Unfortunately, both the general student body and law enforcement don't understand this fundamental right and as a result, law enforcement put Saxton under arrest and escorted him off of University Boulevard, where a basketball game was taking place. Saxton explains how "they [the police] should have protected my rights to free speech in a public area" (Hall). Saxton was seen in a shouting conflict between a man and several others who were watching. Saxton reported, "One guy came over and tried to grab my sign…and there were some women who would punch me in the sides" (Hall). Following these events, University of Arizona Police Department officers arrived to arrest Saxton for disorderly conduct. In expressing his own beliefs and protesting in front of a basketball game, law enforcement favored the public's side after physically abusing him rather than upholding Dean's freedom of speech and assembly. This incident sparks more controversy as to how the First Amendment is to be interpreted and whether or not Saxton's actions were upheld by the law.

Across the country, several universities have set aside zones intended for free speech amongst the students. These "free speech zones" have been deemed by the Supreme Court as unconstitutional since they violate the First Amendment, yet these limitations to free speech still exist on hundreds of college campuses in the United States. These campus policies "send the message to students that freedom of speech is a privilege doled out by administrators—not a fundamental human right" (Haynes). Due to this, students attending the University of Arizona, bring these ideals with them to try and force administration to take disciplinary action on Dean Saxton. These ideals cause them to petition to the administration of the University of Arizona in the attempts to suspend, or expel Brother Dean from the campus. What these students do not realize is that by allowing administration to punish Dean for his statements, students are inadvertently giving the university more power over their own rights to free speech and assembly. In response to these student demands, interim dean of students, Kendal Washington White, forwardly stated that, "We're upholding university policy and law… as much as we don't like it, it's protected speech" (Mejia). While the administration acknowledges that Brother Dean's messages are vile and repugnant, and do not represent the beliefs that students on campus possess, the University of Arizona is a "bastion for free speech, and will uphold the right of this speaker and all others to engage in constitutionally protected speech" (Kingkade).

Several students have gone as far as to petition for the disciplinary action of Brother Dean to the University of Arizona's administration. Most of these students have signed the petition in the belief that Brother Dean has not been practicing free speech, and instead has been verbally abusing students on campus and using methods of hate speech. Samantha Sharman, a gender and women's studies junior, has stated that "The fact that our campus is advertently and implicitly tolerating this kind of behavior is really upsetting… I'm not sure where the line is for the Dean of Students office between free speech and verbal assault, but I feel very clearly that Dean has crossed that line" (Mejia). Hate speech is defined as "speech that offends, threatens, or insults groups, based on race, color, religion, national origin, sexual orientation, disability, or other traits" (Student Central). Of the 2,000 student signatures, most of these claims are that Brother Dean's hate speech is constitutionally unprotected and violates the law. However, executive director of the Student Press Law Center, Frank LoMonte, states that "there is no recognized exception in the law for hate speech" (Mejia). Officials state that the First Amendment protects Saxton "as long as he did not directly threaten another student" (Mejia). As a result, students need to understand that in silencing Brother Dean on the basis that they find his messages offensive and hateful, is unlawful and violates the principle of the First Amendment.

A main reason students feel this way is due to the fact that they disagree with Brother Dean's messages. As pointed out by an article written for the Student Central, "It's always easier to defend someone's right to say something with which you agree." (Student Central) Protecting one individual's right to free speech based on the meaning of the message over another individual's is unconstitutional and doesn't protect everyone's rights to free speech. The university cannot take bias over certain student's beliefs and must act neutrally, as it is a public institution that receives funding from the government. The university, like the government, "may not treat some ideas differently than others because people may find them odious or offensive" (Stone). One example of this comes from the court case of Snyder v. Phelps, where Fred Phelps, founder and pastor of the Westboro Baptist Church, picketed the funeral of Lance Corporal Matthew Snyder. The Westboro congregation held signs with messages such as "Semper Fi Fags" (Stone). While Snyder's family won the case in small-court on the basis that "Phelps' speech was not constitutionally protected in the special circumstance of this case", the Supreme Court ruled it was unconstitutional to the First Amendment law" (Stone). The central principle is that the government cannot base their decisions off of emotions and ignore what the First Amendment specifically forbids. Had Phelps held signs praising the United States Marines, the "Snyder family presumably would not have objected, and even if they had, no jury would have held Phelps liable for intentional infliction of emotional distress" (Stone). Students need to understand that in a university, there will be many conflicting ideas and beliefs, and it is up to the students to defend the rights of all speech, despite instances of strong opposition. Allowing for the university to make decisions that prohibit Dean's abilities to express his opinions and beliefs is precisely what the First Amendment forbids.

While students at the University of Arizona believe that Brother Dean's messages are both offensive and are not protected by the First Amendment, his messages are still guided under the principles of free speech. The students that have knocked signs out of his hands, spat in his face, threw items at him, and continuously physically harass him are unlawful and defying the rights given by off by the Bill of Rights (Kingkade). Students need to understand that strong offensive messages should never result in violence, and every individual living in the United States has the right to express themselves freely. When students favor one message over another and limit others rights to express their message, it shows discord in the rights of others and demonstrates bias of the government and the University of Arizona.

Works Cited

"ABA Division for Public Education: Students: Debating the "Mighty Constitutional Opposites": Hate Speech Debate." *Americanbar*. Student Central. Web. 21 Nov. 2014.

Hall, Jazmine-Foster. "Campus Preacher Arrested Twice over the Weekend." Wildcat Arizona. Arizona Daily Wildcat, 01 Apr. 2014. Web. 24 Nov. 2014.

Haynes, Charles C. "First Amendment Center." First Amendment Center. First Amendment Center, 14 Oct. 2013. Web. 23 Nov. 2014.

Kingkade, Tyler. "'You Deserve Rape' Sign Held By 'Brother Dean' Outrages University Of Arizona Students (VIDEO)." *The Huffington Post*. Huffington Post, 25 Apr. 2013. Web. 24 Nov. 2014.

Mejia, Brittny. "Student's Preaching Sparks First Amendment Debate on UA Campus." *Wildcat Arizona*. Arizona Daily Wildcat, 29 Apr. 2013. Web. 24 Nov. 2014.

Stone, Geoffrey R. "Funerals and Free Speech." The Huffington Post. Huffington Post, 06 Oct. 2010. Web. 24 Nov. 2014.

"The Bill of Rights: A Transcription." National Archives and Records Administration. Charters of Freedom. Web. 23 Nov. 2014.

13.9 Reflective

The Art of Being

By Joshua Rubin Abrams

I have never been much of a writer myself, because many people around me do not appreciate the art of language. It's never been encouraged to sit down and write something for myself in my free time. I believe it's rather therapeutic though. Writing an editorial is a reflection of my thoughts, who I am, and how I feel about a certain subject. But what is the point of language, and communication? Language takes on many forms and its many components allow people to communicate an idea its purest form.

My time in English 101 taught me how to take an idea, define it, and write a paper about it. After that class, I felt that the point of a good essay paper can be summarized by the author's ability to relate one specific topic to another. Writing about how the relationship exists, and changes over time can be used to understand the significance of the subject itself. However, English 102 has taught me how to give an essay, or editorial significance. I now understand that writing a paper that describes how two, or more entities work together may not be very relevant. English 102 has promoted the use of evoking a reaction in an audience. This semester, we had to prepare a speech that would persuade the class to vote for the those worthy of getting into a hypothetical life boat, so that we could be saved in a post-apocalyptic world. After a discussion of what techniques, and mechanisms used in the speeches, I learned that everyone uses a pattern in writing. Every mechanism has an effect on the reader. Therefore, neutral analysis, or rhetorically analyzing the patterns used helps me understand what the author's intentions are.

With practice, I have developed the skills to form, and convey an idea to my audience effectively. My writing process starts with I creating a thesis based on questions that I have come across in my daily routine. I then break down the question into its elementary components, which can be analyzed on a smaller scale. Studying logic to create an argument through the use of the Claim Tree has helped me create deductive arguments. I use small conclusions to result in slightly bigger, medium-sized conclusions, which can be used to justify my larger claim. If I can effectively use deductive, and cogent reasoning, then I can create a strong argument that could influence the way people understand how one subject relates to another.

This skill of organization has been essential in my writing process. I can define a subject, by explaining relevant topics within the subject. By guiding my readers through a flowing essay, I can ensure my readers understand how I formed my large claim. Learning how to collect relevant information effectively has made writing research papers easier. After collecting all relevant information, I write out an annotated bibliography, which is later implement in my essay. The annotated bibliography allows me to see what content will be present in my paper. I have discovered how the use of diction, perspective, organization, and structure of information in an editorial can be used to manipulate the reader's beliefs. To understand a subject, is to understand how that subject relates to the world around you.

Words, their connotation, and denotation all add different levels of meaning to an argument. Similar words can be used to describe the same idea. However, tone, diction, and structure can convey more than just what the idea is, but how a person feels about said idea. Understanding one's approach towards expressing an idea can be used to understand how important that idea is to a person. As a result, I can now conclude a little bit more about the character, beliefs, and values of the people around me. This has been instrumental in developing my social skills, because I understand how to make a conversation flow, while keeping it interesting enough to gain an audience's opinion. Words have more significance, and power than its direct meaning.

Language has many different components that work together in order to understand an idea in its purest form. Our ability to speak is directly related to our ability to write, and read. Developing anyone component of language requires development in all components of language. I believe that language is a reflection of the concepts a person is able to comprehend. We use language as a way of understanding the world around us. A developed vocabulary is important in order to understand intricate concepts. If a word can represent something not tangible, then referring to that word can help communication become more efficient. The existence of said word means one does not have to explain the same idea every time.

Philosophers that we've studied in class have helped me understand the world around me. I now understand the importance of speech and how it is a skill to be able to share an idea effectively. Our class readings about philosophy have taught me how one's writing can be a reflection of what one experiences in life. An individual is a collection of beliefs and those beliefs make up an individual's identity. Albert Einstein said, "If you can't explain it simply, you don't understand it well enough". I like to admire the ethos effect of a quote from Albert Einstein, but I believe his vocabulary is a result of his ability to understand complicated ideas. I find it amazing that I could relate to the ideas that philosophers have articulated hundreds of years ago, because I have had those same ideas. The idea that most stands out to me is that of the whole world being a blur. We subconsciously give objects in our life definition, so that we can separate, organize, and interpret the world around us. The most basic distinction one can make is the one between you, and the rest of the world.

Language, and communication exist, so that knowledge, the only thing we truly possess, can be shared. The techniques I have learned in my English classes have been implemented in my writing process. I completed my research paper on the effect that sanctions on the Russian economy will have on the global economy. I have a thorough understanding of how the politics, and history result in that specific situation and I am able to neutrally analyze the situation, so that I can take a stand in it. My skills in research allow me to teach myself about any topic, or subject that I am interested in. My skills in rhetorical analysis allow me to see what effect a message has on me and therefore, I can write a message to evoke a specific response in my audience. Language is a means to understanding the world around you.

Glossary

Academic writing: Writing that follows discipline-specific style guidelines and genre conventions and may incorporate academic research to support arguments and/or observations.

Alliteration: The repetition of consonant sounds in a sequence of words. For example, "Peter Piper picked a peck of pickled peppers."

Allusion: An indirect reference, often to a person, event, statement, theme, or work. Allusions enrich meaning through the connotations they carry, or the associations that they evoke in a reader's mind. For example, authors may allude to a historic event by mentioning its name or to a play by Shakespeare by using similar language in their writing.

Analysis: The act of explaining how and why a written or visual text does something and whether or not it does so effectively. Analysis goes beyond summary/ description; as summary/description explains what is happening with a topic, while analysis explains how and why something is happening. Analysis is the act of breaking a text into parts and examining how those parts create a message and affect a reader's or viewer's response. Analytical statements reveal a careful consideration of the text beyond just its main point and open up a space for dialogue.

Angle: In visual analysis, the vantage point from which the viewer is seeing the image. An angle can be high or low and can be exaggerated for a pronounced effect.

Annotated bibliography: Alphabetical lists of topic-related sources in MLA format, each with a summary paragraph.

Annotation: The process of writing notes and comments about a text. These notes can include first impressions, questions, summaries, associations, strategies used, analysis, and more.

Argument: The overall claim that your essay makes. An essay's argument should be summarized in its thesis statement. Arguments must be debatable, meaning that they must make a claim which a reasonable person could object to.

Audience: The person or people who are reading, listening to, or viewing a text. An author targets an intended audience by using strategies that will be particularly effective for that person or people. An audience might be a primary audience (the person for whom the text is generated) or a secondary audience (the person who has an interest in the topic because that person is connected to/interested in the speaker, the primary audience, or the topic).

Author/Speaker: In a rhetorical situation, the author/speaker is the person or people seeking to communicate a specific message.

Balance: In visual analysis, the "visual weight" of crowded or attention-grabbing items in the image. For example, an image with most of its important focal points on one side of the image could be described as off-balance and weighted to the left.

Blogging: Compiled from the two terms "web" and "logging," blogging refers to personal or reflective writing that is published online. Blogs can have very limited or very broad audiences, and they can cover virtually any area of interest.

Claim: Assertions made in support of the argument a writer is advocating. An essay's thesis is often referred to as its "primary claim."

Cliché: An expression used so often that it has become hackneyed and lost its original impact. For example, "since the beginning of time," and "throughout history" are both clichés.

Close reading: Focusing attention on the aspects of a text that seem most important. Close reading involves first scanning a text to get a basic sense of the text and its purpose. Then you should read more closely for content and meaning, considering how the text is constructed. In addition, you should consider your reactions to the text. Finally, you should review the text and your responses to form some general conclusions.

Connotations: The associations evoked by a word beyond its literal meaning. Connotations can be unique to a particular individual. For instance, a victim of near-drowning may associate water with terror.

Context: The circumstances surrounding the creation and reception of a text. For example, the personal associations of readers, the biographical backgrounds of writers, related historical events, and political purposes can all contribute to a text's context. The best contexts to study are those that illuminate the meanings and uses of the text.

Contextual analysis (see Text-in-Context)

Contrast: Strong juxtapositions of opposites, such as light and dark, depressing and cheerful, rigid and soft, frantic and calm, etc.

Controversy: A contentious social issue that has a larger relevance for a society and those living within it.

Controversy analysis: An analytical essay that incorporates research to trace the key arguments made by people who have a stake in an issue. Controversy analyses evaluate the validity of key claims, examine the persuasive strategies employed by various groups or individuals, and explore the similarities and distinctions between diverse viewpoints.

Counterclaim: An argument presented in opposition to the argument a text is making. When making a claim, it's important to consider the counterclaims that might arise against your own arguments.

Database: An electronic collection of a wide variety of resources, such as newspapers, magazines, and scholarly journals that have been compiled electronically and are searchable by keyword, author, title, subject, and more. Examples of databases include *Academic Search Complete*, *JSTOR*, and *ProQuest*.

Debatable topics: Appropriate topics for a researched argument. Debatable topics must fulfill two criteria. First, they have to stimulate some sort of argument or disagreement, meaning they go beyond reporting the "facts." Second, debatable topics are issues that other researchers have investigated enough for you to be able to locate sufficient resources to inform your understanding of the topic.

Discourse community: A group of people who share a specific set of writing and speaking practices, as well as specialized vocabulary that is understood by members of the group.

Dominance: In visual analysis, the first thing that your eye is drawn to in an image is the dominant part of that image.

Ethos: A rhetorical strategy in which a writer/speaker attempts to build credibility and character in a text.

Figurative language: Language that employs one or more figures of speech, such as metaphor, simile, synecdoche, or personification.

Focus: In visual analysis, refers to whether a section of the image is clear (in focus) or blurry (out of focus).

Foreshadowing: The technique of introducing material into a narrative that prepares the reader for future events or revelations. Examples of foreshadowing could include mentioning a gun early in the narrative that will later shoot someone, or implying that a character is threatening through suggestive language before his actions become villainous.

Form: The patterns and structure associated with a specific genre. For example, poetry is a genre. Poetic patterns such as rhythm, rhyme, meter, repeated words and images, line breaks, stanza breaks, spatial organization on the page, and more create the form of a poem.

Framing: In visual analysis, what is included in the field of the image (what is visible to the viewer) and what is not included. For example, an artist can frame his or her image to only show part of an item and therefore call attention to it.

Freewriting: A prewriting technique designed to help a writer develop ideas. Freewriting involves designating a set amount of time (e.g., fifteen minutes), and writing whatever comes to your mind, without pausing or rereading, until the set amount of time has expired.

Gender criticism: Rhetorically analyzing a text in terms of gender involves examining the ways that a text seeks to reinforce, challenge, or disrupt systems of inequality based on gender.

Gender performance: Behavior that performs femininity or masculinity in culturally appropriate ways, such as wearing a skirt and high heels to emphasize femininity.

Genre: A category grouping texts based on their content, form, techniques, and social function.

Global revisions: The changes you make to an essay's argument, organization, or style. These changes will have a greater impact on your essay as a whole than local revisions.

Hyperbole: Employing deliberate, emphatic exaggeration, sometimes intended for ironic effect. Saying something is "the very *best* in the world" could be a hyperbolic statement. The opposite of this is understatement.

Idea mapping: As a method of organizing analysis, a visual representation of how the ideas in a text are related to both the main point(s) and each other. An idea map emphasizes the interconnectedness of ideas. This is also called "webbing" or "clustering."

Identification: A rhetorical strategy in which an author/speaker works to identify with the members of an audience by pointing out the qualities, characteristics, assumptions, beliefs, and goals that they share with one another. It's important to keep in mind that identification does not mean "sameness," and an author/speaker must define and explain the importance of any type of identification he or she establishes with the audience.

Ideology: Ideology involves the beliefs that people hold, the prominent ideas that tell us what should be, must be, or what seems normal. Sometimes called "cultural values" when in reference to a popular or widely held belief. For example, the idea of democracy in the United States is an ideology—it assumes that everyone should have a voice and that everyone's voice should be equal. Other ideologies include capitalism, religion, and education.

Ideological criticism: A strategy for rhetorical analysis that examines the ways that an author/speaker uses language to reinforce, challenge, or modify an audience's ideological understanding of the world.

Inquiry: A line of investigation into an issue, topic, or problem. This narrows your scope of analysis to focus on certain aspects of your subject.

Irony (ironic): A contradiction or incongruity between appearance or expectation and reality. This could be the difference between what someone says and what s/he actually means, between what appears to be true and what actually is true, or between what someone expects to happen and what actually happens. This is often subtly comic or tongue-in-cheek.

Literacy: Generally refers to the ability to understand a system of language. Literacy usually refers to the competent understanding and use of written language, including abilities in reading and writing. However, literacy can also refer to one's level of knowledge of a particular culture (cultural literacy).

Literacy narrative: A personal narrative that focuses on an event or events in the author's acquisition of literacy. Literacy narratives can explore a specific, significant experience with writing, reading, and/or language, or they can discuss how writing, reading, and/or language have played a role in the author's past experience.

Local revisions: Changes made at the sentence and paragraph level. Local revisions include revising grammar, typos, misspelled words, and awkward sentences. This includes changes in tense or tone that may impact a whole paper, but occur on the sentence level.

Logical fallacies: Arguments in a text that are questionable or invalid because they rest on faulty logic. Logical fallacies may be persuasive even if they are not logically valid.

Logos: A rhetorical strategy in which a writer/speaker appeals to an audience by making logical arguments. The most basic analysis of *logos* considers whether claims are developed using inductive or deductive reasoning. Analyzing the logical fallacies in an argument is another way to consider a text's *logos*.

Metaphor: Associates two distinct things without using a connective word such as "like" or "as." "That child is a mouse" is a metaphor.

Narrative: Can refer to any story that describes events or experiences, whether fictional or factual. Thus newspaper articles that describe recent events or novels that describe a character's journey follow a narrative structure. When you are telling a group of friends about your most recent camping trip, you are telling a narrative as well.

Paraphrase: A rephrasing of a text or a part of a text that is more specific than summary but is less precise than a quotation. Writers paraphrase in order to include specific information and ideas from other writers in their own work. While a paraphrase does not have to retain all of the content from the original, the meaning and intent of the original passage should not be changed. You should cite page numbers for the sections of text you are paraphrasing.

Pathos: A rhetorical strategy in which a writer/speaker appeals to an audience's emotions in order to move the audience toward the author's position.

Persona: Refers to the ability to present yourself differently according to different situations.

Personal writing: A nonfiction genre of writing that focuses on the writer's personal experience(s) as the main subject of the work. Reflective writing is a kind of personal writing.

Personification: Involves giving human characteristics to anything nonhuman. For example, "Father Time" is a personification.

PIE: An acronym for Point, Illustration, and Explanation. PIE is a helpful way to think about paragraph development, especially for analysis essays and persuasive arguments. Remember, however, that PIE is just one of several ways to develop a paragraph.

Point of view: The vantage point from which a narrative is told, either first-person, third-person, or second-person. First-person narratives are told by a narrator who refers to himself or herself as "I" and is often a part of the action. Third-person narrators can either be omniscient, all-knowing and reliable, or limited, restricted to a single character at a time. Second-person narrators speak directly to the reader as "you."

Popular source: A text written for a public audience rather than for an audience of experts. You may think of a popular source as a text written by a non-expert (or occasionally by an expert) for a broad audience of non-experts.

Prewriting: The stage of composition that generally involves thinking about your writing situation, exploring possible topics to write about, choosing a topic, generating ideas about the topic, researching the topic, and outlining the essay.

Primary source: This term is used to refer to original materials on which other research is based. Primary sources are often the result of primary research, where the writer gathers firsthand information directly him or herself through observation, experimentation, interviews, or other research methods.

Primary text: This is the text that you, or another writer is analyzing—it is the main focus of analysis. It might be a book, an article, a movie, a photograph, a painting, or even a place, or any other kind of "text" as that word has been used throughout this book.

Purpose: Refers to the reason and objective for writing. As a writer, your purpose, usually determined before you begin writing, can be as varied as persuading an audience to change his/her opinion on an issue, to do something, or to feel a certain way. Your purpose can also be to report facts and information, to entertain a reader, or to simply express your feelings, as you would in a diary. Much writing has more than just one purpose.

Quotation: Uses the exact words from a writer's original source, with no changes in language or punctuation. You may quote an entire sentence or a part of a sentence, depending on what is most useful for your writing purpose. Quotations must always be cited.

Reflective writing: A kind of personal writing that focuses on a writer's responses to a particular experience or text.

Rhetor: Refers to any person who is using rhetoric.

Rhetoric (rhetorical): Any type of communication that seeks to move an audience toward a specific position, understanding, or action.

Rhetorical analysis: An analysis of how writers and speakers use language in particular situations to achieve predetermined goals. Rhetorical analysis involves evaluating the effectiveness of a speaker/author's rhetorical strategies.

Rhetorical situation: A communication event in which the author/speaker attempts to communicate some message to an audience for a specific purpose and within a specific context.

Rhetorical strategies: The rhetorical methods an author uses to construct a text, develop ideas, and persuade an audience.

Rubric: A tool that your instructor may use to grade essays. It often resembles a chart with rows for categories of writing criteria and columns that describe achievement levels. These columns usually progress from the highest level of achievement on the left to the lowest level on the right.

Scale: In visual analysis, the size of objects within an image. If all objects seem to be of a normal size, then the scale of the image is natural. If some seem larger or smaller than normal, the scale of the image could be exaggerated.

Scholarly source: A text written for an audience with specialized knowledge about a particular subject. You might think of a scholarly source as a text written by an expert for an audience of experts in a given field.

Secondary source: Sources that comment on and have a direct relationship to the primary text. Some common examples of secondary sources are an analysis of a literary text, a critique of a painting or photograph, a movie review, or an opinion about an interview.

Secondary text: Sources used to enable or extend an analysis of a primary text. Secondary tests may not comment directly on the primary text.

Signal phrase: Words that identify the original speaker your text is borrowing from. Signal phrases make it clear that you're borrowing from someone else's ideas. Example signal phrases include "As Author L writes," "According to Author L," and "Author L argues."

Simile: Compares two distinct things by using words such as "like" or "as." "That child is like a cyclone" is a simile.

Style: Refers to specific traits in a written work, including elements such as word choice, sentence/paragraph structure, sentence/paragraph ordering, or genre conventions. When instructors grade an essay for "style," they are often looking for a combination of the conventions of academic writing and comfortable, readable diction/sentence structure.

Summary: An abbreviated version of a longer text—your statement of what you see to be the major points of a text *using your own words*. A summary can be one sentence long, one paragraph long, or one page long, depending on the length of the text and your purpose as a writer.

Symbolism: The sustained use of symbols to represent or suggest other things or ideas. For example, you could say that an author "uses symbols of nature" to evoke certain associations for the reader.

Synecdoche: A part of something used to represent the whole, such as referring to a car as "wheels."

Text: In analysis, any artifact or object that you analyze—whether written or visual. In your first-year writing courses, you'll be dealing with a variety of texts. For example, a text might refer to a book, a newspaper article, a short story, a poem, a speech, a movie, a picture, a video game, a person, an event, a space, a place, and so on.

Text-in-context: Focuses on a text and its relationship to a larger context, such as the author's biography, the historical or cultural situation surrounding the text, a particular theoretical approach such as feminism or psychoanalysis, the literary tradition to which the work belongs, or a related set of texts.

Textual analysis: An argument for how and why a written or visual text works to make meaning using concrete examples from the text with an emphasis on strategies. Textual analysis emphasizes close reading and usually means looking at a text in isolation of outside factors such as context.

Thesis: A one (sometimes two) sentence declaration of the central point of an essay. The thesis helps to inform the reader of what to expect, and therefore usually comes toward the beginning of an essay. Some writers like to think of the thesis statement as a sort of "contract" with the reader; as a writer, you're making a promise to readers that the paper they're about to read is about what the thesis says the paper is about.

Tone: As a textual strategy, this is an author's attitude toward the reader, audience, or subject matter. An author's tone can be optimistic, morbid, humorous, excited, etc. As a writing strategy, tone refers to the attitude that you, the writer, develop toward your own audience.

Topic: In a researched essay, a topic is a general area of inquiry, the overall subject of your essay. A topic is not an argument; rather, it's the more general subject about which your essay argues.

Topic sentence: One sentence that states the main point of the paragraph. Sometimes, the topic sentence is the first sentence of your paragraph. Regardless of where it is placed, every paragraph should include a topic sentence, while other sentences in the paragraph develop, illustrate, or define the idea in that topic sentence.

Visual rhetoric: A form of communication in which visual elements create meanings and arguments.

Index

About the Editors

Brad Jacobson is a PhD student in Rhetoric, Composition, and the Teaching of English. He teaches first-year composition in the Writing Program. Brad is interested in issues of access in higher education, and his current research focuses on composition pedagogy and the high school to college writing transition. When he is not on campus, Brad likes to dig in his garden and spend time with his family.

Madelyn Tucker Pawlowski is a PhD student in Rhetoric, Composition, and the Teaching of English. She teaches first-year composition in the Writing Program. In both her teaching and research, she seeks to understand the complexities of language and the social actions made possible through writing. More specifically, her current research interests include rhetorical genre studies, print culture, and a rhetorical approach to social movement studies. Madelyn hosts a weekly radio show, loves thrifting, and hopes to someday master the art of calligraphy.

Emma Miller is an MA student in Literature. She received an MFA in Creative Writing from California College of the Arts and her MPhil in Scottish Literature from the University of Glasgow. She also served two years as a Peace Corp volunteer in the education sector in Panama. She currently teaches first-year composition in the Writing Program. Emma's research focuses on 19th-century Scottish literature, Romanticism, monstrosity, and folklore. When not working, Emma can be found sniffing old books and dreaming about Scotland.